D0916722

Family Values in the Old South

UNIVERSITY PRESS OF FLORIDA

Florida A&M University, Tallahassee
Florida Atlantic University, Boca Raton
Florida Gulf Coast University, Ft. Myers
Florida International University, Miami
Florida State University, Tallahassee
New College of Florida, Sarasota
University of Central Florida, Orlando
University of Florida, Gainesville
University of North Florida, Jacksonville
University of South Florida, Tampa
University of West Florida, Pensacola

Family Values
in the Old South

∾

EDITED BY

CRAIG THOMPSON FRIEND AND ANYA JABOUR

UNIVERSITY PRESS OF FLORIDA

Gainesville Tallahassee Tampa Boca Raton
Pensacola Orlando Miami Jacksonville Ft. Myers Sarasota

First cloth printing, 2010
First paperback printing, 2010
Library of Congress Cataloging-in-Publication Data
Family values in the Old South / [edited by] Craig Thompson Friend and Anya Jabour.
p. cm.
Includes index.
ISBN 978-0-8130-3418-8 (cloth, alk. paper)
ISBN 978-0-8130-3676-2 (paperback)
1. Families—Southern States—History. 2. Social values—Southern States—History.
3. Southern States—Social conditions—History. I. Friend, Craig Thompson.
II. Jabour, Anya.
HQ541.F36 2009
306.8509759–dc22   2009026485

The University Press of Florida is the scholarly publishing agency for the State University
System of Florida, comprising Florida A&M University, Florida Atlantic University,
Florida Gulf Coast University, Florida International University, Florida State University,
New College of Florida, University of Central Florida, University of Florida, University
of North Florida, University of South Florida, and University of West Florida.

University Press of Florida
15 Northwest 15th Street
Gainesville, FL 32611-2079
http://www.upf.com

Contents

Figures

Families, Values, and Southern History

CRAIG THOMPSON FRIEND AND ANYA JABOUR

❧

"Ef you doan care 'bout how folks talks 'bout dis family, Ah does."
Mammy, *Gone with the Wind* (1936)

Courtesy of David O. Selznick and the Turner Broadcasting System, almost everyone is familiar with the fictional life of Scarlett O'Hara, the heroine of Margaret Mitchell's epic novel, *Gone with the Wind*. Early in the story, as the young woman threatens to "have a good time today and eat as much as I can," Scarlett's impetuousness drives Mammy to the point of chastising her "spirited" individualism and her neglect of the family's reputation. Of course, as we find out throughout the story, Scarlett cared deeply for her family and suffered greatly to protect and preserve not only the home at Tara but the people who inhabited it. But in this confrontation between mistress and slave, young and old, white and black, daughter figure and maternal figure, nuclear family member and extended family member, Margaret Mitchell made an important point about the southern family: appearances meant everything, and everyone had an investment in it. The family's inner dramas were to remain inside the household, beyond the purview of the neighbors. When neighbors were watching, the family followed established rules of conduct. Scarlett, for example, had every intention of being a glutton at the Wilkes family's barbeque, an action that would have stigmatized her and her upbringing, consequently reflecting on her mother's parenting skills and her father's honor. As Mitchell phrased it, "What a young miss could do and what she could not do were as different as black and white in Mammy's mind" and in the minds of most southerners.[1]

Mammy's steadfast determination to protect the family still resonates today. There is a widespread sense in the United States that the social upheavals of the

1960s and 1970s corrupted "traditional" family values, which conservative commentators define as a set of coherent ideals rooted in early American history and envision as having been universally cherished and carefully maintained well into the twentieth century. As family historian Stephanie Coontz pointed out in her 1992 book, *The Way We Never Were: American Families and the Nostalgia Trap*, both social critics and Americans in general exhibit tremendous ignorance about the realities of the history of family life. What most nonspecialists have in mind when they describe a "traditional" family—one defined by heterosexual marriage, a nuclear household structure, and a male breadwinner/female homemaker economy—is actually a fairly recent historical development dating to the twentieth century. Historians describe this family type as a "modern" family, differentiating it from a "traditional" family defined by patriarchal authority, an extended household structure, and a household economy to which all members contributed. Moreover, they view the "modern" family as a fleeting form, one that is quickly being altered by "new family values" or even "queer family values" in a postmodern age in which young people embrace the "age of independence" to form a variety of unions characterized by "liberty, equality, [and] diversity" rather than by formal or informal rules about gender, ethnicity, or sexuality. In short, while they agree that marriage and family are here to stay, historians of family life also argue that families and "family values" are—and always have been—in a constant state of flux. The real "American tradition," these historians assert, is "family diversity."[2]

Nonetheless, what Coontz calls "the nostalgia trap"—a tendency to measure contemporary families against an illusory yardstick of "traditional" family values—still exerts a powerful force in the United States. As family historian Steven Mintz expressed it in 2004, "Americans are prone to romanticizing the past and confusing historical fantasy and reality," especially where family is concerned. This magnetic pull toward an imagined past may be particularly strong in the American South, where both history and family enjoy close to mythical status as well as interpretation. According to some southerners as well as conservative commentators, in both the region and the nation, the current generation is morally adrift, having abandoned the family values of our ancestors. As a blogger using the moniker "Not Your Typical Southerner" posted in 2007, "When you have REAL family values, not pretend ones, then nothing can come between you and your family. . . . It all is a reflection of a major cultural paradigm shift we're experiencing here in the South: how to maintain the values of the Old South while progressing into a modern New South without taking all the racism and superstition with us."[3]

What "Not Your Typical Southerner" failed to realize, however, is that racism and superstition were so deeply embedded in the "values of the Old South" that abandoning these negative aspects of southern tradition threatens to expose how questionable those values were. After all, traditional family values in the Old South framed a culture in which women who openly expressed interest in sex were shunned as immoral, men could set aside their marital vows and visit prostitutes and slave quarters for sexual fulfillment, abortion and infanticide were persistent if not widespread practices, rape and incest were commonplace, alcoholism was rampant, spousal and child abuse went unregulated, millions of human beings were denied freedom to move and work as they pleased, and slave owners regularly sold off darker-skinned blood relatives.[4]

No, the disturbing side of family values is often overlooked out of a longing for the more romantic notions of the Old South, both out of ignorance and because of purposeful neglect by those who should know better. Consider, for example, historian Eugene Genovese, who spent much of his career demonstrating the degradation of slavery and its deleterious effects on the black and white South. In 1974, he wrote how this "special sense of family [the authoritarianism of fathers over extended and subservient families] shaped southern culture. In its positive aspect, it brought white and black together and welded them into one people with genuine elements of affection and intimacy that may yet, as a black historian has prayerfully suggested, blossom into a wholesome new relationship. But in its overwhelmingly negative aspect—its arrogant doctrine of domination and its inherent cruelty toward disobedient 'children'—it pitted blacks against whites in bitter antagonism and simultaneously poisoned the life of the dominant white community itself."[5]

One has to wonder, then, what familial model Genovese thought he would find in the "southern tradition" when, some two decades later, he decried the modern "collapse of the family" and asked, "How do we recover a sense of national purpose and moral consensus while reinvigorating family and community autonomy?" Genovese did not answer that question, although he vaguely situated southern family and community in "a southern conservatism that has, from its origins, constituted America's most impressive native-born critique of our national development, of liberalism, and of the more disquieting features of the modern world." Unlike his work in his earlier scholarship, Genovese did not bother to examine the "disquieting features" of the southern tradition that he championed.[6]

Genovese's critique of American family values and his celebration of southern family values were neither original nor unique. Rather, the South has a long tradition of decrying modern family life and praising the "traditional" southern family. In the 1930s, for example, twelve writers formed the core of a conservative version of southern populism, and their works contributed to a revival of southern literature known as the Southern Renaissance. These Vanderbilt Agrarians praised the role of family as a conservator of communal order, linking the morality of southern ancestors—as constructed in thousands of agricultural households—to contemporary families living in an increasingly industrialized society. When combined with their claims for the importance of regional identity and connection to the land, the Agrarians' vision was one of familial and regional continuity despite generational change. Still, the Agrarians bemoaned that the "Southerner must know, and in fact he does very well know, that his antique conservatism does not exert a great influence against the American progressivist doctrine." Anticipating later social critics, the Agrarians posited that progressive liberalism corrupted and eroded southern families. Industrialism, individualism, urbanism, consumerism, competition, sexual liberation—all were (and seemingly remain, according to some critics) great liberal threats to the stability of family, community, region, and identity.[7]

Similarly, the Dixiecrats of the 1940s and 1950s were concerned with the disintegration of domestic order, particularly a vaguely defined "family" as the fundamental unit of the state. In opposing the elimination of segregation and the repeal of anti-miscegenation statutes, the Dixiecrats argued against the validity of interracial families, which were taboo for a variety of reasons ranging from blatant claims of white supremacy to more nuanced arguments about mixed-race relationships subverting the social order and making a mockery of the institution of marriage. Of course, the theoretical position of the Dixiecrats could not bear the weight of the sins of the southern past or even those of its own members. When faced with the exposure of his interracial daughter in 2003, South Carolina senator Strom Thurmond—who had campaigned as the Dixiecrats' presidential candidate in 1948—dismissed the incongruence between his public segregationist stances and his long-standing private relationship with his daughter as "Well, that's the way things have always been done."[8]

Southern social critics continue to refer to what Thurmond defended as "the way things have always been done" to criticize everything from family life to government policies. Consider the American Family Association, founded in Tupelo, Mississippi, in 1977 as "a Christian organization promoting the biblical ethic of decency in American society." In reaction to a 2005 *Newsweek* article on the closing of abortion clinics in Mississippi, the AFA denounced 1960s liberal politicians for expanding the welfare state to provide aid to single mothers and their families—what AFA writer Matt Friedeman called "compassion in the form of cash." The result, he asserted, was "more out-of-wedlock children, fewer dads in the home, and less work," as well as burgeoning crime rates, skyrocketing drug use, and rampant sexually transmitted diseases. According to the AFA, that old bugaboo, "liberal social compassion," destroyed Mississippi's society, families, and—in its embrace of abortion rights—children.[9]

Given the passion with which such critics have argued on behalf of Old South family values, one has to wonder exactly what they believe they have lost and why they choose to emphasize what they do. Writing in the 1970s, latter-day agrarian Wendell Berry imagined that we had lost the familial model of "a household welcoming to neighbors and friends . . . a marriage bond that would bind a woman and a man not only to each other, but to the community of marriage . . . [and] all living things and the fertility of the earth." Like the Agrarians, Berry and all who believe in the Agrarian Myth imagine family and morality as inseparable from agricultural economy and ecology. The Agrarians thought that the loss of traditional patterns of household economies meant that southern families and indeed the entire South had lost its moral footing. The Dixiecrats defined morality through racial lenses, interpreting the legal and economic privileges (and resulting psychological advantages) that southern whites enjoyed as requisite to the maintenance of southern culture and morality. They imagined southerners and all Americans as losing the familial model of the homogenous white family and the patriarchal family values that it represented. Without the explicit racism, this is the lynchpin to the AFA's denunciation of liberalism: that the weakening of patriarchy, facilitated by liberal government programs, has led to teen pregnancy, drug abuse, criminal violence, and the degradation of a southern state.[10]

Southerners are not alone in their nostalgic view of the past. Many American politicians and commentators have refused to deal with "the way we really are" and prefer "looking for someone to blame" instead of "working with what we've got," as Stephanie Coontz urges policymakers to do.[11] But the public commentary on family values arising from the South makes it abundantly evident that no one does utopian idealism or unrealistic nostalgia quite as well as southerners do. One of the region's most influential commentators, W. J. Cash, knew this well. In *The Mind of the South* (1941), Cash not only recognized southerners' "tendency toward unreality, toward romanticism, and, in intimate relation with that, toward hedonism." He also identified the mechanism by which southern idealism was perpetuated: "nothing is so certain as his [the southerner's] remarkable tendency to seize on lovely words, to roll them in his throat, to heap them in redundant profusion one upon another until meaning vanishes and there is nothing left but the sweet, canorous drunkenness of sound, nothing but the play of primitive rhythm upon the secret springs of emotion."[12] The southern rhetoric of family values throughout the twentieth century and into the twenty-first century is laden with the primitive and emotive impulses of romantic and pastoral idealism. Are the visions of family embraced by the Agrarians, Dixiecrats, the American Family Association, and even "Not Your Typical Southerner" rooted in the historical reality of the southern family, or are they products of what Cash dubbed Cloud-Cuckoo-Town? In imagining Old South families in an unrealistic and ahistorical fashion, do critics make it impossible for today's families to identify historically accurate "southern family values" and to recognize that the structures that created and supported so-called traditional family values—sexism, racism, and heterosexism—run counter to American values such as democracy, opportunity, and equality?

Family Values in the Old South is a collection of original essays by a diverse and innovative group of scholars, some of whom are steeped in family history and others who are just beginning to explore the field. Our collective goal is to uncover more about southern family life and values than we have previously known. The authors have been charged with raising new questions about how southerners conceptualized family from demographic structures, power relations, and gender roles to affective experience, economic significance, and the relationship of family to society. Most basically, these essays ask: what was the nature of family, and what values did it inspire in the Old South?

The first section of the collection offers articles exploring southerners' definitions of family. These essays take up important questions about household structure and power dynamics. In doing so, they remind us that change often happens in fits and starts. While there is near-universal agreement among scholars that antebellum southern families were "modern" insofar as they adopted the nuclear family ideal, families in the Old South remained "traditional" in their adherence to patriarchal authority. Moreover, since the authority of the planter-patriarch often extended over both his own (white) family and his enslaved (black) family, the plantation household was a peculiar amalgam of tradition and modernity, containing both a modern nuclear family characterized by affection and a traditional extended family governed by authority.

Clearly the nuclear family was an important ideal in the Old South. At a 1989 conference at Clemson University on "Women, Family, and Marriage in the Victorian South," for example, participants recognized patterns of extended kinship and slave dependency among their subjects. In general, however, they all assumed a nuclear structure to the families that they studied. Hence, their emphasis on "intimate family relationships" meant family relationships built around a conjugal unit, usually one containing and limited to a husband/father, wife/mother, and children. Most historians of southern family life continue to assume the importance of the nuclear family. This assumption has been most commonly applied to elite white planter families, but it has also been the underlying supposition when exploring white and black families across the Old South's socioeconomic spectrum. The prevalence or absence of the two-headed, co-resident, nuclear family has been especially significant in framing questions as to the purported "problems" of maternal authority and extended kinship among enslaved families.[13]

Alongside this general agreement on the importance of the nuclear family— a characteristic of "modern" family life—southern historians also point to the continued preeminence of the plantation patriarch. From the colonial era forward, elite southern men proudly proclaimed themselves the masters of all they surveyed. Family was the basic unit of the patriarch's world. As Virginian William Byrd II expressed it in 1726: "Like one of the [biblical] Patriarchs, I have my Flocks and my Herds, my Bond-men and Bond-women," as well as "a large Family of my own." Less wealthy individuals in the early national and antebellum South adopted a similar model. Casting themselves as "masters of small worlds," white landholding men of all ranks established their leadership on the basis of heading a household that did not distinguish between kin and non-kin. Among the southern elite, planter-politicians and proslavery writers celebrated the idea of "our family, white and black," under the supposedly benevolent guidance of the master.[14]

So powerful and pervasive are these images of planter-patriarchs and "our family, white and black," that many historians have argued that the conflation of household and family is what made families in the antebellum South different from those in the North. Retaining a "traditional" relationship between family and household, southerners situated the head of household—almost always a patriarch—as "not only the principal governor of the family but also its sole representative to the larger world beyond the household," as historical demographer Daniel Scott Smith phrased it.[15]

What, then, can the essays in this collection contribute to this confusing quagmire of "tradition" and "modernity"? As the authors in part 1 reveal, the modern ideal of the nuclear family was strong in the Old South, reverberating beyond marital, nuclear, and male-headed families to organize extended, augmented, and female-headed families as well. Still, circumstances either incidental or purposeful kept many southerners from replicating that ideal. High childhood mortality rates, the difficulties of pregnancy and labor, and short life expectancies made creating and maintaining nuclear families problematic. Even many apparently nuclear families were often stepfamilies wrought with their own complicated dynamics. In addition, the pervasive imagery of "our family, white and black"—a popular phrase that described the reality of black and white families coexisting within a slaveholding household while masking the harsh power dynamics of slavery—testified to the continued importance of "traditional" notions of patriarchal power alongside the antebellum elevation of a "modern" affectionate family.

The essays in part 1 demonstrate the range of responses southerners displayed toward their region's uneven transition from "traditional" to "modern" family life. The many types of families that southerners formed, while mimicking the nuclear structure to some degree, also negotiated the gender roles, power relationships, and compulsory heterosexuality implied in the patriarchal system. The southern family was not always father, mother, and children. It could be mother, mother, and many children; or woman, woman, and girls; or father, mother, and children under different roofs on different plantations. In examining these alternatives, these articles raise worthwhile questions: Beyond demographic structure and power relations, what contributed to defining family? What challenges faced families that were not nuclear in structure or patriarchal in governance? Why might such families have been perceived to threaten southern society and culture? What challenges faced families that were nuclear in structure or patriarchal in governance? How did society ensure the perpetuation of such families in times of crisis? How much space did a rigidly hierarchical society like that found in the Old South offer for individuals to create alternative types of families? Ultimately, what was the southern family?

Part 2 offers three articles exploring another aspect of family values: the economics of family life. Historians of the antebellum North generally concur that the shift from "traditional" to "modern" family life coincided with the linked processes of industrialization and urbanization and contributed to the rise of "separate spheres" for women and men, commonly referred to as "the home" and "the world." While a "cult of domesticity" granted women increased influence in the home, "self-made men" were released from domestic responsibilities to engage in marketplace competition. At the same time, the value of home and family came to be measured in terms of affect rather than economics. Rather than a locus of production, the home became a site of consumption for the comfort of its inhabitants. While money may have made "the world" go round, the home was celebrated as a "haven from a heartless world," where affection reigned supreme.[16]

In the Old South, however, agriculture remained the primary economic activity and kept the household bound to the family; as a result, home retained its economic importance as a place where men governed their domestic dependents and women contributed to the family economy through both productive and reproductive labor. In a 1986 survey of the state of family history, John Demos described the function of the pre-modern family, which he characterized as "a hive of instrumental activity: of production (e.g., the 'family farm'), of schooling, of worship, of medical practice, and of care for all sorts of 'dependents' (orphans, elderly people, the insane, even criminals)." In function, then, even if not in form, many antebellum southern families remained "traditional."[17]

As the contributors to part 2 demonstrate, however, the "traditional" economic value of southern households under patriarchal authority often ran counter to the value that "modern" families placed on affectionate relationships. Whether in the household production of cloth, the family enterprise of tavern keeping, or in the plantation business, domestic disorder could spell economic disaster—and both were indicative of a patriarch's failure to exert effective control. The articles included in this section raise interesting questions about the inner workings of southern families: How did economic values mesh with—or undermine—affective relationships? What challenges to the modern ideal of the nuclear family were raised by economic activity within the household? Why did families in the antebellum South continue to engage in household production? How did the persistence of the "traditional," economically oriented household shape the emergence of "modern," affective nuclear families? In short, what were families worth in the Old South?

The first two sections of this collection examine structure, power, and function in family life and examine the complicated relationship between the "traditional" household and the "modern" family. The articles in the collection's final section, however, move beyond both the boundaries of the family and the walls of the household to explore ways in which the family had broader cultural and social meanings. An intimate and influential relationship between family and society was not a new idea to antebellum southerners; indeed, the notion of the family as "a little commonwealth" prevailed in colonial America and shaped both northern and southern culture, although in vastly different ways. But as with so many other "traditional" aspects of family life, the cultural significance of the family carried particular weight in the Old South. As historian Elizabeth Fox-Genovese explained in a 1991 essay, "family figured as a central metaphor for southern society as a whole."[18]

But it was much more than a metaphor: family served as a microcosm of society, the essential building blocks upon which southern culture—including slavery—was founded. As secessionist firebrand Reverend Benjamin Morgan Palmer explained years after the demise of the slaveholding South, family was "the original society from which the State emerges, and the Church, and every other association known among men." While Palmer, like other proslavery authors, had in mind families headed by elite white men, as the last three contributors demonstrate, whether the historical actors were white, black, or Native American, family had important political and legal consequences in southern society.[19]

The articles in the final section raise thoughtful questions about the role of families in southern society: How did family, even in communities like those of the Creek Nation that were structurally different from the rest of the South, create economic and political significance through familial identity? How was kinship limited in demarcating familial identity and racial sovereignty? How, despite an emerging division between "public" and "private," was family a presence in society? At the most basic level, why did family matter in the Old South?[20]

Taken together, the essays in this collection suggest that however defined, southern families and family values were crucial in shaping the Old South. But have we lost core values of the sort that critics of modern families yearn to recover? The articles herein offer a variety of possibilities for readers to consider.

If there was a set of core values, *Family Values in the Old South* suggests that those values were rooted in the common experience of racial slavery. Slavery in the American South was a system of absolute power in which one race, and specifically the male gender of that race, ruled over another race. In proslavery discourse, patriarchal power emanated from the New Testament, which dictates, "Servants, be obedient to them that are your masters according to the flesh, with fear and trembling." While slavery became the justification for patriarchal dominance, such power was not limited to relations with slaves. "Wives, submit yourselves unto your own husbands" preceded the command to slaves in the book of Ephesians, extending the principle of racial and gendered hierarchy into the household and family.[21]

While slaves lived and worked in a minority of southern households, slavery was ubiquitous in the South, creating inordinate power for white men by emphasizing the need for control over slaves and, by extension, all dependents. John Demos has argued that early American families were shaped by "both a system of gender relations *and* a system of age relations. Power, status, and responsibility within the family are defined by the second no less that the first." Clearly, Demos did not take the South into consideration. In the South, race played an equally significant, and possibly more critical, role in defining power, status, and responsibility in households and families. The articles in all three sections, whether directly addressing slavery or not, attest to the constant pressure exerted on southern families by slavery's existence.[22]

Whether Old South families offer examples of appropriate family values is for each reader to decide. Our hope is that in offering *Family Values in the Old South* we can contribute to a vibrant dialogue about how our ancestors shaped their lives and their families and how their efforts created historical and moral precedents for us to use or dismiss.

Notes

1. Margaret Mitchell, *Gone with the Wind* (1936; reprint, Garden City, N.Y.: International Collectors Library, 1964), 54.

2. See esp. Stephanie Coontz, *The Way We Never Were: American Families and the Nostalgia Trap* (New York: Basic Books, 1992); Coontz, *The Way We Really Are: Coming to Terms with America's Changing Families* (New York: Basic Books, 1997); Coontz, ed., *American Families: A Multicultural Reader* (New York: Routledge, 1999); Coontz, *Marriage, a History: How Love Conquered Marriage* (New York: Viking, 2005); Nancy F. Cott, *Public Vows: A History of Marriage and the Nation* (Cambridge: Harvard University Press, 2000); Valerie Lehr, *Queer Family Values: Debunking the Myth of the Nuclear Family* (Philadelphia: Temple University Press, 1999); Michael J. Rosenfeld, *The Age of Independence: Interracial Unions, Same-Sex Unions, and the Changing American Family* (Cambridge: Harvard University Press, 2007), Judith Stacey, *In the Name of the Family: Rethinking Family Values in the Postmodern Age* (Boston: Beacon Press, 1999); Karen Struening, *New Family Values: Liberty, Equality, Diversity* (New York: Rowman and Littlefield, 2002).

3. Steven Mintz, "Does the American Family Have a History? Family Images and Realities," *OAH Magazine of History* 15 (summer 2001); Not Your Typical Southerner [pseudo.], post to City-Data.com discussion list, 9 April 2007, www.city-data.com/forum/alabama/2604—relocating-alabama-small-town-family-values-4.html. For more on southern values and attitudes vis-à-vis American ones, see John Shelton Reed, *The Enduring South: Subcultural Persistence in Mass Society* (Lexington, Mass.: Lexington Books, 1972); John Egerton, *The Americanization of Dixie: The Southernization of America* (New York: Harper's Magazine Press, 1974).

4. Lorri Glover, "The Myth of Better Times: America's Real Family Values," *Proceedings of Conference on Values in Higher Education*, Knoxville, Tenn., 16–18 April 1998, http://web.utk.edu/~unistudy/values/pres98.htm.

5. Eugene D. Genovese, *Roll, Jordan, Roll: The World the Slaves Made* (New York: Pantheon Books, 1974), 74.

6. Genovese, *The Southern Tradition: The Achievement and Limitations of an American Conservatism* (Cambridge: Harvard University Press, 1994), 1–2, 99–101.

7. Donald Davidson, "Still Rebels, Still Yankees," *American Review* 2 (November 1933): 58–72 and (December 1933): 175–88; John Ransom Crowe, "Reconstructed but Unregenerate," in Twelve Southerners, *I'll Take My Stand: The South and the Agrarian Tradition* (1930; reprint,

Baton Rouge: Louisiana State University Press, 1977), 1–27, quote on 3. For similar arguments by a latter-day Agrarian, see Wendell Berry, *The Unsettling of America: Culture and Agriculture* (San Francisco: Sierra Club Books, 1977), 97–142; Berry, "A Jonquil for Mary Penn," *Fidelity: Five Stories* (New York: Pantheon Books, 1992).

8. Platform of the States Rights Democratic Party, 14 August 1948; "Trent Lott's Wish List: Thinking About What the Nation Would Have Been Like under *President* Strom Thurmond," *Journal of Blacks in Higher Education* 42 (Winter 2003/2004): 24–26; Jon Meacham, "Southern Family Values," *Newsweek,* 29 December 2003, 25. As political scientist Julie Novkov has demonstrated, "To the extent that the law could successfully bar mixed-race sexual relationships, the state could maintain the color line and prevent the growth of a class of dissatisfied and rebellious mulattoes. Such mulattoes were a threat to whiteness, because they could be expected to challenge constantly both in their overt actions and in their very existence the permanent division between social and political equality that early interpretations of the Fourteenth Amendment had endorsed." See Julie Novkov, "Racial Constructions: The Legal Regulation of Miscegenation in Alabama, 1890–1934," *Law and History Review* 20 (Summer 2002): 225–78, quote on 276.

9. Matt Friedeman, "Saving the South by Killing Its Babies: Liberal Logic, Liberal Compassion," 2 February 2005, http://www.afa.net/church/GetArticle.asp?id=217.

10. Berry, *Unsettling of America*, 120; Cheryl Harris, "Whiteness as Property," *Harvard Law Review* 106 (June 1993): 1709–95.

11. Coontz, *The Way We Really Are,* chaps. 7 and 9.

12. W. J. Cash, *The Mind of the South* (1941; reprint, New York: Vintage Books, 1991), 44, 51.

13. Carol Bleser, ed., *In Joy and in Sorrow: Women, Family, and Marriage in the Victorian South, 1830–1900* (New York: Oxford University Press, 1991), xi. For the pervasiveness of historians' assumptions about the nuclear nature of southern families, see Joan Cashin, "The Structure of Antebellum Planter Families: 'The Ties that Bound us Was Strong,'" *Journal of Southern History* 56 (February 1990): 56n2. Also see Orville Vernon Burton, *In My Father's House Are Many Mansions: Family and Community in Edgefield, South Carolina* (Chapel Hill: University of North Carolina Press, 1985); Jane Turner Censer, *North Carolina Planters and Their Children, 1800–1860* (Baton Rouge: Louisiana State University Press, 1984); Daniel Blake Smith, *Inside the Great House: Planter Family Life in Eighteenth-Century Chesapeake Society* (Ithaca: Cornell University Press, 1980); Brenda Stevenson, *Life in Black and White: Family and Community in the Slave South* (New York: Oxford University Press, 1996); Catherine Clinton, *The Plantation Mistress: Woman's World in the Old South* (New York: Pantheon Books, 1982).

The most significant argument for the importance of the nuclear family ideal among black southerners is Herbert G. Gutman, *The Black Family in Slavery and Freedom, 1750–1925* (New York: Pantheon, 1970). While many historians have argued that blacks had great difficulty in meeting that ideal, few have questioned the ideal itself as the organizing model. See John W. Blassingame, *The Slave Community: Plantation Life in the Antebellum South* (New York: Oxford University Press, 1972); Genovese, *Roll, Jordon, Roll*; Charles Joyner, *Down by the Riverside: A South Carolina Slave Community* (Urbana: University of Illinois Press, 1984); Kenneth M. Stampp, *The Peculiar Institution: Slavery in the Ante-Bellum South* (New York: Vintage, 1956). For claims that the structure of the black family evolved abnormally (i.e., with a weakened patriarchy), see Daniel Patrick Moynihan, *The Negro Family in America: The Case for National*

Action (Washington, D.C.: Office of Policy Planning and Research, Department of Labor, 1965); see also Stanley M. Elkins, *Slavery: A Problem in American Institutional and Intellectual Life* (Chicago: University of Chicago Press, 1959); E. Franklin Frazier, *The Negro Family in the United States* (Chicago: University of Chicago Press, 1939); Steven Ruggles, "The Origins of African-American Family Structure," *American Sociological Review* 59 (February 1994): 136–51; Clair Robertson, "Africa into the Americas? Slavery and Woman, the Family, and the Gender Division of Labor," in *More than Chattel: Black Women and Slavery in the Americas*, ed. David Barry Gaspar and Darlene Clark Hine (Bloomington: Indiana University Press, 1996), 9–20; Jacqueline Jones, *Labor of Love, Labor of Sorrow: Black Women, Work, and the Family, from Slavery to the Present* (New York: Basic Books, 1985); Ann Patton Malone, *Sweet Chariot: Slave Family and Household Structure in Nineteenth-Century Louisiana* (Chapel Hill: University of North Carolina Press, 1992). Deborah Gray White, *Ar'n't I a Woman? Female Slaves in the Antebellum South* (1985; reprint, New York: W. W. Norton, 1999) is one of the few treatments to argue for a non-nuclear, non-male-headed family among slaves.

One of the few historians to recognize variations in black and white family structures has been Orville Vernon Burton, who described nuclear, nonnuclear (extended or augmented), and irregular families; see *In My Father's House Are Many Mansions*, esp. 109–10. Joan Cashin has demonstrated on several occasions southerners' difficulties in successfully forming nuclear families; see, for example, "Households, Kinfolk, and Absent Teenagers: The Demographic Transition in the Old South," *Journal of Family History* 25 (April 2000): 141–57; and *A Family Venture: Men and Women on the Southern Frontier* (New York: Oxford University Press, 1991).

14. William Byrd to Lord Orrey, 5 July 1726, in *Correspondence of the Three William Byrds of Westover, Virginia, 1684–1776*, ed. Marion Tinling, 2 vols. (Charlottesville: University Press of Virginia, 1977), 1:354–55; Stephanie McCurry, *Masters of Small Worlds: Yeoman Households, Gender Relations, and the Political Culture of the Antebellum South Carolina Low Country* (New York: Oxford University Press, 1995). For further explication of the contexts in which Byrd wrote, see David Hackett Fischer, *Albion's Seed: Four British Folkways in America* (New York: Oxford University Press, 1989), 274–332. For the primacy of patriarchy in scholarly depictions of the antebellum South, see Anne Firor Scott, *The Southern Lady: From Pedestal to Politics, 1830–1900* (Chicago: University of Chicago Press, 1970); Catherine Clinton, *The Plantation Mistress: Woman's World in the Old South* (New York: Pantheon Books, 1982); Steven M. Stowe, *Intimacy and Power in the Old South: Ritual in the Lives of the Planters* (Baltimore: Johns Hopkins University Press, 1987); Victoria E. Bynum, *Unruly Women: The Politics of Social and Sexual Control in the Old South* (Chapel Hill: University of North Carolina Press, 1992); Bertram Wyatt-Brown, *Southern Honor: Ethics and Behavior in the Old South* (New York: Oxford University Press, 1982); Kathleen M. Brown, *Good Wives, Nasty Wenches, and Anxious Patriarchs: Gender, Race, and Power in Colonial Virginia* (Chapel Hill: University of North Carolina Press, 1997); Mary Beth Norton, *Founding Mothers and Fathers: Gendered Power and the Forming of American Society* (New York: Vintage, 1997). On the perpetuation of social values that promoted the patriarchal order, see Steven M. Stowe, "The Rhetoric of Authority: The Making of Social Values in Planter Family Correspondence," *Journal of American History* 73 (March 1987): 916–33; Lorri Glover, *Southern Sons: Becoming Men in the New Nation* (Baltimore: Johns Hopkins University Press, 2007); Robert F. Pace, *Halls of Honor: College Men in the Old South* (Baton Rouge: Loui-

siana State University Press, 2004); Jon L. Wakelyn, "Antebellum College Life and the Relations between Fathers and Sons," in *The Web of Southern Social Relations: Women, Family, and Education*, ed. Walter J. Fraser Jr., R. Frank Saunders Jr., and Jon L. Wakelyn (Athens: University of Georgia Press, 1985), 107–26.

15. Daniel Scott Smith, "The Meanings of Family and Household: Change and Continuity in the Mirror of the American Census," *Population and Development Review* 18 (September 1992): 421–56, quotation on 430; David Herlihy, "Family," *American Historical Review* 96 (1991): 2–5; Carl N. Degler, *At Odds: Women and the Family in America from the Revolution to the Present* (New York: Oxford University Press, 1980), 8–9; Cashin, "The Structure of Antebellum Planter Families," 55–70; Peter W. Bardaglio, *Reconstructing the Household: Families, Sex, and the Law in the Nineteenth-Century South* (Chapel Hill: University of North Carolina Press, 1995); Bynum, *Unruly Women*.

16. On separate spheres, the cult of domesticity, and self-made men, see esp. Jeanne Boydston, *Home and Work: Housework, Wages, and the Ideology of Labor in the Early Republic* (New York, 1990); Nancy F. Cott, *The Bonds of Womanhood: "Woman's Sphere" in New England, 1780–1835* (New Haven: Yale University Press, 1977); Linda K. Kerber, "Separate Spheres, Female Worlds, Woman's Place: The Rhetoric of Women's History," *Journal of American History* 75 (June 1988): 9–39; and E. Anthony Rotundo, *American Manhood: Transformations in Masculinity from the Revolution to the Modern Era* (New York: Basic Books, 1993). The phrase "haven from a heartless world" comes from a historian cum cultural critic, Christopher Lasch, *Haven in a Heartless World: The Family Besieged* (New York: Basic Books, 1977).

17. John Demos, *Past, Present, and Personal: The Family and the Life Course in American History* (New York: Oxford University Press, 1986), 17; see also Elizabeth Fox-Genovese, *Within the Plantation Household: Black and White Women of the Old South* (Chapel Hill: University of North Carolina Press, 1989).

18. John Demos, *A Little Commonwealth: Family Life in Plymouth Colony* (New York: Oxford University Press, 1970); Mary Beth Norton, *Founding Mothers and Fathers: Gendered Power and the Forming of American Society* (New York: Random House, 1996); Elizabeth Fox-Genovese, "Family and Female Identity in the Antebellum South: Sarah Gayle and Her Family," in *In Joy and in Sorrow*, ed. Bleser, 19.

19. For elaborations on the connections between kinship, identity, and the political sphere, see Christopher J. Olsen, *Political Culture and Secession in Mississippi: Masculinity, Honor, and the Antiparty Tradition, 1830–1860* (New York: Oxford University Press, 2000); McCurry, *Masters of Small Worlds*; Bynum, *Unruly Women*; J. William Harris, *Plain Folk and Gentry in a Slave Society: White Liberty and Black Slavery in Augusta's Hinterlands* (Middletown, Conn.: Wesleyan University Press, 1985); Robert Kenzer, *Kinship and Neighborhood in a Southern Community: Orange County, North Carolina, 1849–1881* (Knoxville: University of Tennessee Press, 1987); Burton, *In My Father's House Are Many Mansions*. For connections with tribal sovereignty, see Claudio Saunt, *A New Order of Things: Property, Power, and the Transformation of the Creek Indians, 1733–1816* (New York: Cambridge University Press, 1999); Benjamin W. Griffith, *McIntosh and Weatherford, Creek Indian Leaders* (Tuscaloosa: University of Alabama Press, 1985); Gary E. Moulton, *John Ross, Cherokee Chief* (Athens: University of Georgia Press, 1978).

20. Benjamin Morgan Palmer, *The Family in Its Civil and Churchly Aspects* (Richmond, Va.:

Presbyterian Committee of Publication, 1876), 9–10. Also see Amy Murrell Taylor, *The Divided Family in Civil War America* (Chapel Hill: University of North Carolina Press, 2006); James Marten, "Fatherhood in the Confederacy: Southern Soldiers and Their Children," *Journal of Southern History* 63 (May 1997): 269–92; Elizabeth R. Varon, *We Mean to Be Counted: White Women and Politics in Antebellum Virginia* (Chapel Hill: University of North Carolina Press, 1998); Kirsten E. Wood, *Masterful Women: Slaveholding Widows from the American Revolution through the Civil War* (Chapel Hill: University of North Carolina Press, 2004).

21. Ephesians 5:22, 6:5; Eugene Genovese, "'Our Family, White and Black': Family and Household in the Southern Slaveholders' World View," in *In Joy and in Sorrow*, ed. Bleser, 69–87.

22. Demos, *Past, Present, and Personal*, 11.

I

Defining (and Defying)
Southern Family Values

∽

Many southern planters secretly fathered children with slave women. Kentucky's Richard Mentor Johnson, however, openly lived with Julia Chinn, one of his slaves, with whom he fathered two daughters, Adaline and Imogene. His nomination as Martin Van Buren's running mate in 1836 raised questions about his form of family: a common-law marriage to a mulatto slave. This political cartoon ridiculed Johnson's biracial family for defying American society's insistence on racial hierarchy even as it suggested another meaning for the popular proslavery phrase "our family, black and white."

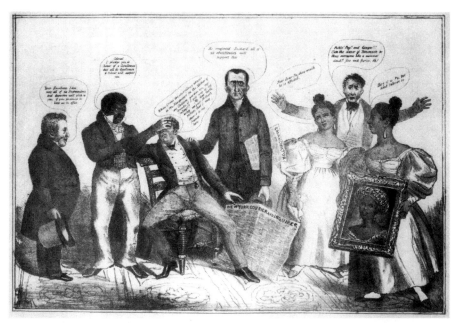

Fig. 1. "An Affecting Scene in Kentucky," 1836. Courtesy of Library of Congress, Washington, D.C.

1

"Every Thing but a Parent's Love"

Family Life in Orphan Asylums of the Lower Mississippi Valley

NANCY ZEY

∾

During the autumn of 1819, yellow fever struck Mississippi and Louisiana, killing thousands and sending countless others to the countryside fearing for their lives. The ravages of disease left a number of children homeless, among them William Gregory O'Neill, an infant from Adams County, Mississippi. Legally, the boy was the responsibility of the overseers of the poor, yet somehow he came into the protection of the Natchez Female Charitable Society. Founded a few years before the epidemic, this voluntary association of white, affluent, evangelical women had initially organized a charity school. However, the steady stream of needy boys and girls who survived the yellow fever prompted members to call for the creation of an orphan asylum, which was built shortly after the crisis.[1]

Years later, in April 1840, the officers of the Natchez Orphan Asylum convened their monthly meeting and "resolved that Gregory O'Neill be offered $10 a month and his board in compensation for services rendered, as he is now of age, and entitled to leave the institution." Very likely the William Gregory O'Neill from the yellow fever epidemic, the young man was now twenty-one, an extraordinarily mature age compared with the other orphans. The boys and girls in the asylum averaged between eight and nine, and when they reached age ten, the asylum usually placed them with local families as laborers. Sometimes the asylum expelled young males sooner for rebuffing female governance or causing other unpleasant distractions.[2] Gregory's situation, therefore, was unique. Most children in the asylum remained for a relatively short duration, though a number of them endured repeated stays when placements failed to work out or when impoverished parents found themselves once again unable to provide for their children. At the same time, O'Neill's extended stay at the orphanage raises intriguing questions about what it was like to grow up in an orphan asylum rather than in a single-family home.

In many ways, the Natchez Orphan Asylum, like other orphan asylums in the antebellum United States, functioned as what one historian has characterized as a "second home": a sometimes long-term but almost always temporary shelter for children whose parents had died or fallen on hard times. These shelters resembled large middle-class households, both in their outward appearances and their internal managements. To begin with, the "inmates" received room and board and schooling. Furthermore, the women who ran these residences strove to cultivate religious and moral principles through pious study as well as enforcement of strict discipline.[3] Despite the homelike qualities of orphan asylums, however, they have received only scant attention in discussions of southern households and families.[4] Could it be said that children who spent time in an asylum—whether two months, two years, or twenty years, like Gregory O'Neill—still experienced "family life" while there?

Families and orphanages have usually been considered by scholars as mutually exclusive entities—in other words, a child left a family upon entering an asylum. Moreover, asylum inhabitants, including staff and inmates, typically did not share natural or conjugal ties, ties that define the normative household. Because blood and marriage have dominated as criteria for what constituted a family, it is understandable that historians have tended to view orphanages within an institutional rather than a familial context.[5] Yet the founders of asylums saw more in those buildings than a motley and ever-changing crew of destitute boys and girls. "She will be required to instruct in all the common branches of education, to prepare and assist in the sewing for the family," wrote the managers of the Natchez Orphan Asylum when discussing the qualifications required of a new governess. "She will also be expected to attend to family worship." Down the Mississippi River in New Orleans, the ladies of the Poydras Female Orphan Asylum also cast their institution in domestic terms, declaring that "all the family, except the governess, must be in bed at half after nine o'clock." Such references were not peculiar to the early nineteenth century. Decades earlier, in 1740, evangelical minister George Whitefield built an orphanage in Savannah and frequently wrote of its occupants as his "family."[6] How people referred to themselves and others deserves careful consideration as we strive to make sense of the past. We must also examine how people acted. What about orphan asylums led them to be cast in familial terms?

While pauper apprenticeship had long been the principal method of child welfare, by the opening of the nineteenth century, affluent evangelical women led the way in promoting orphan asylums as a better form of relief for both the child and society. These benevolent women sought to create a refuge for the casualties of fractured households as well as a model abode, one that would rear boys and girls to be industrious, upstanding adults. Apprenticeship declined while institutional relief emerged as the preferred form of juvenile relief in the Lower Mississippi Valley, especially for white children.[7] A closer look at the origin and organization of orphan asylums expands our understanding of the southern household by revealing how they functioned as homes in every sense of the word—with parents, siblings, and a family life all their own.

The Ursuline convent in New Orleans is widely held to be the first orphanage in what is now the United States, and its founding was accidental. In 1727, a group of Ursuline nuns ventured from France to Louisiana to educate young females, but the sisters were soon caring full-time for a number of girls. A few years later, an Indian attack on the French settlement in nearby Natchez left more children homeless. The boys quickly found new families upon reaching New Orleans because male labor was particularly valuable on the frontier. Young females, however, were often seen more as burdens than assets. "The little girls whom none of the colonists wished to adopt have swelled the cherished troop of orphans that the nuns are rearing," reported a local priest at the time, adding that "there is not a single one of this saintly community who is not delighted to have crossed the seas, nor believes she can do greater good here than to keep the children in innocence, and to give the young French a polite, Christian education, since these are in danger of being hardly better reared than slaves." The same citizens who had declined to take the homeless girls gladly entrusted them to the Ursulines. By raising orphaned girls to be useful and respectable women—in a manner that befit their gender, race, and social station—the nuns contributed to the colony's growth and enhanced its prosperity.[8]

Ecclesiastical residential relief for young minors was the customary practice in Catholic communities, but throughout Protestant North America, the English civil system of apprenticeship had been the preferred form of child welfare since the earliest days of colonial settlement. In this patriarchal system, prominent men served as county overseers of the poor and bound out those destitute and orphaned children who were free and settled within the county. Through the terms of indenture, masters and mistresses became the legal guardians of pauper apprentices, giving them basic support, rudimentary education, and vocational training in exchange for labor. But ultimate authority for indigent minors rested in the hands of county officials. Upon discovering instances of juvenile neglect, they held the power to break familial bonds—both contractual and natural—and place minors with new guardians. Although southern Protestant men had founded a few "orphan houses" in the eighteenth century, such institutions remained rare until the early nineteenth century when associations of evangelical women began to gather poor minors into "orphan asylums."[9] Bolstered by the rising perception of mothers as the primary caretakers of small children and the growing belief in female charity as a moral and social duty, these women created not only a juvenile sanctuary but a new, matriarchal system of relief.[10]

Mirroring the Ursulines, evangelical benevolent women primarily assisted children of their own sex, as females seemed especially vulnerable. In 1817, a group of affluent Anglo-American women in New Orleans founded the Poydras Female Orphan Asylum while the Ursulines were still caring for orphans in their convent. However, the city council transferred all the children under the nuns' charge to the Poydras Asylum in 1824 on the grounds that the girls were better off with Protestant mothers. A few years earlier, the charitable women of Natchez had founded an orphan asylum that, unusual for such institutions, welcomed boys as well as girls. Whether in New Orleans or Natchez, benevolent women who formed juvenile residences acted as "civic mothers," asserting that poor white children were better off living in a central household under their management. These assertions met with some ridicule early on, but generally the public supported the notion that small children fared better when reared under a female hand.[11]

Although patriarchy prevailed in families of the antebellum South, evangelicalism and the ascendancy of motherhood empowered benevolent women to construct a separate matriarchal system to govern themselves, the adults in their employ, and the children in their care.[12] The formation of early female voluntary associations has been well chronicled by scholars, including the intricacies of their operations.[13] While disenfranchised and legally impotent, under the auspices of charity, women created a hierarchical administrative structure and held elections for officers. At the top was a panel of "directresses" who headed the enterprise, chairing meetings and issuing orders. A secretary kept minutes; a treasurer maintained an accurate account of donations and expenditures; and a rotating committee of managers sought out needy children, supervised the staff, and made regular inspections of the asylum. Decades before Progressive women launched a maternalist reform of American child welfare, civic mothers of the early republic impinged upon the authority of male officials and appropriated responsibility over certain minors in the community.[14]

The women who founded orphan asylums in the Lower Mississippi Valley had not set out to displace pauper apprenticeship. At first, they presented their charitable endeavors as supplements to the existing system, but soon benevolent women replaced county officials as the primary source of juvenile relief. To be sure, civic mothers cultivated this role for themselves by advocating female institutional care as a more effective and efficient means of rearing young white paupers than what the county had been providing. Openly decrying "the cheerless support allow'd by our laws," the women of Natchez established a civic household under their governance in 1821. Then in 1825, the Mississippi legislature granted asylum officers full rights of guardianship over resident minors, an extraordinary provision considering that mothers did not automatically possess such rights over their own children. Indeed, when founder Eliza Burling lost her husband, she became guardian over their four daughters only upon the consent of the orphans court, which also designated two gentlemen as joint custodians. The state showed greater willingness to give affluent white women authority over the children of the poor, as the managers of Poydras Asylum discovered. In 1819, the Louisiana legislature prohibited the removal of inmates by relatives without the governesses' permission or reimbursement for the care provided. The statute came about after a girl was snatched from the asylum by a woman claiming to be her guardian; in the ensuing effort to reclaim her, the officers realized the necessity of having "some legal hold on the objects of their institution" and eventually persuaded lawmakers of the same. On the whole, male officials seemed glad to hand over the bulk of juvenile relief work, but sometimes they bristled at this newfound female interference in public matters. "During the delay some of the city lawyers put it into the heads of the Directresses of the Poydras Female Orphan Asylum to pray the Court of Probates here to open the will and have it recorded," wrote one New Orleans gentleman to a judge in a nearby parish. He expressed great relief when the court denied their meddlesome request.[15]

In the family of the civic household, asylum officers served as collective head and viewed matriarchal authority as essential to shaping young inmates into moral, industrious adults. The officers of the Natchez Orphan Asylum controlled who entered and exited, and in some cases, they even superseded the traditional family patriarch. Early in 1838, for example, the asylum managers declared the father of William and John Gray "intemperate, and totaly [sic] unfit to have the children with him." On another occasion, they found Eliza James's father "not qualified to have the care of her." All three children remained in the asylum. In the early nineteenth century, the paterfamilias still held considerable sway over his "little commonwealth," but class could trump gender and limit his rule if benevolent women found the habits of indigent fathers inconsistent with their notion of proper child rearing.[16] By positioning themselves as matriarchs of poor white children, benevolent women in Natchez and New Orleans restructured the southern family.

This is not to say that civic mothers shunned male participation in their charitable efforts. Only women could join the societies that governed orphan asylums, but—in an interesting reversal of the South's patriarchal order—men were permitted or even encouraged to help in an auxiliary capacity. In fact, the women of the Poydras Asylum named their institution after planter and statesman Julien Poydras, whose donation of property made the asylum possible and whose annual gifts composed its primary support for several years. The women of Natchez did not similarly honor the local merchant, Samuel Postlethwaite, who contributed both lands and funds, yet they gratefully accepted the assistance that he and other philanthropic men bestowed.[17]

Though casting themselves as natural caretakers, civic mothers did not attend to the daily management of charity children. Instead, they devoted themselves to raising funds, making decisions, promulgating and enforcing regulations, and serving as liaisons between the institution and the public—in short, all the masculine tasks ordinarily undertaken by the (male) head of household. Meanwhile, the direct care of the inmates fell primarily to white women who labored out of necessity rather than from a spirit of charity. Some were widows with small children; others were spinsters. The Poydras Asylum officers once hired a married couple to run the orphanage, but "after *having tested the experiment* of having a gentleman at the head," they dropped it altogether. Four months was sufficient to convince them of "the propriety and necessity of returning to their original plan by placing the proper authority in the hands of a respectable Female."[18]

Although wages and orders placed matrons and housekeepers in a separate, subordinate class from managers and officers, the well-to-do women who ran orphan asylums hesitated to tend poor children themselves. So they hired individuals who would oversee "charitable objects" according to their vision of proper, matronly upbringing. The officers of the Poydras Asylum seemed especially pleased with Mary Clark, whom they considered "highly qualified for the situation." And what were those qualifications? According to the clergyman who recommended her, she was "well acquainted with housekeeping, with grooming and instructing the rising generation." Of still greater import, she had once served as a Sunday school mistress, taking charge of sixty children "to whom she admirably and affectionately explained the leading doctrine and duties of Religion."[19] Upon her engagement, Clark became responsible for around eighty girls and apparently excelled in her custodianship. Whether the children viewed her and other governesses as loving surrogate mothers remains a matter of speculation, but the prodigious size of the household suggests that firm discipline necessarily outweighed tender affection.

Publicly, asylum officers presented governesses in the best light, and they also crafted idealized images of the orphans. To convince patrons that they did not assist the offspring of the undeserving poor, the managers of the Natchez Orphan Asylum always portrayed their charges sympathetically—indeed, sometimes romantically. "There is nothing which would afford the widowed mother, without fortune or friends, more earthly consolation in her last moments, than the thought, that there existed a Society of her own sex, which would feed, clothe, protect, and educate her helpless children, after she had left them." No mention of drunken fathers, unreliable mothers, and ill-mannered brats appeared in this or other annual reports, yet as with any other home, orphan asylums were by no means immune to familial strife. For example, one "widowed mother" hired as a matron continually irked the officers with her spendthrift ways. The asylum managers also complained about the charity children. Eliza Ellison ran away, and Ann Barrow was "discharged from all further care" for refusing to do as she was told. An unnamed boy was "disobedient to orders given him." The officers even decreed that "Mrs. Benedict's children be excluded from all further care of the Society as ungovernable subjects," one of several indications in the records that the asylum served minors who were not true orphans, despite public professions to the contrary. But even when maternal authority ceased to affect certain inmates, asylum officers did not completely abandon them. Determining that Kennedy Ford had "arrived at an age when he seems no longer amenable to female control," the officers made arrangements to place him elsewhere.[20]

While males on the brink of adolescence seem to have been disproportionately disobedient to managers and matrons, they posed other, more serious problems, as hinted in the 1829 annual report of the Natchez Orphan Asylum. The officers announced that "for many reasons, which need not be detailed, it is their intention to appeal to the public for aid in erecting an additional building, for the residence of the orphan boys." Even childless citizens could imagine the inappropriate encounters that might arise from mixing girls and boys under the same roof. The house maintained a discreet separation, down to the divided privies out back, yet the officers sought to create a more controlled arrangement through the construction of a separate facility. By welcoming children of both sexes, the asylum extended the benefit of residential care to a greater pool of minors and more closely resembled normative households. However, the taboos that precluded physical intimacy among brothers and sisters did not constrain asylum siblings, who tended to be unrelated. Sibling groups appeared among the inmates, and sometimes the matrons had their own children with them, but family ties in the civic household were usually situational rather than natural. The Poydras Asylum eschewed the numerous problems attendant with mixed relief by focusing solely on girls, a path taken by most orphanages in the early republic.[21]

Despite variations, asylums in the Lower Mississippi Valley shared a common goal of improving the home life experience for poor white children. Under the old system of relief, apprentices could expect shelter, meals, and clothing along with basic education and vocational instruction. Mississippi law required masters and mistresses to furnish "a sufficiency of good and wholesome provisions," but the interpretation of that clause could vary widely. Although apprentices had the right to lodge complaints against their guardians, such occurrences were rare. For the most part, county officials stood back and let household heads determine how best to rear indigent wards. Benevolent women regarded this hands-off approach as deficient, even dangerous, for minors. After all, households were the primary site of learning. The kind of food, the condition of clothing, the organization of time—every quotidian aspect of home life instilled habits and expectations that would persist into adulthood. How could county officials guarantee that apprentices were being reared as virtuous citizens and pious Christians? How could they ensure that destitute boys and girls were not being exploited or abused? County officials could not, in the opinion of female charitable societies. Encouraged by the increasing belief that women were responsible for the moral and religious upbringing of the young, civic mothers therefore sought to gather poor children into a household of their making—a household whose physical structure and internal management would impart vital lessons for a new generation of laborers.[22]

Early on, it was difficult to distinguish orphan asylums from the refined habitations of the elite women who ran them. The original Poydras Asylum sat at the corner of Julian and St. Charles streets in the Faubourg Sainte Marie, the predominately Anglo-American suburb on the western edge of New Orleans, where many of the officers themselves lived. Those who sauntered through this elegant neighborhood would have been hard pressed to spot the asylum among the other houses, for it was a house. The eponymous patron donated his old abode early in 1817, and the managers filled it with orphaned girls. After years of boarding out girls and boys with various "matrons," the benevolent women of Natchez finally raised enough money to establish an orphan asylum in 1821. With the assistance of a local merchant and orphans court justice whose wife served as an asylum officer, the women bought the former town residence of a wealthy judge.[23]

Private homes could not long meet the needs of orphans. Benevolent women in New Orleans and Natchez soon designed new structures to accommodate their ever-increasing brood. Normally haphazard about their record keeping, the managers of the Natchez Asylum were especially thorough in noting construction details, and from them we can sketch a clear image of the place that children like Gregory O'Neill called home. Built in 1822, the new orphan asylum stood just outside the city on five acres of land enclosed by a tall cypress fence. The wood-frame house appeared neat inside and out, but a discerning eye would not have mistaken it for an affluent residence. Three levels high and four thousand feet square, the structure featured two stacks of chimneys, allowing a total of six fireplaces to heat the large building. The weatherboarded exterior was painted white, and the interior walls were covered with brown plaster. While commodious and clean, the asylum was not elegant; the officers made no mention of wallpaper, moldings, or other decorative accoutrements typical in the homes of the well-to-do. Furnishings were spare, and rooms served as chambers for study, work, and sleep. In short, the Natchez women designed the civic household not for display or entertainment but for comfort and instruction.[24]

From the painted gutters to the tongue-and-grooved floors to the washboards scattered about, each mundane characteristic of the asylum modeled the type of domestic environment the children should emulate as adults. Indeed, the whole house operated as an educative device, conditioning inmates to a humble yet respectable environment. Civic mothers eschewed opulent trappings due to the firm conviction, common among the elite, that the laboring classes were better off remaining in their station. Improving the material surroundings of poor children was humane, but encouraging them toward consumption on the level of their patrons' sons and daughters subverted the social order and rendered everyone miserable as a result.[25] Hence inmates lived comfortably but not luxuriously, even with respect to meals. "Conceiving a proper attention to the fare of their charge, as a part of their duty," the officers of the Poydras Asylum itemized all the food to be served there:

Bill of Fare

Breakfast
coffee with milk—wheat bread or corn bread and butter

Dinner
Sunday
roast meat—vegetables—bread
Monday, Wednesday, Saturday
soup, boiled meat—hominy or rice
Tuesday, Thursday
gumbo—meat—rice or hominy—boiled or baked pudding
Friday
fish—potatoes

Supper
Sunday, Wednesday
tea—bread and butter
Monday, Tuesday, Thursday, Friday, Saturday
mush or rice with molasses[26]

Meals were ample, nutritious, and plain. No cakes or other delicacies appeared on the bill of fare, although inmates received a comparatively sumptuous dinner after church on Sundays. And while most of the weekly menu seems to have been standard American victuals, local dishes like "gumbo" also appeared. We do not know what utensils the children used or where they sat while eating, but asylum managers generally demanded that matrons maintain decorum at meal-times, including the saying of grace.[27]

Apart from the house, the children's clothing was perhaps the most obvious manifestation of sound domestic management. Pauper apprentices could expect only one new suit, and it came as "freedom dues" at the expiration of their term of service. By contrast, orphan asylum managers continually supplied their charges with newly fashioned garments to maintain a tidy appearance—no small feat given that most inmates fell between ages six and twelve and quickly outgrew their clothes. Furthermore, the officers wanted each child to have at least two different outfits: one for daily wear and another for Sundays. Christ may have embraced the beggar, but civic mothers refused to send orphans to church in anything less than their Sunday best.[28] In fact, the Natchez Asylum officers began sending inmates to divine services only when they could be "neatly clad in a suitable dress all of one colour." Evidence suggests that the color may have been blue, the traditional color of charity.[29] In England, charity children had worn blue for centuries, and the officers of the Boston Female Asylum, the first established by Protestant women in the United States, followed suit by clothing their orphans in blue uniforms.[30] The color signaled the children as under the "protection" of benevolent women and also may have aroused sympathy, for blue-clad boys and girls reminded affluent citizens of their duty to help the poor and the fatherless.[31] Moreover, plain uniforms cost less to make than individualized outfits. Patrons and prospective donors could therefore see that asylum officers spent funds economically and steered charity children away from the material excess that ruined families of all classes.

While officers prepared many garments themselves, the task mainly fell to the matrons and female inmates. Even though county courts regularly apprenticed boys as tailors, shoemakers, and hatters, the managers of the Natchez Orphan Asylum relegated sewing to the girls. According to the schedule, all inmates devoted the mornings to reading, writing, spelling, and basic arithmetic, and then the girls spent the afternoon on that most feminine of accomplishments. By plying the needle, they met an immediate need as well as developed an employable skill. The girls probably also assisted with cooking and cleaning in order to learn housekeeping, the other occupation benevolent women thought fitting for their social station. Although the records do not specify how male children in the Natchez Asylum spent their afternoons, they likely engaged in "masculine" work: tending the garden, feeding livestock, chopping wood, fetching water, cleaning gutters, and countless other heavy chores required of a large household. Indeed, the absence of boys caused problems for the Poydras Asylum. Restricting girls to activities that befit their gender necessitated hired hands for the more rigorous tasks. The arrangement worked only as long as hands were available. "The Managers regret the unproductive state of the garden during the last year," wrote the officers in their 1823 annual report. "The great difficulty of procuring labourers on advantageous terms will oblige them to reduce the plan of cultivation to a sufficiency of vegetables for the supply of the Establishment." Boys sometimes outnumbered the girls in Natchez Orphan Asylum, thus leading to an occasional surfeit of labor. One boy worked outside the orphanage for a while, thus raising additional income for the institution.[32]

Civic mothers strove to set poor children on trajectories they considered appropriate to class as well as gender. Compared with the sons and daughters of the wealthy, asylum inmates enjoyed little leisure or idleness. Instead, officers filled their days with lessons, work, and pious study to cultivate good moral habits and inure them to a lifetime of industry.[33] Residential care largely supplanted pauper apprenticeship for white minors in the Lower Mississippi Valley, yet asylum managers incorporated their own form of binding out in this new system of relief. Above all, women strove to ensure that prospective homes corresponded with their concept of proper family life for charity children. Ten-year-old Olivia Wrice was among the first to be placed out by the Natchez Orphan Asylum. Officers drew up articles of agreement with Mr. and Mrs. Alfred Green, who promised to give the girl "a good plain education, clothe her genteelly, and instill into her mind moral and religious principles." They also pledged to allow her regular attendance at church and Sunday school and to teach her "those useful acquirements which will enable her to get an honest living." In short, the Greens agreed to rear Olivia as she had been in the asylum. Two months later Olivia appeared once again in the asylum's roster, the meticulous arrangement for some reason having failed to work out. Benevolent women did not hesitate to exert their matriarchal prerogative, especially when a potential destination appeared unsuitable for inmates. After examining one residence, the officers decided that they did "not approve of placing the girls from the asylum in a boarding house." They also refused to send a man his own children, for he lived in the poorhouse located just outside town. Finding it "manifestly an improper home," the managers determined that "they shall remain in the Asylum." The women shunned promiscuous places where males and females cohabited with scant supervision, sometimes with insidious consequences.[34] Reluctant to remove poor boys and girls from the sanctuary of the civic household only to plunge them into dire straits, officers released charity children only upon finding comparable or superior family environments.

In the early nineteenth century, the home—first the father's, then the husband's—was woman's sphere. Nonetheless, even in the South, women managed to carve a public presence. Women who established orphan asylums created a separate domestic environment under their control, a radical child welfare innovation that passed muster largely because many viewed the civic household as a natural extension of the female milieu. Nevertheless, benevolent women did not take public support for granted. The Poydras Asylum managers downplayed their intrusion into the civil system of juvenile relief through the language of female modesty. "They were asked for their aid in the name of the orphan," stated the first annual report. "That sacred name went straight to the heart; they gave their mite . . . to the relief of those who had no natural earthly guardian." Quietly omitting county officials as a source of assistance, the ladies attributed the asylum's founding not to their own initiative but to the heart-melting appeals of desperate, faceless others. Like their counterparts in New

Orleans, the women of Natchez took care to deflect attention from the public (read masculine) nature of their charitable enterprise by emphasizing the maternal aspects of their work: "to confer the benefit of moral and religious instruction—to arrest profligacy, cherish virtue, strengthen the feeble, as well as to bestow the tender guardianship of a parent on the bereaved orphan." The tender guardianship of a mother is what orphan asylums in Louisiana and Mississippi offered in the early nineteenth century, and the women who ran them continually stressed that their charitable work stood well within the female sphere. Indeed, the ladies implied that the establishment of a civic household strengthened southern womanhood and manhood by rearing poor white children more conscientiously according to prevailing expectations of their gender, their class, and their race.[35]

That one Poydras Asylum inmate returned for her wedding suggests that this novel domestic arrangement succeeded in instilling "proper" virtues. An orphaned female of the laboring classes could have easily slipped into a life of prostitution, but the managers had guided her toward self-sufficiency through more respectable means. Marriage to a white carpenter enhanced her respectability as well as her future prospects. Although weddings frequently took place in orphan asylums, the institution's officers would not have hosted the nuptials of their former charge unless they approved of her choices. They may have viewed the event as an opportunity for instruction, as the excitement of a wedding could further impress upon current inmates the happy outcome of good behavior and dutiful compliance with the officers' directives. Unfortunately, we have no evidence from the girl herself. As is usually the case with the poor—and also with children—this incident survives only because someone else made note of it. Children in particular rarely left behind written records. When they did, their words were almost always filtered, sometimes through their own adulthood.[36]

Such was the case in 1827, when the editor of a Natchez newspaper printed an advertisement from a former inhabitant of the orphan asylum there. In a previous notice, the same editor had attempted to drum up financial support by referring to pitiful waifs at the "Female Orphan Asylum," a name which inspired greater pathos despite its inaccuracy. Because the former inmate making this announcement was male, he had to explain that the managers accepted "such orphans of the other sex under their protection as they may deem worthy." Clearly, the editor was not above spinning a little yarn to help raise funds for the institution, but it seems unlikely that he would have entirely fabricated the following story:

A Lost Son. PHILANDER BOYCE was brought from Kentucky, as he believes, to Natchez about 14 years ago, being then about 4 years old. He knows nothing of his father who brought him here but that his name was *John Boyce*, or of his mother but that her name was *Mary*, and she was living when he was taken from her; and had no other child living.

Philander, snatched from his affectionate mother in tender infancy, owes lasting obligation, to the Female Orphan Asylum, which for many years afforded him every thing but a parent's love.

He has now arrived at manhood, and he would gladly return to alleviate the cares and comfort the declining years of his mother, if she be living. Should she see this, or should it meet the eye of a relation or of a remaining friend of the family, and would she or they communicate the place of their residence to him, or to the Editor of the *Ariel*, Natchez, it will be met with inexpressible joy; and Philander, poor as he is, will travel to any part of the United States to meet them.

The Editors of the Newspapers in Kentucky will please to copy this.[37]

Supposing for a moment that this account contains more truth than fiction, it offers a glimpse into the perspective of an orphan looking back on his childhood and his multiple families. His first home was in Kentucky, where he was part of a "typical" nuclear household of a father, mother, and at least one living child. Then, at around four years of age, Philander and his father became a separate household, relocating to the bustling port community of Natchez, Mississippi. Judging by the asylum records, the boy entered the care of civic mothers when he was about eight years old. Now at age eighteen, he currently resided with a local gentleman (according to the editor) and sought to form a new household with his long-lost natural mother.[38]

Through these brief details about his life, Philander offers glimpses of his sentiments toward his several households. John Boyce was the household patriarch as well as his legal guardian, yet Philander describes his mother as the rightful parent, especially given his "tender infancy." Having left Kentucky at such an early age, he probably barely remembered Mary Boyce. It could have been that she was the real villain in the story and that her husband "snatched" away their son in order to protect him. Regardless of what actually happened, the impulse to reunite with his natural mother was so strong that Philander seemed willing to endure considerable hardship to achieve it. Of course, prolonged interactions with matrons and female managers may have shaped the favorable impression of his mother at the expense of his father.

Benevolent women did not always have the same favorable impression of Philander. Institutional records show that the Natchez officers enrolled him in a local school in 1818, but even after two years of instruction, one manager reported that Philander was "very backward" in his studies. In November 1820, the officers placed Philander, then around ten years of age, with a local silversmith and repairer of clocks and watches, presumably to learn his trade. How long he remained in this new household is impossible to determine, for he disappeared from the records. He may have been like Olivia Wrice, one of many charity children who found themselves back in the asylum. However long Philander Boyce resided in the "Female Orphan Asylum," the newspaper editor characterized him as "interesting evidence" of the institution's usefulness to this child and to the community at large. Though reared for long stretches of time by a group of women while he was an "infant," Philander now proclaimed himself as "arrived at manhood" and ready to assume the duties of a man. In particular, he sought to return the familial dynamic to its traditional form and become the provider for females, rather than their ward. His attempt to find his mother after so many years' separation demonstrated that benevolent women had cultivated a strong sense of filial duty in this "lost son" as well as manly virtues.[39]

In his reference to the orphan asylum, Philander proclaimed that he had received there everything he needed—except "a parent's love." Assuming this was not the editor's fabrication but Philander's own statement, he probably did not intend to slight his former caretakers. Indeed, benevolent women shared the view that surrogate families could not provide children everything, for some relationships had no substitute. Asylum managers were not alone in advancing the notion that children belonged with their natural parents, particularly their mothers. Philander Boyce implies this in his account. So strongly did he desire a natural maternal connection that he was willing to abandon the community of his upbringing and spare no expense in the attempt to reunite with the mother he had never known.

This story serves as a potent reminder that "family" is no static entity. Households were formed—and reformed—several, sometimes many, times over the course of a person's life. The dangers and vicissitudes of the frontier South, especially in port communities like Natchez and New Orleans, only increased domestic volatility. While Philander Boyce may not have regarded the orphan asylum as his "true" home, he professed greater affection for it than the household of his own father. To discount the years Philander spent with benevolent women simply for the lack of conjugal or natural ties, or because terms like *asylum* and *institution* sound anything but homelike, is to discount one of this young man's family lives.

Over the course of the nineteenth century, orphanages would acquire the unsavory reputation that compelled a new generation of reformers to seek child welfare alternatives. Nevertheless, the women who founded orphan asylums in the early republic saw themselves as innovators and endeavored first and foremost to create homes for distressed white children. For most inmates, the civic household was a temporary abode and thus easier to overlook in considerations of "the southern family." But for those like Gregory O'Neill, who spent his entire childhood in an orphan asylum, it seems absurd to conclude that asylum life deprived him of family life altogether. Stretching the traditional definition of "family" to include the childhood experiences of Gregory, Philander, and their fellow inmates enriches our understanding of southern households and complicates the picture of antebellum southern family life.[40]

In particular, a close look at orphan asylums in the antebellum South offers an instructive alternative to southern patriarchy within the plantation household. With officers as matriarchs, governesses as mothers, and inmates as children, the power dynamics in the asylum hierarchy both reflected and inverted the normative nineteenth-century southern family governed by a planter-patriarch. At the same time, the southern orphanage served as an alternative family, providing food, clothing, shelter, discipline, and instruction—in short, "every thing but a parent's love"—to its residents. In civic households in southern cities, benevolent women shaped a new domestic order based on female control and a shared residence rather than on patriarchal power and ties of blood and marriage.

Notes

1. One contemporary mortality record numbered the deaths in New Orleans alone at three thousand. *American Medical Recorder* 3 (January 1820): 135. A Natchez resident reported to the Academy of Medicine in Philadelphia that "the summer and autumn of 1819 were the most sickly ever known in this country." A. Perlee, "An Account of the Yellow Fever in Natchez," *Philadelphia Journal of the Medical and Physical Sciences* 3 (1821): 7. While the precise date the infant was received by the asylum is not recorded, it was probably between 20 December 1819 and 6 March 1820 given the location of the reference to him in Minutebook I (1816–22), Natchez Children's Home Records, Center for American History, University of Texas at Austin. First adopted when Mississippi was a territory, Chapter 36: "A Law Pertaining to the Binding of Apprentices" outlined the procedure for relieving all destitute minors; reprinted in P. L. Rainwater, comp., "Sargent's Code," *American Journal of Legal History* 11 (July 1967): 312–13. The story of the organization of the Natchez Female Charitable Society and its transformation into the Female Orphan Asylum is the subject of my dissertation, "Rescuing Some Youthful Minds: Benevolent Women and the Rise of the Orphan Asylum as Civic Household in Early Republic Natchez" (University of Texas at Austin, 2007).

2. See 1 April 1840, Minutebook III (1835–40), Natchez Children's Home Records. Unfortunately, Minutebook II has long been missing. Among thirteen instances when children and their ages are specified, the average age was 8.5 years. Data compiled from Minutebook I, Natchez Children's Home Records. Daniel Griffin and Philander Boyce were placed out at age ten, as was Olivia Wrice, whose case will be discussed in more detail later with cases of boys expelled from the asylum; see entries for 6 November 1820 and 14 May 1822, Minutebook I, Natchez Children's Home Records.

3. Thomas Hacsi writes that "orphan asylums were touted by their managers as 'homes,' and probably did succeed in being more 'homelike' than other institutions, such as insane asylums, whose managers made similar claims. However, most failed to be homes to their children in the most positive senses of the word." Thomas A. Hacsi, *Second Home: Orphan Asylums and Poor Families in America* (Cambridge, Mass.: Harvard University Press, 1997), 2. His is the most recent comprehensive work on the history of American orphanages, although he devotes relatively brief attention to their origins. Much of his information regarding their early development is drawn from Homer Folks, *The Care of Destitute, Neglected, and Delinquent Children* (New York: Macmillan, 1902), which contains one of the first general histories of orphan asylums in the United States. David Rothman broke new ground in examining early institutional care by itself, and his *Discovery of the Asylum: Social Order and Disorder in the New Republic* (Boston: Little, Brown, 1971) remains a seminal work.

4. Peter W. Bardaglio briefly discusses orphan asylums not as households unto themselves but as impersonal entities with the "authority to intervene in family life," in *Reconstructing the Household: Families, Sex, and the Law in the Nineteenth-Century South* (Chapel Hill: University of North Carolina Press, 1992), 159.

5. "An increasing percentage of the children who entered orphan asylums had families to which they could hope to return, and most asylum children did in fact rejoin their families after being institutionalized for a few years": Hacsi, *Second Home*, 1. Hacsi is by no means alone in regarding asylums and families as two separate entities. In one of the most influential works on the subject, Peter Laslett categorized "persons not evidently related" but living under the same roof as "no family": *Household and Family in Past Time: Comparative Studies in the Size and Structure of the Domestic Group over the Last Three Centuries in England, France, Serbia, Japan, and Colonial North America, with Further Materials from Western Europe* (New York: Cambridge University Press, 1972), 31. Laslett went on to say that "a concept is needed to cover the relationships between such people" and that "such a concept must be of a neutral or even of a suspensive character" (35). Other scholars have moved toward the more inclusive concept of "households" to allow for the consideration of non-relatives while still focusing their study on "homes" rather than "institutions." For example, see Tamara K. Hareven, *Families, History, and Social Change: Life-Course and Cross-Cultural Perspectives* (Boulder, Colo.: Westview Press, 2000), and Carole Shammas, *A History of Household Government in America* (Charlottesville: University of Virginia Press, 2004). A leading historian of early American families, John Demos likewise defined them almost entirely as individuals bound by natural and conjugal ties; see *A Little Commonwealth: Family Life in Plymouth Colony* (New York: Oxford University Press, 1970), as well as the essay "Digging Up Family History: Myths, Realities, and Works-in-Progress," in John Demos, *Past, Present, and Personal: The Family and Life Course in American History* (New York: Oxford University Press, 1986), 3–23.

6. See 14 February 1838, Minutebook III, Natchez Children's Home Records; 22 February 1817, Minutebook, Poydras Home Collection, Manuscripts Department, Tulane University, New Orleans; George Whitefield, *An Account of the Money Received and Disbursed for the Orphan-House in Georgia* (London: W. Strahan, 1741), 3, 4; as well as his *A Further Account with God's Dealings with the Reverend Mr. George Whitefield . . . to Which Is Annex'd a Brief Account of the Rise, Progress, and Present Situation of the Orphan-House in Georgia* (London: W. Strahan, 1747), 32, 33.

7. In New Orleans, at least ten orphan asylums emerged in the decades after the founding of the Poydras Female Orphan Asylum; only one is listed for "colored" children. See Emma C. Richey and Evelina P. Kean, *The New Orleans Book* (New Orleans: L. Graham, 1915), 104–6. At the same time, the number of minors bound out as apprentices declined, reflecting the increasingly important role that residential care assumed during the nineteenth century. For an analysis of New Orleans apprenticeship indentures, see Paul Lachance, "Index to New Orleans Indentures, 1809–1843," New Orleans Public Library, www.nutrias.org/~nopl/inv/indentures/ ind-intr.htm#resource. Apprenticeship as child welfare also declined in Natchez, which saw two additional orphanages in the nineteenth century: one for Catholic boys and another for Catholic girls. D. Clayton James, *Antebellum Natchez* (Baton Rouge: Louisiana State University Press, 1968). For a detailed analysis of the emergence of institutional relief as the dominant form of child welfare in Natchez, see Nancy Zey, "'Rescuing Some Youthful Minds.'" David Rothman argues that the colonial almshouse, a precursor to the nineteenth-century orphan asylum, followed a family model both in physical setting and domestic governance, though he also seems to regard residential juvenile institutions as separate and apart from families. *The Discovery of the Asylum*, 41–43.

8. Mathurin Le Petit, *The Natchez Massacre*, trans. Richard H. Hart (New Orleans: Poor Rich Press, 1950), 30. Homer Folks was one of the earliest scholars to make this claim, in *The Care of Destitute, Neglected, and Delinquent Children*, 9. Despite its age, this work continues to serve as a key secondary text on the historiography of early orphan asylums. On the significance of female education to the French colonial project, see Clark Robenstine, "French Colonial Policy and the Education of Women and Minorities: Louisiana in the Early Eighteenth Century," *History of Education Quarterly* 32 (summer 1992): 193–211.

9. Daniel C. Vogt, "Poor Relief in Frontier Mississippi, 1798–1832," *Journal of Mississippi History* 51 (August 1989): 181. On poor relief in the antebellum South as well as early "orphan houses," see Barbara L. Bellows, *Benevolence among Slaveholders: Assisting the Poor in Charleston, 1670–1860* (Baton Rouge: Louisiana State University Press, 1993); and Edward J. Cashin, *Beloved Bethesda: A History of George Whitefield's Home for Boys, 1740–2000* (Macon, Ga.: Mercer University Press, 2001). For a more focused discussion on the pauper apprenticeship system, see Karin L. Zipf, *Labor of Innocents: Forced Apprenticeship in North Carolina, 1715–1919* (Baton Rouge: Louisiana State University Press, 2005). An example of child confiscation by county officials took place in Adams County in 1819. Orphans court justices bound out the children of Elisha Crosby, "a pauper," because he was determined to be "unfit to take care of or bring up his children." Orphans Court Minutebook II (February 1815 to January 1820), 232, Adams County Courthouse, Natchez, Miss.

10. Hacsi, *Second Home*, 17–20. For more on changing perceptions and self-perceptions of

southern women's place in the home and society, see Cynthia A. Kierner, *Beyond the Household: Women's Place in the Early South, 1700–1835* (Ithaca: Cornell University Press, 1998). Though looking at a narrower slice of time, Anya Jabour also examines the importance of charity work to Southern womanhood in *Scarlett's Sisters: Young Women in the Old South* (Chapel Hill: University of North Carolina Press, 2007). On early republic female benevolence and women's roles in founding orphan asylums at the turn of the nineteenth century, see Anne M. Boylan, *The Origins of Women's Activism: New York and Boston, 1797–1840* (Chapel Hill: University of North Carolina Press, 2002).

11. Emily Clark, *Masterless Mistresses: The New Orleans Ursulines and the Development of a New World Society, 1727–1834* (Chapel Hill: University of North Carolina Press, 2007), chap. 7. Female charitable societies widely reported receiving public criticism for their ventures. In their 1818 annual report, for example, the officers of the Poydras Asylum stated that "amidst many discouraging circumstances, these ladies still proceeded; the voice of ridicule, which frequently assailed them, was unheeded; they pressed on with a firm step in the path of duty": 16 January 1818, Minutebook I, Poydras Home Collection.

12. Peter W. Bardaglio argued that the persistence of slavery fortified the traditional patriarchal familial order and strengthened the power of fathers, husbands, and masters over their subordinates, a power that the judiciary and southern state legislatures upheld; see *Reconstructing the Household*. Joan E. Cashin echoed this view while noting that the relative isolation of frontier southerners rendered wives and daughters all the more dependent on male guidance and governance: *A Family Venture: Men and Women on the Southern Frontier* (New York: Oxford University Press, 1991). However, as Blair A. Pogue contended, Southern evangelical women carved a certain degree of public authority for themselves under the auspices of organized religion. See Pogue, "'I Cannot Believe the Gospel That Is So Much Preached': Gender, Belief, and Discipline in Baptist Religious Culture," in Craig Thompson Friend, ed., *The Buzzel about Kentuck: Settling the Promised Land* (Lexington: University Press of Kentucky, 1999). Linda K. Kerber coined the term "Republican Mothers," which has been widely adopted, but early American women are almost never described as "matriarchs" by historians. I do not aim here to establish "matriarchy" as the preferred analytical construct for elite females in early America but instead to point out how some women, through organized benevolence, placed themselves at the top of a hierarchal system of governance in the name of charity.

13. Nancy Cott's *The Bonds of Womanhood: "Woman's Sphere" in New England, 1780–1835*, 2nd ed. (1977; New Haven: Yale University Press, 1997) was one of the earliest works to consider female benevolence in the early republic. In a similar vein, Linda K. Kerber looks at benevolent societies within a broader study of female domesticity in *Women of the Republic: Intellect and Ideology in Revolutionary America* (1980; reprint, New York: W. W. Norton, 1986). For works that focus entirely on early women's organized benevolence, see Lori D. Ginzberg, *Women and the Work of Benevolence: Morality, Politics, and Class in the Nineteenth-Century United States* (New Haven: Yale University Press, 1990); Anne Firor Scott, *Natural Allies: Women's Associations in American History* (Urbana: University of Illinois Press, 1991); Boylan, *The Origins of Women's Activism*.

14. From the beginning, the Poydras Asylum called those in the highest office "directresses," whereas the Natchez society initially had a "president." All organizational details can be found

in the associations' constitutions. See Minutebook I, Natchez Children's Home Records; Administrative Papers, Poydras Home Collection. See Judith N. McArthur, *Creating the New Woman: The Rise of Southern Women's Progressive Culture in Texas, 1893–1918* (Urbana: University of Illinois Press, 1998); Molly Ladd-Taylor, *Mother-Work: Women, Child Welfare, and the State, 1890–1930* (Urbana: University of Illinois Press, 1994).

15. Annual report, 6 March 1820, Minutebook I, Natchez Children's Home Records; *Laws of the State of Mississippi, Passed at the Eighth Session of the General Assembly, held in the Town of Jackson* (Jackson, Miss.: Silas Brown, 1825), 88. Elizabeth Burling's guardianship appointment appears in the entry for 31 October 1812, Orphan's Court Minutebook I (April 1803 to January 1815), 262, Adams County Courthouse; *Acts Passed at the First Session of the Fourth Legislature of the State of Louisiana . . .* (New Orleans: J. C. de St. Romes, 1819), 78. Details of the snatching of a girl by someone not her guardian appeared in entries for 15 and 22 March and 15 April 1817, Minutebook I, Poydras Home Collection; John [ill.] to Peter Dormenson, 17 July 1824, Natchez Trace Collection, Center for American History.

16. Both references appear for the entry on 28 February 1838, Minutebook III, Natchez Children's Home Records. On this characterization of the early American family, see Demos, *A Little Commonwealth*.

17. This exclusion was consistent with polite notions of propriety, but it also served a practical function. If men were members, the ladies would necessarily have to defer to them. By keeping the organization entirely female, they could govern themselves far more freely. Julien Poydras is mentioned repeatedly from the asylum's founding in 1817 until his death in 1824; see Minutebook I, Poydras Home Collection. Samuel Postlethwaite gave a plot of land in town and sold the officers, at a greatly reduced price, a house to move there. His wife, Ann Dunbar Postlethwaite, was a society member and later served as first directress; see 4 June 1821, Minutebook I, Natchez Children's Home Records.

18. See 7 October 1829, Minutebook II, Poydras Home Records. The idea of hiring a married couple to superintend the asylum was mentioned in the entry for 8 May 1829.

19. See 5 December 1818, Minutebook I, Poydras Home Records; Jonathan Homer to unknown, 25 September 1818, Administrative Papers, Poydras Home Records. The Natchez ladies hired a poor widow as their first matron, who was allowed to care for her own two children along with a number of other "orphans." Though focusing on the late nineteenth century, Hacsi discussed asylum "staff" in *Second Home*, 81–85.

20. *Mississippi Gazette*, 19 March 1825; *Mississippi Statesman and Gazette*, 28 March 1829. For example, in annual reports of the Natchez Female Orphan Asylum, governesses were praised for their "affectionate care of the children" as well as the "great sacrifices" made in tending them, as if they were natural rather than hired mothers. Female Orphan Asylum annual report, printed in the *Mississippi Statesman and Gazette*, 28 March 1829. The officers complained about high expenses incurred by "Mrs. Floyd" on 1 July and 7 August 1816, Minutebook I, Natchez Children's Home Records. The minutebook records Eliza Ellison as having run away on 6 May 1816, Ann Barrow discharged on 6 May 1819, the "disobedient" boy on 3 July 1820, and expulsion of the Benedict boys on 5 April 1819. Minutebook I, Natchez Children's Home Records.

21. *Mississippi Statesman and Gazette*, 28 March 1829. Those in Boston, Providence, Portsmouth, N.H., and Canandaigua, N.Y., for example, specified "female children" and set an age

range from about three to ten years of age. See *The Constitution of the Providence Female Society for the Relief of Indigent Women and Children* (Providence, R.I.: John Carter, 1801), 7; Timothy Alden, *A Discourse, Delivered before the Members of the Portsmouth Female Asylum, at a Third Service on the Sabbath, 16 September, 1804. Prepared and Published at the Request of the Managers of This Benevolent Institution* (Portsmouth, N.H.: J. Melcher, 1804), 11; *The Constitution of the Female Charitable Society of Canandaigua, Formed July 17, 1815* (Canandaigua, N.Y.: John A Stevens, 1815), 5.

22. The rights of bound minors were outlined in apprenticeship statutes. See Rainwater, comp., "Sargent's Code," 312–13. According to Phillip N. Mulder, "Mothers played a crucial role in the education of their children, from catechizing to setting pious examples." Indeed, religious instruction began in the home with the assistance of primers such as "A Mother's Catechism." See Mulder, *A Controversial Spirit: Evangelical Awakenings in the South* (New York: Oxford University Press, 2002), 22–23. Ruth H. Bloch discussed the dominant conception of women as "moral mothers" in the early republic, situating that conception within religious and intellectual developments, in *Gender and Morality in Anglo-American Culture, 1650–1800* (Berkeley: University of California Press, 2003). For political influences in shaping views of women, see Kerber, *Women of the Republic*, chap. 7, esp. 210–13, 228–31; also Cott on "Domesticity" in *The Bonds of Womanhood*, chap. 2.

23. See 1 February 1817, Minutebook I, Poydras Home Collection. Although the Natchez ladies initially organized in March 1816 to form a charity school, they had engaged a matron to care for a number of "orphan children" by the meeting on 6 May. At the 4 June 1821 meeting, they discussed buying Judge Taylor's house at a reduced price from Samuel Postlethwaite. On 1 April 1822, the officers of the Female Orphan Asylum began making arrangements to sell the asylum at a substantial profit and then build a new one. Minutebook I, Natchez Children's Home Records.

24. Most of the entries for 1822, the last year covered in the minutes, pertain to the new asylum. Also recorded is the contract made between the asylum officers and carpenter Alexander Smith, which details every aspect of the building's construction. Minutebook I, Natchez Children's Home Records. For an excellent discussion on changes in domestic "built environments" at the turn of the nineteenth century, see John E. Crowley, *The Invention of Comfort: Sensibilities and Design in Early Modern Britain and Early America* (Baltimore: Johns Hopkins University Press, 2001). Judging by the descriptions of houses built at the turn of the nineteenth century, the floor plan and materials used for the orphan asylum mirrored those found in the residences of prosperous artisans and middling merchants elsewhere in the nation.

25. Elite women engaged in organized benevolence during the late eighteenth and early nineteenth centuries were concerned with improving the present situation and future prospects of the poor while maintaining the traditional, deferential social order. Hacsi examined the daily routine of a number of early nineteenth-century orphan asylums and discusses how the women who managed them strove not only to meet the immediate needs of inmates but also to condition their behavior: *Second Home*, 148–72. On the similar tactics employed by the male-run Charleston Orphan House and the aim of its commissioners to cultivate obedience and deference among poor children, see Bellows, *Benevolence among Slaveholders*, 136–39.

26. See 7 March 1818, Minutebook I, Poydras Home Collection.

27. The Salem Female Charitable Society, for example, published the bill of fare served to the orphan girls under its protection as well as the "Rules and Regulations for the Government of the Children" and the copy of a charity sermon. See Lucius Bolles, *A Discourse, Delivered before the Salem Female Charitable Society, September 27, 1810, Being Their Tenth Anniversary* (Salem, Mass.: Thomas C. Cushing, 1810), 16.

28. Statutes pertaining to apprentices always specified the provision of new clothes as "freedom dues" to help the apprentice secure a position as a journeyman or some other respectable, lucrative employment. One of the most thorough discussions of apprentices and clothing remains Ian M. G. Quimby, *Apprenticeship in Colonial Philadelphia* (New York: Garland, 1985), 60–73. Many of the minutebook entries for both institutions pertain to the inmates' clothes. The officers of the Natchez Orphan Asylum eventually designated a manager to regularly inspect the children's appearances and report their needs to the board. Providing outfits for so many girls finally led to the creation of an auxiliary society in New Orleans to assist with providing clothes to the Poydras Asylum.

29. See 2 December 1816, Minutebook I, Natchez Children's Home Records. A notation refers to the purchase of "16 yards blue cloth" for both under and outer garments: 10 October 1822, Minutebook I, Natchez Children's Home Records.

30. From an article detailing the history of a Philadelphia free school founded in 1796 by a group of ladies, which also mentioned the significance of blue as the color of charity: "Free School," *Port-Folio*, 30 July 1803. Susan Lynne Porter discussed the adoption of blue uniforms for the inmates of the Boston Female Asylum in "The Benevolent Asylum—Image and Reality: The Care and Training of Female Orphans in Boston, 1800–1840" (PhD diss., Boston University, 1984), 109.

31. For example, at a special meeting on 1 June 1818, the officers met in part to discuss the removal of Washington White and ascertain "by what authority he was removed from the protection of the 'Society'"; Minutebook I, Natchez Children's Home Records.

32. John Everitt Jr. was apprenticed as a shoemaker in 1804, Henry Wyth as a tailor in 1806, and John Scotthorn as a hatter in 1817. Records for Everitt and Wyth appear in the Orphans Court Minutebook I and those for Scotthorn in the Deed Record Book I, both from the Adams County Courthouse. The Natchez Asylum officers frequently discussed sewing among female inmates, and at the 3 May 1837 meeting, they stipulated that one of the two governesses would lead the girls in sewing from 2 to 6 P.M. Minutebook III, Natchez Children's Home Records. The Poydras Asylum officers even presented silver thimbles as prizes for girls with the best sewing skills. April 1821, Minutebook I, Poydras Home Collection; 16 January 1823, Minutebook I, Poydras Home Collection; annual report, printed in the *Natchez Gazette*, 5 April 1827.

33. In the Natchez Orphan Asylum, the hours between 8 A.M. and noon were "school hours" for inmates, and the girls sewed from 2 to 6 P.M.; 3 May 1837, Minutebook III, Natchez Children's Home Records. The officers of the Poydras Asylum were much more detailed in noting the inmates' schedule: they awoke at dawn, performed chores, then read scripture before breakfast; school (involving the study of reading, spelling, and mathematics) took place from 9 A.M. until noon; dinner was at 1 P.M.; at 2 they returned to the schoolroom for three hours to learn various employments, followed by one or two hours for play ("subject at all times to the restriction of the governess"); and the day closed with the reading of scripture and prayer; 22 February 1817, Minutebook I, Poydras Home Collection.

34. See 5 April 1837, Minutebook III, Natchez Children's Home Records. The placement of Olivia Wrice with the Greens was discussed on 14 May 1822, and the article of agreement was copied into the record on 17 May. Minutebook I, Natchez Children's Home Records. The poorhouse was visited on 7 June 1837, and a decision was made on 5 July 1837. Minutebook III, Natchez Children's Home Records. Christopher L. Stacey discussed the Adams County poorhouse in "The Political Culture of Slavery and Public Poor Relief in the Antebellum South," *Journal of Mississippi History* 63 (spring 2001): 137. For example, in 1818, three-year-old Laura Zane was nearly raped by a lodger in her mother's house. Charges were brought, but then inexplicably Elizabeth Zane dropped them and asked for the accused to be released. Memorandum of Testimony, 14 October 1818, *State of Mississippi v. Jacob R. Thompson*, Historic Natchez Foundation, Natchez.

35. See 16 January 1818, Minutebook I, Poydras Home Collection; 6 March 1820, Minutebook I, Natchez Children's Home Records. Barbara Bellows argued that the Charleston Orphan House served to reinforce white racial superiority while testifying to the public of Southerners' philanthropy. See Bellows, *Benevolence among Slaveholders*, 122.

36. See 19 March 1825, Minutebook I, Poydras Home Collection. Historians of early American children universally lament the dearth of narratives and other written evidence from childhood. On the problem of sources with respect to the history of children as well as a sample from early modern "child diarists," see Linda Pollock, *Forgotten Children: Parent-Child Relations from 1500 to 1900* (New York: Cambridge University Press, 1984); Robert H. Bremner, ed., *Children and Youth in America: A Documentary History*, vol. 1, *1600–1865* (Cambridge, Mass.: Harvard University Press, 1970).

37. *Ariel* (Natchez), 7 September 1827.

38. Philander Boyce is first mentioned in the minutes on 1 June 1818, Minutebook I, Natchez Children's Home Records.

39. See 1 May 1820 and 6 November 1820, Minutebook I, Natchez Children's Home Records, as well as the articles in Craig Thompson Friend and Lorri Glover, eds., *Southern Manhood: Perspectives on Masculinity in the Old South* (Athens: University of Georgia Press, 2004).

40. Recent studies of enslaved family life include Wilma King, *Stolen Childhood: Slave Youth in Nineteenth-Century America* (Bloomington: Indiana University Press, 1995); Marie Jenkins Schwartz, *Born in Bondage: Growing Up Enslaved in the Antebellum South* (Cambridge, Mass.: Harvard University Press, 2001). On middling white families, see Stephanie McCurry, *Masters of Small Worlds: Yeoman Households, Gender Relations, and the Political Culture of the Antebellum South Carolina Low Country* (New York: Oxford University Press, 1997). Poor white and Indian families are among the many domestic topics explored in Walter J. Fraser Jr., R. Frank Saunders Jr., and John L. Wakelyn, eds., *The Web of Southern Social Relations: Women, Family, and Education* (Athens: University of Georgia Press, 1985).

2

"He come sometimes widout de pass"

Rethinking Cross-Plantation Marriages and Enslaved Families
in Antebellum South Carolina

EMILY WEST

⁓

> Well, my pa b'longin' to one man and my mammy b'longin' to another, four or five
> miles apart, caused some confusion, mix-up, and heartaches. My pa have to git a pass
> to come to see my mammy. He come sometimes widout de pass.
>
> Millie Barber

Millie Barber's comments are fairly typical of enslaved children whose parents
resided in cross-plantation or "abroad" marriages. Somewhat neglected in the
historiography of American antebellum slavery, cross-plantation families—
where parents belonged to different owners, children resided with their mothers, and fathers visited when they could—were significant in the Old South.
Cross-plantation marriages offer a fresh way of understanding the construction
of gender roles within enslaved families.

Historians have found it difficult to assess the extent and nature of cross-
plantation marriages among enslaved African Americans, and most scholarship
has dwelt upon the issue of whether women or men dominated family life. In
the 1950s, Kenneth Stampp emphasized absent fathers and the weakness of marriage under slavery, an interpretation that reappeared in the Moynihan Report
of 1965. In the 1970s, revisionist historians attempted to reinstate the husband-
oriented nuclear family. Herbert Gutman's magisterial volume, *The Black Family
in Slavery and Freedom*, and *Time on the Cross*, the controversial work of Robert
Fogel and Stanley Engerman, focused on nuclear families where parents resided
together. Later, in quantitative studies of WPA testimony, Paul Escott and Ste-

phen Crawford both concluded that cross-plantation marriages were numerically significant. Yet their studies often overlooked the emotional dimensions of living in abroad unions.[1]

Historians of female slavery have considered cross-plantation families from the perspective of women, and Deborah Gray White has speculated that from a woman's point of view, abroad marriages might have held benefits. Although they were possibly jealous and suspicious of "absent" spouses, White suggested that enslaved women were strong, independent, and resilient when forced to cope with domestic issues on their own. However, Ann Patton Malone argued there is little evidence that cross-plantation families were common in Louisiana, except on small farms "where marriage choices were so limited as to convince owners that the merits outweighed the risks." Indeed, along with other historians of enslaved families, Malone has tended to conflate cross-plantation families with those that were headed by women.[2]

Thus far, the historical paradigm for the study of enslaved families has been the perceived dominance of one gender over another. Moving away from that paradigm shows that slaves lived within a multiplicity of different family formations, within which those that crossed plantations played an important part. Rethinking enslaved marriages suggests, too, that while living arrangements for abroad spouses could cause stress and anguish, fathers were not "emasculated" by their enforced separations from their families, despite slaveholders' attempts to downplay the importance of marriage to enslaved African Americans. Enslaved men were not only incapable of providing for their wives and children, owners contended, but also were unable to love and comfort their families during the working week. Evidence from South Carolina, however, shows that cross-plantation families permitted men held in bondage to develop patterns of "heroic" behavior that asserted their masculinity and created valuable avenues of autonomy. Enslaved men in South Carolina went to great lengths to visit, protect, and cherish their wives and children. The evidence used for this study also suggests while abroad families can be attributed to practical necessity, rethinking these families from the perspective of the enslaved shows that slaves strove to wed someone not of their masters' choosing but of their own. Cross-plantation families were not, therefore, a type of "single parent" family.[3] Neither were they illustrative of absent husbands and fathers. Instead, cross-plantation unions represented highly resilient institutions desired by the enslaved. Cross-plantation slave families were an important variant of family life in the antebellum South.

Cross-plantation marriages are relatively absent in the plantation records of white slaveholders, although slave management manuals sometimes offer guidance about how visiting rights might be facilitated. In their personal letters and diaries, slave owners discussed the lives of their chattel in detail, including scattered references to their slaves' cross-plantation unions. Most important for this study, the testimony of the enslaved themselves, especially the Works Progress Administration narratives, allow for an estimation of the numerical importance of cross-plantation families in the late antebellum era. When coupled with other primary evidence, such as published autobiographies, these oral histories form a substantial sample from which to explore the character of cross-plantation family life.[4]

Evidence from antebellum South Carolina suggests that cross-plantation families accounted for approximately one-third of all enslaved households and that they were far from weak and nominal relationships. Former slave Louisa Davis told her interviewer: "My husband was a slave of de Sloans and didn't get to see me as often as he wanted to, and of course, as de housemaid then, dere was times I couldn't meet him, clandestine like he want me. Us had some grief over dat, but he got a pass twice a week from his marster, Marse Tommie Sloan, to come to see me. . . . Sam was a field hand and drive de wagon way to Charleston once a year wid cotton, and always bring back something pretty for me."[5]

Davis's reminiscences demonstrate the resilience of enslaved spouses in their fight to court, to marry, and to remain married to the person they loved. Yet they also point to some of the ways in which abroad marriages caused problems. These difficulties included being dependent on owners' whims in granting visiting rights, facing patrollers' wrath when traveling away from home, and assigning household chores. Roles played by men and women within cross-plantation families reveal the gendered expectations of the enslaved. Neither men nor women played a dominant role, yet notions of masculinity and femininity were played out within a unique familial arena. Men frequently risked white anger and punishment to visit their wives and girlfriends, highlighting strong male-female bonding and revealing notions of enslaved manhood. Men, not women, saw it as their role to undertake visits and risk the attendant danger. Despite bondage, enslaved men saw themselves as initiators, protectors, and providers. Women similarly acted upon contemporary norms of feminine obligation in the work they performed within the home. Care of infants and young children, cooking, cleaning, and washing and mending clothes, for example, all primarily devolved upon women.

Living within a cross-plantation family could cause grief and anguish for the enslaved as well as offering a space for love, support, companionship, and a sense of independence. However, while some slaves formed cross-plantation unions from necessity (for example, because they lived on small slaveholdings with no suitable marriage partners), the existence of abroad marriages on large plantations suggests that a desire for autonomy or "social space" from white oversight was equally important.[6] The enslaved strove to make their own marital decisions and to enact particular gender roles. Cross-plantation marriages therefore offer a unique perspective on a very specific type of southern family as well as suggesting how broader ideas about gender were played out within them.

While cross-plantation families reflected the will of the enslaved in striving to marry someone of their own choice, they were also shaped by practical considerations. Slaves on large plantations had a wider pool of potential spouses and were more likely to marry "at home" than those whose owners held only a handful of slaves. For example, Nancy Washington entered an abroad marriage because her master owned only Nancy, her siblings, and her mother. Location was significant, with owners of large lowcountry plantations encouraging slaves to marry "at home" rather than abroad. There was also a relationship between a slave's work assignment and family type. Respondents whose parents were house servants or skilled workers were slightly more likely to live in co-resident households, while those whose parents were field slaves displayed a greater propensity to reside in cross-plantation families. In some cases, owners may have indulged house slaves by buying their chosen partners, while in others, perhaps, the marriages of certain favored slaves would have been protected from sale and separation. Historian Michael Tadman has suggested that the marriages most likely to be protected were not simply those of domestics as a group but a subset of favored "key" slaves with whom owners felt that they had special bonds of affection and respect.[7]

Slaves' desire to marry and to live with a spouse of their own choosing gave slaveholders a useful tool of control because the facilitation or prevention of abroad unions was easily integrated into systems of rewards and punishments. While it is not surprising that masters would perceive cross-plantation families from the perspective of their own convenience rather than slaves' priorities, the extent to which owners generated rules over abroad marriages indicates that these families were commonplace on large plantations. For masters who owned only a handful of slaves, enabling abroad marriages could facilitate the reproduction of the enslaved labor force—at least for the owner of the wife in the union.[8] Many owners resented the fact that cross-plantation unions would lead to more movement among—and perhaps, a greater degree of independence for—their slaves. Yet they were forced to recognize that both social custom and the desire for reproduction meant that abroad relationships should be permitted, thereby establishing some limits over masters' control over the families of those they held in bondage.

Owners often mentioned cross-plantation arrangements in their plantation books in rather disapproving tones. In his "Plantation Rules," for example, Sumter slave owner John B. Miller wrote: "*Marriages:* Not to marry from house if to be avoided. *Meetings and Religion:* Home at night. Not to go from home to them at night." In his list of "Rules for Government of Plantation," he added:

Negroes:
To be kept in good order and at home and not to leave plantation without a ticket and that to express the place they are to go to and how long to be absent and not to be for any greater distance than a few miles without my express orders, except to the nearest church. Tickets to be given alone by me, wife or son. . . . No negro but those connected to my negroes and of good character to be allowed on plantation and they must have a ticket for that purpose from their owners to be brought to me except them that have a wife or husband on the plantation.9

Miller's rules illustrate well how owners sought to reconcile accepted customs and the need for a reproductive workforce with the desire to limit the freedom—especially the geographic movement—of their chattel.

Plantation rules in the Conway-Black-Davis family papers also refer indirectly to the inconvenience of cross-plantation families. Overseers were advised, "Prevent night visits in the week, and put an end to late hours. Let 'early to bed and early to rise' be the word." Slaveholders evidently felt that well-rested workers would be more productive and that cross-plantation unions disrupted slaves' rest. Similarly, Charleston planter Andrew Flinn worried about night visits and the mobility of his property, writing that slaves were not to be allowed out of their houses after nine o'clock at night in summer and eight o'clock in winter. Flinn also compiled a list of punishable offenses, ranked according to severity, as follows: "The following is the order in which offences must be estimated and punished. 1st, running away. 2nd, getting drunk or having spirits. 3rd, stealing hogs. 4th, stealing. *5th, leaving plantation without permission.* 6th, absence after horn blow. 7th, unclean house or person. 8th, neglect of mules. 9th, neglect of tools. 10th, neglect of work. The highest punishment must not exceed fifty lashes in one day." The list illustrates the significance owners placed on illicit visits. A minority of owners simply banned abroad marriages. The majority, though, utilized more subtle tactics of persuasion. Aside from offering better material conditions to those who married "at home," the threat of sale or separation also loomed large. Some owners felt no hesitation in warning those who married off-plantation that their spouses might be sold by "less kindly" masters. For example, in his autobiography, Sumter County ex-slave I. E. Lowery detailed the courtship and marriage rules of his master, Mr. Frierson: "When the boys and girls reached a marriageable age he [Mr. Frierson] advised them to marry, but marry someone on the plantation, and he would see to it that they were not separated. But if they married someone from the adjoining plantations, they might be separated by the 'nigger traders' as they were called in that day and time."[10]

Many slaveholders discouraged their human chattel from marrying off-plantation but did not prohibit cross-plantation unions. However, a minority of masters who owned large plantations took a harsher line. In a letter to his overseer, Charles Manigault simply dictated: "I allow no strange negro to take a wife on my place." Probably feeling the large size of his rice plantation meant he did not need to "indulge" his slaves, Manigault did not permit abroad families. He had approximately one hundred slaves living on his Gowrie Plantation on Argyle Island in the Savannah River, and he believed that the pool of potential spouses was sufficient. However, despite the relatively large numbers of slaves living there, historian William Dusinberre argues that the harshness of plantation life at Gowrie (including disease, death, and enforced separations) meant the number of potential partners was actually rather small, forcing many slaves to form unions with significantly older or younger partners.[11]

Planters who owned more than one plantation sometimes permitted cross-plantation families involving slaves on their own plantations. James Henry Hammond wrote in his plantation diary: "Negroes living on one plantation and having wives at the other can visit them only between Saturday night and Monday morning." However, he also directed, "No marriage will be allowed with negroes not belonging to the master." In his attempts to limit cross-plantation families to those he owned, Hammond exerted control over his slaves. Other, less wealthy owners attempted similar kinds of rules, such as permitting abroad marriages only between their own slaves and those owned by white relatives. The former slave Jacob Stroyer detailed in his autobiography how his sisters, Violet and Priscilla, married two men belonging to the brother of Stroyer's master.[12] Such marriages fulfilled two functions: They heightened the owners' control, and they enabled masters to reaffirm their benevolent self-image. Slaveholders could take a paternalist pride in the existence of enslaved family ties within their own extended family networks.

The testimony of the enslaved suggests, however, that it was not the norm for those who lived in cross-plantation families to belong either to the same owner or to owners who were related. Out of fifty-three cross-plantation marriages in the South Carolina WPA narratives, only four involved spouses whose owners appear to have been related. In one of these cases, John Franklin of Spartanburg County lived with his mother on the plantation of Benjamin Bobo, whereas his father lived on the plantation of Bobo's brother-in-law, Henry Franklin. Bill Leitner and his mother, both from Winnsboro, belonged to Robin Brice, while his father belonged to John Partook Brice. Leitner recalled: "Daddy have to have pass to come to see mammy" but commented no further on the owners' relationship. Lucinda Miller and her mother belonged to Mat Alexander, while her father was the property of Mat's brother who "lived two or three plantations away." Finally, Sam Polite, although not explicit about the relationship between owners, testified that: "My fadder b'long to Mister Marion Fripp and my mudder b'long to Mister Old B. Fripp."[13] In the South Carolina sample, however, few cross-plantation families formed their unions within the context of white families.

Cross-plantation families also affected the ways in which enslaved communities coped with local forced separations, be it through sale, the giving away of slaves, or estate division. Historian Thomas Russell has argued that local (as well as long-distance) sales caused a high rate of family separations. However, abroad marriages often diminished the impact of local sales on slave families. Family members could maintain contact with each other following such separation, albeit in an attenuated way. Thus the enslaved drew a distinction between separations they perceived to be "local" and those which were "long distance," and they feared the latter more. In his autobiography, Charles Ball explained that his enslaved wife was a chambermaid to Mrs. Symmes, while Ball belonged to Jack Cox, for whom he labored in the field. The couple's marriage was cross-plantation. However, Cox's ownership was called into question by a lawsuit, and Ball was eventually passed onto Levin Ballard: "One day, whilst I was at work in the cornfield, Mr. Ballard came and told me I was his property. . . . I accordingly went with him," Ball detailed his own local sale. Significantly, he added, "as he lived near the residence of my wife's master, my former mode of life was not materially changed by this change of home."[14] Ball asserted a degree of independence in choosing a wife and living as full a family life as possible within a cross-plantation environment. Despite gaining a new master, Ball could carry on his family life in much the same way as he had before. Experiences such as these convey the underlying resilience of enslaved southern families and their multiple formations.

However, the severity of bondage should be remembered. Although living outside of South Carolina, Missouri slave autobiographer Mattie Jackson described how her parents lived in a cross-plantation union but managed to maintain their relationship following the sale of her mother twenty miles away: "My father thereafter visited my mother once a week, walking the distance every Saturday evening and returning on Sunday evening."[15] Walking twenty miles weekly to see his wife and children conveys Jackson's father's commitment to his familial role. Unfortunately, he was later subjected to a long-distance sale, and neither Mattie nor her mother ever saw him again.

WPA respondents from South Carolina conveyed similar sentiments about the impact of local separations on cross-plantation families. Sylvia Cannon, eight years old in 1860, was sold locally. She testified: "Father en mother belong to old Bill Greggs en dat whe' Miss Earlie Hatchel buy me from. After dat, I didn' never live wid my parents any more, but I went back to see dem every two weeks. Got a note en go on a Sunday evenin' en come back to Miss Hatchel on Monday."[16] Families that were "abroad" in scope therefore had different permutations. While in the majority of cases fathers did the visiting, children might also be granted permission to visit parents elsewhere.

The local sale of a parent often meant that slaves who had previously lived in nuclear households then became cross-plantation families. Mack Taylor explained that all his family members were owned by the Clarks, who lived on the Wateree River in Winnsboro. Although his father was sold to a man in Columbia, he managed to remain in regular contact with his family in Winnsboro. Likewise, Lucinda Miller and her mother were sold from their home in Spartanburg, leaving her father behind. Their new master was the brother of their former owner and lived only "two or three plantations away." Hence, the Miller family maintained familial contact. Other respondents maintained cross-plantation families both before and after local sales. Lucretia Heyward and her mother, for instance, were able to keep in regular contact with Lucretia's father, Tony MacKnight, who belonged to Stephen Elliot, both before and after their sale from Joe Eddings to Edward Blunt, because all three masters resided in the Beaufort area.[17]

White owners often gave their slaves to other family members as gifts. This practice helped slaves maintain familial ties because such exchanges were often local. Bill McNeil was enslaved in York County and was bequeathed (along with his mother and brother) to his master's daughter upon marriage. McNeil's father subsequently received a pass to visit his family in their new home. Similarly, Adeline Jackson explained: "When my younges' mistress, name Marion Rebecca, married her second cousin, marster Edward P. Mobely, I was give to her and went wid them to de June place. It was called dat because old Doctor June built it and sold it to Marster Ed."[18] In expressing familiarity with the geography of the area, Jackson suggested that the June place was relatively close to her previous home. Geographical proximity among white families therefore facilitated cross-plantation familial relationships among the enslaved.

Estate divisions also followed the interests of white families; consequently, slaves divided among heirs were often dispersed locally. Moses Roper, the son of his "young master," described in his autobiography that when "old master" died, his heirs divided the slaves among themselves with little regard to the slaves' sentiments: "The way they divide their slaves is this: they write the names of different slaves on a small piece of paper, and put it into a box, and let them all draw. I think that Mr. Durham drew my mother, and Mr. Fowler drew me, so we were separated a considerable distance, I cannot say how far." Roper later lost touch with his family when he was sold long-distance to a trader headed south.[19]

Provided the distances involved were not insurmountable, spousal and broader familial interaction could be maintained following local separations. While all slaves feared being forcibly separated from their families, their relative lack of concern regarding local separations is significant. Cross-plantation family networks ensured that local moves had less impact upon family and community ties than long-distance separations. Moreover, the maintenance of marriages despite the upheavals of sale, gift, and estate division represents a significant achievement by enslaved family members in seeking to create and sustain autonomous family and community lives.

The relative absence of references to voluntary separation in slave testimony is another indication of slaves' attachment to family. The South Carolina WPA narratives contain only two rather oblique references to this occurrence, when two respondents spoke of their parents living apart. Will Dill, his mother, and his father all lived on the plantation of Zeek Long in Anderson County, but his parents resided in different houses. Ryer Emmanuel simply said that "Daddy somewhe' on de plantation."[20] While another ten respondents lived with stepparents, eight of these testified this was due to circumstances other than voluntary separation. For example, three had white fathers, and John C. Brown had a white mother.[21] The death of a parent accounted for two other examples, and another two interviewees had had a parent sold away.[22] In the remaining two cases there was no testimony concerning the circumstances in which natural parents had been lost.[23] Most familial separations were the result of owner actions rather than the choice of the enslaved.

WPA interviewees' explanations for female-headed families also suggest that

voluntary separation was rare. Of twenty such families reported, two interviewees gave no details other than that they, as children, lived only with their mothers.[24] Seven respondents testified that they and their mothers had been sold or
given away, thus separating children from fathers.[25] Another five, one of whom
was Robert Smith, enslaved in Union County, revealed that their father had been
sold away.[26] Smith testified, "My ma was Chlorrie Greer, and my pa was Bob
Young. His white folks ca'ed him off somewhars and I never see'd him [again]."[27]
Of the remaining six female-headed families in the sample, the respondents had
white fathers and unmarried mothers.[28] Female-headed families in the South
Carolina WPA narratives, therefore, can be best defined as broken two-parent
families, where owners initiated the breaking.

Occasionally, enslaved families adapted to the hardships imposed by bondage in unusual ways. Emmanuel Elmore, who lived with his father and step-
mother, conveyed the adaptability of enslaved family formation under desperate circumstances. His father had remarried a woman named Jenny following
Elmore's mother's sale from their home in Spartanburg to Alabama. Eventually,
and probably during or following the turmoil of the Civil War, Elmore's mother
returned: "When she did get back to Col. Elmore's [the master's] place, she was
lanky, ragged, and poor, but Col. Elmore was glad to see her and told her he was
not going to let anybody take her off. Jenny had cared so well for her children
while she was off, that she liked her. They lived in the same house with pa till
my mother died." A desire to provide a stable environment for children appears
to have taken precedence among members of Elmore's family. Alternatively,
this family could have been engaged in the practice of polygamy. Although
historians generally agree that polygamous relationships among the enslaved
had mostly died out by the antebellum era, they were more common in states
such as South Carolina, especially in the lowcountry, where large plantations
predominated.[29]

Whatever the explanation for this situation, the experiences of Elmore's family
demonstrate resilience and diversity among enslaved families, which took on a
multiplicity of forms in response to slaves' efforts to maintain them. Cross-plantation marriages were malleable and adapted to owners' actions. However, they
also provided the enslaved with a space in which they could act out traditional
gendered expectations. Men, not women, were expected to visit their wives and
families, usually on weekends but occasionally during the week. While owners'
rules were sometimes followed, at other times men risked "illicit" visits to see
their families. Millie Barber was the only interviewee to mention the distances
involved, claiming her father lived four or fives miles away.[30] However, her tes-

timony appears to be representative, since traveling much farther would have been difficult.

This gendered behavior within cross-plantation families meant that men were much more at risk than women of being caught and punished by patrollers. Slave men's willingness to face up to this threat illustrates that enslaved men placed their families above other considerations. Former slaves recalled the patrollers with a sense of dread, and many children remembered the beatings that their fathers or other men had endured. Many informants were familiar with masters' rules on visitation. Julia Woodberry of Marion County explained that enslaved husbands had to carry a permit: "You see, de nigger men would want to go to see dey wives en dey would have to get a 'mit from dey massa to visit dem." Manda Walker vividly recalled the slaves' dread of the patrollers, testifying: "Him [her father] stayed over his leave dat was writ on de pass. Patrollers . . . come ask for de pass. They say, 'De time done out, nigger.' Pappy try to explain but they pay no 'tention to him. Tied him up, pulled down his breeches, and whupped him right befo' mammy and us chillun. I shudder, to dis day, to think of it."[31]

Many former slaves recalled the dread of patrollers and testified to the courage of lovers, husbands, and fathers in running the gauntlet of patrols. Will Dill, enslaved in Anderson County, had an uncle who used to sneak off at night to visit a girl, trying to give the patrollers the slip. Charlie Grant of Mars Bluff stated he would not dare leave his home to visit anyone without a permit for fear of being caught and whipped by patrollers. Ben Horry explained that when visiting girls on another plantation in the lowcountry, a pass was vital: "Got to have paper. Got to carry you paper. Dem patroller put you cross a log! Beat you to death."[32]

Decrees that slaves should have a pass when leaving their farms and plantations seem to have been universal among owners, although rules varied both in terms of level of detail required and punishments inflicted upon those who did not comply. In his autobiography, Sam Aleckson described the visit of a slave man named Mingo to his sweetheart, Dolly. Mingo had to show his pass to Dolly's owner, Mr. Ward: "Mingo produced the desired article. Mr. Ward read it, his brows—contracting a little. 'This is all right' he said, returning the paper. 'Except that it does not say where you are to go. Now I never allow anyone on my place with such a ticket. The next time you visit Dolly you must have a different ticket. Ask your master to give you one stating plainly that you are to visit my plantation.'" John Edwin Fripp's plantation journal contained the blunt entry: "Gave Peter 25 lashes for going to the [St. Helena] island without permission." Less harshly, Darlington slave owner Ada Bacot wrote in her diary: "I find some of my young negroes have been disobeying my orders, they were found away from home without a pass. I hope I may be able to make them understand without much trouble that I am mistress and will be obeyed. I have never had any trouble with them until now. Even now I don't apprehend much."[33]

Being without a pass represented "disobedience" and undermined slaveholders' authority. Enslaved men's determination to visit their wives, children, and girlfriends also countered the notion that enslaved families, especially those that crossed plantations, were weak. Furthermore, the fact that men took the role of visitors, with its attendant risks and hardships, suggests the position of slave husbands and fathers as heroic protectors and risk-takers. Rather than being emasculated by the constraints that owners placed upon family life or by systematic efforts to undermine black manliness thorough whippings and other physical punishments, enslaved men involved in cross-plantation marriages played a strong and visible role within their families. Some risked their own safety to protect their loved ones from external assault.[34]

Philip Evans recalled how his uncle defended his wife after her beating by an overseer, despite the repercussions that this would bring: "Pears like he [the overseer] insult my aunt and beat her. Uncle Dennis took it up, beat de overseer, and run off to de woods. Then when he git hungry, he come home at night to eat sumpin'. Dis kept up till one day my pappy drive a wagon to town and Dennis jined him. Him was a settin' on de back of de wagon in de town and somebody point him out to a officer. They clamp him and put him in jail. After de 'vestigation they take him to de whippin' post of de town, tie his foots, make him put his hands in de stocks, pulled off his shirt, pull down his britches and whip him terrible." In a similar fashion, Henry Gladney recalled how his father, known as "Bill the Giant," once broke the leg of another enslaved man for "looking" at his wife on their plantation near White Oak. Also, in the published narrative of the South Carolina slave "Wild Tom," Tom killed the overseer who whipped his wife to death. The defiance of these men in trying to protect their wives shows courage, yet it also helps define a regime characterized by volatility, violence, and aggression, in which defending and displaying their masculinity was highly important for enslaved men.[35]

In contrast, with their day-to-day childcare responsibilities, enslaved wives in abroad marriages received rather than initiated visits. Although some historians have argued that slave families were "unusually egalitarian," South Carolina evidence suggests that cross-plantation and nuclear enslaved households followed what can be described as conventional norms in gendered expectations and behavior. While most couples found marriage a place of refuge and a mechanism of support under adversity, married life was far from idyllic. Enslaved partnerships, and in particular those that crossed plantations, were subject to discord. All slave wives were responsible for performing hard labor for owners as well as working on behalf of their families, but this problem was particularly acute for those women in cross-plantation unions. The stresses caused by raising children without the presence of one parent raised tension levels and conflict, as did loneliness and jealousy. For example, sometimes enslaved men who married abroad had to "lodge" with other women and children during the week, perhaps causing friction between spouses.[36]

Many disputes arose from gendered norms about domestic responsibilities. Fishing and hunting were the preserve of men and boys. Men also often acquired skills useful for making and selling supplementary goods to support their families. Women were expected to raise the children, cook the meals, clean the cabin, and wash and mend clothing. Tending garden patches was a family enterprise in which all household members participated.[37]

Work performed by slaves for their families therefore conformed to conventional gender roles. As was the case in both white American society and in pre-colonial West Africa, men undertook more arduous physical labor, while the bulk of women's work revolved around the home. The majority of the enslaved worked a long day in the field or in the Big House under the task or gang system, in addition to performing familial labor after "sundown." However, the extra burdens of pregnancy, birth, and child rearing may have increased enslaved women's levels of exhaustion and perhaps contributed to friction between spouses. Enslaved females worked the "double day" before many other women in American society.[38]

Conflict ensued when a partner failed in his or her household responsibilities. Charles Ball cited the unhappiness of his friend Lydia, married to a man who claimed he was once a priest in Africa. Unaccustomed to labor, he performed no work within the home, to the chagrin of both his wife and the rest of the enslaved community. However, the response of Greenville mistress Elizabeth Franklin Perry to the news that her slave, Maria, was a poor housekeeper, was different. Jim beat his wife and then informed his mistress that Maria would not clean the couple's cabin, refused to wash or mend his clothes, and served meals in dirty plates "with peas all sticking to them." Because Maria did not fulfill her gendered obligations, both Maria's husband and her mistress viewed her abuse as justifiable.[39]

The enslaved may have placed a great emphasis on gender roles, at least in part, because the system of bondage so often worked to undermine them. It was masters, not husbands, who provided food, shelter, and clothing. Likewise, slave women engaged in hard physical labor that eroded popular notions of femininity, defined by piety, purity, submissiveness, and domesticity. Slaves' adoption of accepted masculine and feminine roles, therefore, were a form of resistance. Within their own families, the enslaved tried to strengthen gender conventions that were constantly being undermined elsewhere.[40]

South Carolina WPA respondent Charlie Davis recalled proudly how his father evaded the patrollers when visiting his family. His testimony gives a sense of how enslaved fathers were perceived as both heroes and protectors:

> Mammy said dat de patrollers was as thick as flies 'round dese plantations all de time, and my daddy sho' had to slip 'round to see mammy. Sometime they would ketch him and whip him good, pass or no pass. De patrollers was nothin' but poor white trash, mammy say, and if they didn't whip some slaves, every now and then, they would lose deir jobs. My mammy and daddy got married after freedom, 'cause they didn't git de time for a weddin' befo'. They called deirselves man and wife a long time befo' they was really married, and dat is de reason dat I's as old as I is now. I reckon they was right, in de fust place, 'cause they never did want nobody else 'cept each other, nohow. Here I is, I has been married one time and at no time has I ever seen another woman I wanted.[41]

Davis's account also conveys the significance of romantic love among the enslaved. Slaves testified to strong ties of affection between couples who snatched private moments of romance. Take John Collins, who recalled how his father "used to play wid mammy just lak she was a child. He'd ketch her under de armpits and jump her up mighty high to de rafters in de little house us lived in."[42] Enslaved children who witnessed their parents' affections must surely have gained a sense of the happiness that marriage based on romantic love could bring. Falling in love with another person and choosing one's spouse, was of paramount importance to the enslaved; cross-plantation marriages increased the likelihood that slaves could make their own choices about their romantic lives.

Cross-plantation families were both numerically and culturally significant. They were not "broken" or "female-headed" families, but widely accepted and highly resilient. Faced with the prospect of spending considerable time apart, enslaved men and women created strategies of survival that maintained kin networks and maximized the importance of family as a tool of autonomy. They strove to live their domestic lives according to the gendered norms followed by couples in co-resident households as well as in white families. Abroad families gave women their own space and female support networks, yet their primary loyalty was to their husbands. Women looked forward to their husbands' visits and cherished time spent together. For men, residing in a cross-plantation family meant periods of loneliness and lodging with other families during the week. Men risked capture and punishment to spend time with their wives and children. Despite the tensions from within and the obstacles from without, South Carolina's slaves maintained long-term cross-plantation marriages. The hardships that they endured to maintain their unions demonstrates the importance of cross-plantation marriage to South Carolina slaves. Such families were not only remarkable examples of family resilience; they also represented one form of slave resistance. Enslaved men and women wanted to distance themselves as much as possible from slaveholders and plantation life.[43] The intimate space that enslaved men and women created for themselves within cross-plantation families facilitated survival within and resistance to the oppression of bondage.

Notes

1. Kenneth M. Stampp, *The Peculiar Institution: Slavery in the Antebellum South* (New York: Knopf, 1956); Robert Fogel and Stanley Engerman, *Time on the Cross: The Economic of American Negro Slavery* (Boston: Little, Brown, 1974); Daniel Patrick Moynihan, *The Negro Family: The Case for National Action* (Washington, D.C.: Office of Policy Planning and Research, U.S. Department of Labor, 1965); Herbert G. Gutman, *The Black Family in Slavery and Freedom, 1750–1925* (Oxford: Basil Blackwell, 1976); Paul D. Escott, *Slavery Remembered: A Record of the Twentieth-Century Slave Narratives* (Chapel Hill: University of North Carolina Press, 1979), 50–52, 62; Stephen Crawford, "Quantified Memory: A Study of the WPA and Fisk University Slave Narrative Collections" (PhD diss., University of Chicago, 1980), 149–54.

2. Deborah Gray White, *Ar'n't I a Woman? Female Slaves in the Plantation South* (New York: W. W. Norton, 1985), 154; Ann Patton Malone, *Sweet Chariot: Slave Family and Household Structure in Nineteenth-Century Louisiana* (Chapel Hill: University of North Carolina Press, 1992), 202n3, 227. Brenda Stevenson's detailed study of George Washington's slaves in Loudoun County, Virginia, concludes that, while around 72 percent of his slaves had abroad spouses, such families can be regarded as "single parent." See *Life in Black and White: Family and Community in the Slave South* (New York: Oxford University Press, 1996), 212. Likewise, in her case study of enslaved families belonging to Lindsey Durham of Piedmont, Georgia, Carole Merritt similarly claimed that by 1860, the majority of Durham's slaves resided in abroad families where women regarded themselves as single parents. See "Slave Family and Household Arrangements in Piedmont, Georgia" (PhD diss., Emory University, 1986), 112, 131, 221.

3. Notions of enslaved masculinity and ideas of "heroism" in the face of attempted emasculation by owners are explored in Edward Baptist, "The Absent Subject: African American Masculinity and Forced Migration to the Antebellum Plantation Frontier," in *Southern Manhood: Perspectives on Masculinity in the Old South*, ed. Craig Thompson Friend and Lorri Glover

(Athens: University of Georgia Press, 2004), 136–73. I would argue that historians have been imposing contemporary norms about family formation upon the enslaved. If one were forced to look for a present-day parallel, a more appropriate example would be families split by the demands of work, where one parent resides away from the familial home during the working week and returns only at weekends. For more detailed arguments on cross-plantation marriages and enslaved family formation, see Emily West, *Chains of Love: Slave Couples in Antebellum South Carolina* (Urbana: University of Illinois Press, 2004), chap. 2; and West, "The Debate on the Strength of Slave Families: South Carolina and the Importance of Cross-Plantation Marriages," *Journal of American Studies* 33 (August 1999): 221–41.

4. I believe WPA interviewees who mentioned family formation were representative. They were not prompted to answer questions on families, so comments came in the natural flow of conversation. The respondents were more likely to show reticence in discussing "difficult" topics such as sexual abuse or physical punishment. Moreover, the fact that the majority of interviewees were trying to recall childhood memories does not render their reminiscences on families obsolete. Most clearly recalled their family formations and the relationships of their parents. Nonetheless, writings on methodological issues associated with use of the WPA narratives are extensive. See, for example, John Blassingame, *Slave Testimony: Two Centuries of Letters, Speeches, Interviews, and Autobiographies* (Baton Rouge: Louisiana State University Press, 1979); and Blassingame, "Using the Testimony of Ex-Slaves: Approaches and Problems," *Journal of Southern History* 41 (November 1975): 473–92; John B. Cade, "Out of the Mouths of Ex-Slaves," *Journal of Negro History* 20 (July 1935): 294–337; Stephen Crawford, "Quantified Memory" and "The Slave Family: A View from the Slave Narratives," in *Strategic Factors in Nineteenth-Century American Economic History: Essays to Honor Robert W. Fogel*, ed. Claudia Goldin and Hugh Rockoff (Chicago: University of Chicago Press, 1992), 331–50; James West Davidson and Mark Hamilton Lytle, *After the Fact: The Art of Historical Detection* (New York: Knopf, 1986), chap. 7; Charles T. Davis and Henry Louis Gates Jr., eds., *The Slave's Narrative* (New York: Oxford University Press, 1985); Escott, *Slavery Remembered*; Donna J. Spindel, "Assessing Memory: Twentieth-Century Slave Narratives Reconsidered," *Journal of Interdisciplinary History* 27 (autumn 1996): 247–61.

5. George P. Rawick, *The American Slave: A Composite Autobiography*, 24 vols. (Westport, Conn.: Greenwood Press, 1972), 2: 300. From Rawick's collection, 334 South Carolina respondents (190 men and 144 women) were entered into a spreadsheet where comments on their own lives and those of their parents were recorded. In ascertaining that a given family was cross-plantation rather than female-headed or broken by sale, I required certain criteria be met. These related primarily to the marriages of the respondents' parents, as few were themselves of an age to be married during bondage. I included cases whereby respondents stated that although their father lived elsewhere or belonged to a different owner, he maintained contact with his family during enslavement. I also included cases where respondents explained how their fathers "visited" the family home. In total, out of a sample of 158 who commented on family structure, 73 (46.2 percent) apparently lived within standard "nuclear" households consisting of both parents and their offspring; 53 (33.5 percent) resided in cross-plantation families; and 20 (12.7 percent) lived in families with their mothers and sometimes siblings but did not mention fathers. A further 10 (6.3 percent) lived with a parent and a stepparent; and finally, 2 respondents (1.3 percent)

appear to have had parents who had separated. The overall results therefore suggest a significant minority living in cross-plantation families.

6. On the concept of social space between the lives of slaves and slave owners, see Larry E. Hudson Jr., "'All That Cash': Work and Status in the Slave Quarters," in *Working toward Freedom: Slave Society and Domestic Economy in the American South*, ed. Larry E. Hudson Jr. (New York: University of Rochester Press, 1994), 77–94.

7. Rawick, *American Slave*, 3: 184–87. For more information on how categories of "skilled," "house," and "field" workers are defined among enslaved communities, see West, *Chains of Love*, 82–84. On the protection of the marriages of favored "key" slaves from sale, see Michael Tadman, *Speculators and Slaves: Masters, Traders, and Slaves in the Old South*, 2nd ed. (Madison: University of Wisconsin Press, 1996), xix–xxxvii.

8. Eugene Genovese claimed that owners "knew that a man who fell in love with a woman off the place would be a poor and sullen worker, and probably soon a runaway, if deprived of his choice." See *Roll, Jordan, Roll: The World the Slaves Made* (1972; reprint, New York: Vintage, 1974), 473. Similarly, Richard H. Steckel has argued that owners benefited from slave marriages, including cross-plantation unions, since "the slaves were probably better workers when connected to a desirable home life and [for the owner of the wife] the marriages also yielded offspring." See Steckel, *The Economics of U.S. Slave and Southern White Fertility* (New York: Garland, 1985), 229. Owners' perceptions of cross-plantation families are also considered in Emily West, "Masters and Marriages, Profits and Paternalism: Slave Owners' Perspectives on Cross-Plantation Unions in Antebellum South Carolina," *Slavery and Abolition* 21 (April 2000): 56–72.

9. "Negro Rules for Government," Cornhill Plantation Book, 1827–1873 [plantation of John B. Miller], McDonald-Furman Papers, William R. Perkins Library, Duke University, Durham, N.C.

10. List of Plantation Rules, February 1815, Conway-Black- Davis Family Papers; List of Plantation Rules, Andrew Flinn Plantation Book (italics added), both in South Caroliniana Library, University of South Carolina, Columbia; Rev. I. E. Lowery, *Life on the Old Plantation in Ante-Bellum Days; or, A Story Based on Facts* (Columbia, S.C.: State Company, 1911), 42.

11. Charles Izard Manigault to J. F. Cooper [overseer at Gowrie], 10 January 1848, Letterbook, 1846–48, Charles Izard Manigault Papers, South Caroliniana Library. For more on Manigault's plantations, see James M. Clifton, ed., *Life and Labor on Argyle Island: Letters and Documents of a Savannah River Rice Plantation* (Savannah, Ga.: Beehive Press, 1978); Jeffrey R. Young, "Ideology and Death on a Savannah River Rice Plantation, 1833–1867: Paternalism amidst 'a Good Supply of Disease and Pain,'" *Journal of Southern History* 59 (November 1993): 673–706. William Dusinberre wrote that several abroad marriages existed at Manigault's Gowrie plantation when he bought it in 1833. However, through his enforcement of the above rule, cross-plantation unions became rare with dire consequences for the slave population. Manigault, he argued, prioritized plantation discipline over the family life of those he held in bondage. See Dusinberre, *Them Dark Days: Slavery in the American Rice Swamps* (New York: Oxford University Press, 1996), 106.

12. Orville Vernon Burton, *In My Father's House Are Many Mansions: Family and Community in Edgefield, South Carolina* (Chapel Hill: University of North Carolina Press, 1985), 163n50,

169n69; Jacob Stroyer, *My Life in the South* (1879; reprint, Salem, Mass.: Newcombe and Gauss, 1898), 39.

13. Rawick, *American Slave*, 2: 84; 3: 100–101, 191, 271.

14. See Thomas Russell, "Sale Day in Antebellum South Carolina: Slavery, Law, Economy, and Court-Supervised Sales" (PhD diss., Stanford University, 1993); Russell, "South Carolina's Largest Slave Auctioneering Firm," *Chicago Kent Law Review* 68 (1993): 1241–82; Russell, "Articles Sell Best Singly: The Disruption of Slave Families at Court Sales," *Utah Law Review* 4 (Winter 1996): 1161–1209; Charles Ball, *Fifty Years in Chains; or, The Life of an American Slave* (1858; reprint, New York: Dover, 1970), 25. The relationship between abroad marriages and local sales is also considered in West, *Chains of Love*, chap. 5, and West, "Surviving Separation: Cross-Plantation Marriages and the Slave Trade in Antebellum South Carolina," *Journal of Family History* 24 (April 1999): 212–31.

15. *The Story of Mattie J. Jackson* (Lawrence, Mass., Sentinel, 1866; reprinted in *Six Women's Slave Narratives*, ed. Henry Louis Gates [New York: Oxford University Press, 1988]), 7. Although enslaved in Missouri, not South Carolina, Jackson's autobiography is included to provide a female voice.

16. Ibid., 2: 188.

17. Ibid., 2: 279–80; 3: 158, 191.

18. Ibid., 3: 1–2, 164.

19. Moses Roper, *A Narrative of the Adventures and Escape of Moses Roper from American Slavery* (London: Harvey and Darton, 1840), 2–4. As Michael Tadman has noted, when estates were sold or divided, the lots in which slaves were distributed tended to include those of all ages. Therefore, probate sales and non-sale divisions between heirs often enabled families to stay together. See Tadman, *Speculators and Slaves*, 136.

20. Rawick, *American Slave*, 2: 23, 319.

21. These were Adeline Brown (Rawick, *American Slave*, 2: 127), Isiah Jeffries (3: 17), and Alexander Robertson (3: 31). John C. Brown's testimony can be found in Rawick, *American Slave*, 2: 127.

22. Andy Brice and George Fleming both suffered the death of a parent. See Rawick, *American Slave*, 2: 75 and 11: 126. Emanuel Elmore and Sena Moore both witnessed a parent being sold away. See Rawick, *American Slave*, 2: 6 and 3: 209.

23. These were Charlie Davis and Hunter Hester. See Rawick, *American Slave*, 2: 245, 331.

24. These were Jane Bradley and Pauline Worth. See Rawick, *American Slave*, 2: 74 and 3: 260.

25. These included Francis Andrews (Rawick, *American Slave*, 2: 17); Thomas Campbell (2: 176); Thomas Jefferson (3: 20); Emma Jeter (3: 33); Jimmie Johnson (3: 53); Mary Scott (3: 81); and Josephine Stewart (3: 151).

26. Included here were John Collins (Rawick, *American Slave*, 2: 224); Sim Greely (2: 290); Andrew Means (3: 182); Robert Smith (11: 294); and Aleck Woodward (3: 253).

27. Rawick, *American Slave*, 11: 294.

28. These were Ed Barber (Rawick, *American Slave*, 2: 34); John Davenport (2: 240); Henry Davis (2: 260); Thomas Dixon (2: 324); Jack Johnson (3: 41); and Victoria Perry (3: 260).

29. Rawick, *American Slave*, 2: 9. Allan Kulikoff, in his study of the Chesapeake colonies,

argued some Africans would have brought polygamy to America. However, far too few African women (in relation to the number of men) immigrated to make it common. Philip Morgan has noted how, along with many other African cultural traits, polygamy was more common among lowcountry slaves, despite the admonition of owners and religious ministers. See Kulikoff, "The Beginnings of the Afro-American Family in Maryland," in Aubrey C. Land, Lois Green Carr, and Edward C. Papenfuse, eds., *Law, Society, and Politics in Early Maryland* (Baltimore: Johns Hopkins University Press, 1977), 173; Morgan, *Slave Counterpoint: Black Culture in the Eighteenth-Century Chesapeake and Lowcountry* (Chapel Hill: University of North Carolina Press, 1998), 553–54. Drew Gilpin Faust claims that there may have been a couple of polygamous marriages on James Henry Hammond's Silver Bluff plantation; see *James Henry Hammond and the Old South: A Design for Mastery* (Baton Rouge: Louisiana State University Press, 1982), 84.

30. Rawick, *American Slave*, 2: 39. The proposition that it was generally only male slaves who traveled to visit wives and girlfriends is supported by Burton, *In My Father's House*, 163. For a more detailed analysis of slave patrols, see Sally E. Hadden, *Slave Patrols: Law and Violence in Virginia and the Carolinas* (Cambridge, Mass.: Harvard University Press, 2001).

31. See Rawick, *American Slave*, 3: 170–71, 238. Conversely, Deborah Gray White focused on the negative consequences of cross-plantation marriages for female slaves, in that they were geographically more restricted than men. See *Ar'n't I a Woman?* 76.

32. Rawick, *American Slave*, 2: 174, 304, 3: 319.

33. Sam Aleckson, *Before the War and after the Union: An Autobiography* (Boston: Gold Mind, 1929), 56; John Edwin Fripp Plantation Journal, 2 September 1858, Southern Historical Collection, Wilson Library, University of North Carolina at Chapel Hill; Ada Bacot, Diary, 11 February 1861, South Caroliniana Library.

34. On enslaved masculinity, see Baptist, "The Absent Subject," 136–73.

35. Rawick, *American Slave*, 2: 36, 129–30; Tom Jones, *Experience and Personal Narrative of Uncle Tom Jones, Who Was for Forty Years a Slave. Also the Surprising Adventures of Wild Tom, of the Island Retreat, a Fugitive Negro from South Carolina* (Boston: H. B. Skinner, 1855). Larry Hudson has argued that the willingness to use violence and brute force could bring power and respect to slave men; see "'The Average Truth': The Slave Family in South Carolina, 1820–1860" (PhD diss., University of Keele, 1989), 181.

36. White, *Ar'n't I a Woman?* 158. Disputes between enslaved couples are considered in Emily West, "Tensions, Tempers, and Temptations: Marital Discord among Slaves in Antebellum South Carolina," *American Nineteenth-Century History* 5 (June 2004): 1–18. Charles Ball details how his owner required him to lodge with an enslaved family in *Fifty Years in Chains*, 145.

37. For example, Charles Ball made wooden trays and bowls that he sold in order to support financially the family he lodged with. See *Fifty Years in Chains*, 134. For more on slave men hunting and fishing, see West, *Chains of Love*, 100. On female roles within enslaved homes, see West, *Chains of Love*, 100–101. Tending gardens or patches of land had become common in South Carolina from the 1820s onwards among slaves on both large and smallholdings. Larry E. Hudson, *To Have and to Hold: Slave Work and Family Life in Antebellum South Carolina* (Athens: University of Georgia Press, 1997), 10, 32–33; Julie Saville, *The Work of Reconstruction: From Slave to Wage Laborer in South Carolina, 1860–1870* (New York: Cambridge University Press, 1994), 7; Betty Wood, *Women's Work, Men's Work: The Informal Slave Economies of Lowcountry Georgia* (Athens: University of Georgia Press, 1995), 41.

38. Leslie Schwalm has warned historians against romanticizing the family life of enslaved women, writing that their "social and reproductive" labor should be examined as critically as the work they performed for their owners. See *A Hard Fight for We: Women's Transition from Slavery to Freedom in South Carolina* (Urbana: University of Illinois Press, 1997), 47. The idea that enslaved women worked a "double-day" before others was put forward by Bonnie Thornton Dill in "Fictive Kin, Paper Sons, and *Compadrazgo*: Women of Color and the Struggle for Family Survival," in *Women of Color in U.S. Society*, ed. Maxine Baca Zinn and Bonnie Thornton Dill (Philadelphia: Temple University Press, 1994), 153.

39. Ball, *Fifty Years in Chains*, 197; Elizabeth Perry to Benjamin Franklin Perry, 11 May 1846, Benjamin Franklin Perry Papers, South Caroliniana Library.

40. Despite its ideological importance, black women often found the notion of separate spheres bore little resemblance to their lives. Linda Kerber, "Separate Spheres, Female Worlds, Woman's Place: The Rhetoric of Women's History," *Journal of American History* 75 (June 1988): 9–39. For more on the polarity between ideologies of black and white womanhood under slavery, see Hazel Carby, *Reconstructing Womanhood: The Emergence of the Afro-American Woman Novelist* (New York: Oxford University Press, 1987), chap. 2; Elizabeth Fox-Genovese, *Within the Plantation Household: Black and White Women of the Old South* (Chapel Hill: University of North Carolina Press, 1988), 50–51. Also significant here is Angela Davis's claim that slavery could not infer privilege on black men vis-à-vis black women: "The attainment of slavery's intrinsic goals was contingent upon the fullest and most brutal utilization of the productive capacities of every man, woman, and child. They all had to 'provide' for the master." See "Reflections on the Black Woman's Role in the Community of Slaves," *Black Scholar* 3 (winter 1971): 7.

41. Rawick, *American Slave*, 2: 252.

42. Ibid., 2: 224–25.

43. Social space is considered in Hudson, "All That Cash," 80. In his summary of slavery historiography, Peter Kolchin questioned whether historians have been too optimistic in assessing resilience among enslaved families: *American Slavery* (Penguin: London, 1993), 137–38. So did Wilma Dunaway in *The African-American Family in Slavery and Emancipation* (Cambridge: Cambridge University Press, 2003), 4–5. However, I believe that emphasizing resilience and autonomy does not necessarily mean that exploitation by owners (through sale, separation, physical punishment, or sexual abuse) was not significant. Rather, that slaves *strove* for this autonomy despite adversity is of crucial significance.

3

Little Eva's Last Breath

Childhood Death and Parental Mourning
in "Our Family, White and Black"

CRAIG THOMPSON FRIEND

~

The most famous Old South childhood deathbed scene was not southern at all. As Little Eva lay dying, the young heroine of Harriet Beecher Stowe's *Uncle Tom's Cabin* (1852) began clipping her locks and distributing them as *memento mori* to those she loved, an act memorialized in a stanza of the poem "Death of Eva":

> . . . Oh sweet and sad were the tears that fell
> As her gifts among them passed
> And Tom, he got the first fair curl
> And Topsy got the last. . . .

With Topsy, Tom, and the other slaves that comprised the extended plantation family surrounding her in mourning, the brave child reached out to ease their pain and fears: "I sent for you all, my dear friends, because I love you. I love you all; and I have something to say to you, which I want you always to remember. . . . I am going to leave you." Contrasted to the unrestrained grief of the slaves, Eva's Christ-like benediction was peaceful and composed. Once the slaves left the room, she turned to her immediate family and assured them of eternal life with her final words: "O, love—joy—peace!" Then Eva "slept."[1]

Little Eva's deathbed was and remains a powerfully symbolic version of the self-abnegating Victorian culture of the mid-nineteenth-century South; it is what the white planter-class childhood deathbed supposedly entailed. The "beautiful death," as historian Philippe Ariès labeled such scenes, enabled the bereaved (and Stowe certainly desired her readership to grieve as deeply as Eva's fictional family) to supplant the painful image of a dying child with an attractive and even appealing portrait that was "both comforting and exalting." Ideally, Eva's death, as representative of any child's death, was a "moment of ecstasy bordering on the visionary." As many scholars have demonstrated, Stowe's rhetoric and imagery were culminations of the era's evangelical impulse and rising romantic sentimentalism, manifested most acutely among the northern middle class to which she belonged. But did her portrait truly represent the antebellum South, or was Stowe's representation of dying child and comforted family more an interpretation than a representation?[2]

Few scholars have attempted to answer that question. Like other subdisciplines of social history, the history of death and dying originated with studies of northern urban and middle-class life. Historian Sylvia Hoffert, for example, argued that grieving white parents in the antebellum North resigned themselves to the possibility of childhood death, refraining from expressing guilt or questioning the reasons for their children's deaths and consciously employing such occasions to demonstrate submission to God's will by satisfying themselves that "their children had gone to Him in heaven." Although Hoffert focused specifically on responses to infant death, many other historians who have studied death shared her conclusions: parents and other survivors accepted the inevitability of childhood death, and they used children's deaths to reassure their own sense of salvation. By living with a strong sense of moral purpose, applying scriptural dictates to their lives and expected afterlives, and demonstrating self-control when faced with these lowest moments of life, northern middle-class Americans epitomized the Victorianism of their era.[3]

Southern children's deaths rarely resembled Eva's serene, controlled, and sentimentalized deathbed scene. From the violence of the whooping cough and dysentery to the tragedy of agricultural accidents, childhood death permeated the Old South, and the deathbed was more often heartbreaking than romantic. Few southern parents accepted childhood deaths with the stoicism that Little Eva's parents displayed. Instead, they often grieved deeply over deceased children, expressing guilt, confusion, and frustration at their helplessness. Some emotionally shut down as their losses became unbearable. Neither did parents believe that they were helpless in preventing their children's deaths. While they did find comfort in imagining their children in Heaven, they were not hesitant to express anger with or openly question God's will. Southern parents seldom became introspective until long after the child had passed—if ever.[4]

Such disparity in approaches to childhood death does not mean that southern and northern mourning ways were dramatically different. They were both thoroughly Victorian and reflected long familiarity with high childhood mortality rates. Despite improvements in diet and medicine, American children's death rates remained high throughout the nineteenth century. The mortality rate for infants in particular varied remarkably little from region to region and compared poorly with rates in Victorian England.[5] Historian Lawrence Stone once argued that, familiar with such high mortality rates in earlier centuries, parents became emotionally detached from young children (especially "such ephemeral creatures as infants") and conserved their "emotional capital" for older youth. Historians have relied heavily on Stone's conclusions to argue for Victorians' resignation and emotionally restrained attitude toward childhood death. But, as this essay explores, childhood death elicited a great range of emotional responses from parents. With a tendency toward sentimentalizing the victim's passing and their own mourning, antebellum southerners were as "Victorian" as their northern counterparts in their attitudes toward childhood death—and that is not really surprising.[6]

So, then, was there anything particularly "southern" about childhood death in the Old South? Glancing back on Little Eva's deathbed scene, it is difficult to overlook the extended plantation family that surrounded her. "Our family" was the phrase that white slave owners employed to describe the white *and* black residents of their households. Every expectation was that blacks, as members of "our family," would fully participate in the emotional milestones of the white family's life—childbirths, weddings, and deathbed scenes. Despite this apparent intimacy, however, an emotional distance existed in the household between the two races. Whereas planters or plantation mistresses may have attended the death of a slave child, whites generally were not found at the emotional milestones of the black family's life. More important, the sentimental value that Victorian culture assessed to white children's deaths did not extend to southern black children's deaths. When it came to families and childhood deaths, then, the South was different not in practicing mourning ways and conceptualizing children's deaths in a manner particular to its regional needs, but rather in the emotional intersection of family with the racial constructions of southern households. When it came to antebellum southern childhood death, race mattered.[7]

Before leaving Little Eva, let us take one last glance at her deathbed. In an elegiac salute to the child, Stowe declared, "There is no death such as thou, dear Eva! neither darkness nor shadow of death; only such a bright fading as when the morning star fades in the golden dawn. Thine is the victory without the battle,—the crown without the conflict." In speaking of victories and crowns,

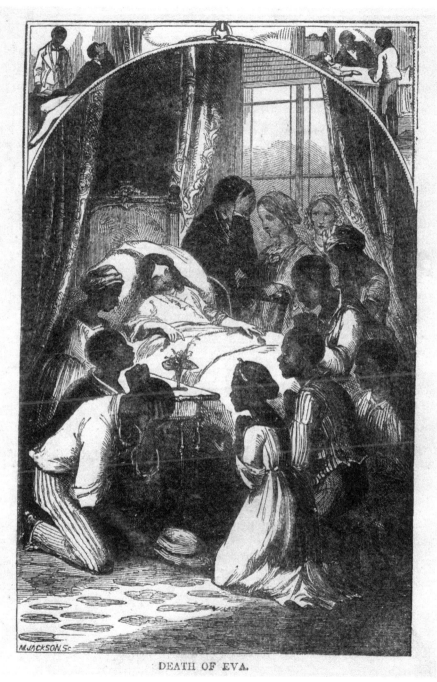

DEATH OF EVA.

Fig. 2. Harriet Beecher Stowe, *Pictures and Stories from Uncle Tom's Cabin* (Boston: John P. Jewett, 1853), 27. Courtesy of Harriet Beecher Stowe Center, Hartford, Conn.

Stowe paralleled Eva's death to that of the Christ and, in so doing, sanctioned childhood death with the power to redeem those left behind, to reinforce their faith, to overcome death itself, and to strengthen the family as a social and sentimental institution. Of course, *Uncle Tom's Cabin* was as much about the United States as it was about the white and black families who peopled its pages, and as literary historian Mary Louise Kett explained, Stowe employed an "economy of sentiment" in her pages to fortify "the constitutions not just of the individuals concerned but of the nation." Stowe imagined the nation as a family, and her purpose in *Uncle Tom's Cabin* was national reconstitution formulated on a familial model. Sentiment, then, was not important solely at the child's deathbed but in continuing to influence family/national development, symbolized in the novel by Eva's locks of hair as mystic relics with powers sufficient to free two of the slaves—Cassy and Emmeline—from slavery and return them into a reconstituted family, representative of national healing. At Little Eva's deathbed with black and white family surrounding her, or at her last moments with the immediate family awaiting her ecstatic passage, or at the reunion of Cassy's family, the economy of sentiment employed childhood death to reinforce the ideal of family, both national and intimate.[8]

The association of childhood death with familial reconstitution was not uncommon. Antebellum fiction and poems abounded with such Victorian notions of childhood death, offering solace to grieving parents and postulating that God's purpose in taking children was to redeem family on earth and welcome family into the afterlife. Sentimental letters and diaries relating hopefulness and anticipation of having the deceased child prepare the way to heaven evidenced the nation's romantic culture. As an example, circa 1858, the *American Agriculturist* published "Steer Straight to Me, Father," a short story of a man who went fishing but became trapped by the fog, only to hear his young boy's voice from the shore guiding him home. Days later, the fictional boy died, but the words echoed after his death, guiding the father to Christianity and salvation.[9]

Salvation—as in the mid-nineteenth-century North, the South was wracked by evangelicalism and its emphasis on conversion and deliverance. Theologically, evangelicals promoted the immanence of God and His revealed law while encouraging perfectionism, purity, and virtue in countering temptation. At the heart of the faith was conversion leading to salvation. As they constructed new congregations, evangelicals turned to the family as the model for community. Under the patriarchy of God, unrelated believers found support and fellowship as "brothers and sisters in Christ"—a model that Stowe emphasized in using the family metaphor for national reconstitution. Within the patriarchal atmosphere

of nineteenth-century America, the familial model of community re-created expectations of domestic dependence upon the ultimate patriarch: God. Several
lines of a poem circulated in the late 1850s expressed how childhood death was
meant to force individual submission to the Father:

> . . . I loved them so,
> That when the elder Shepherd of the fold
> Came, covered with the storm, and pale and cold,
> And begged for one of my sweet lambs to hold,
> I bade him go. . . .

> . . . "Is it thy will?
> My father, say, must this pet lamb be given?
> Oh! Thou hast many such, dear Lord, in heaven";
> And a soft voice said, "Nobly hast thou striven;
> But—peace, be still!" . . . [10]

The Patriarch's will was unquestionable; acquiescence to it permeated similar
poems and letters of sympathy sent to mourning parents. "God will not be a *Rival*," wrote a friend to Anne Swann of Pittsboro, North Carolina, "and we know
that he is jealous of every thing which robs him of his Glory." [11]

Of course, this same type of language can be found in condolence letters and
literature throughout the antebellum North as well. What made these words
particularly pertinent in the South was the acceptance of earthly patriarchal will
as a central facet of household life. God as patriarch fit very nicely with white
southerners' ideas about the *unrivaled* dominance of the man in familial, communal, political, economic, social, and religious contexts. In masculine qualities, southerners boasted they were second to none, and no quality was more
cherished than family protectiveness (which, in turn, exhibited multiple manly
characteristics, including bravery, physical skill, ferocity of will, and honor).
Portraying God as jealous and insistent on primacy had plenty of precedent in
the Old Testament, but it also engaged southern conceptualizations of mastery,
patriarchal prerogatives, and the subordination of white dependents—his wife,
his children, and on occasion his widowed mother or unmarried sisters—and
black slaves. [12]

Consider, for instance, the death of and mourning for little Phereba Hinton Bethell of Rockingham County, North Carolina. In late 1852, three-year-old
Phereba moved too close to a pile of burning leaves. The fire caught her clothes
and badly burned the child; she lingered for thirty-six hours as her mother,

Mary, tried to ease the pain—both the child's and her own. Unlike Little Eva, Phereba said nothing, leaving her mother to search for meaning in her child's violent and painful demise. Unlike Little Eva's mother, who interpreted her daughter's death as a passing from here to the hereafter, Mary Bethell believed that Phereba's death had little to do with passage or even the child. "The Lord afflicted me for *my* good," she feared: her personal joy in Phereba had angered the vengeful Patriarch of her faith, who in turn challenged her to become more Abrahamic than Abraham in sacrificing her own child.[13]

Bethell's approach to childhood death applied as well to childbirth. In the fall of 1853, she gave birth to John Hinton Bethell, predictably attributing his healthy arrival to a smiling deity who rewarded her for maintaining faithfulness in the aftermath of Phereba's death. But seven months later, John took ill and died within twenty-four hours. Bethell's diary barely acknowledges the event, suggesting either her shock or an absence of emotional investment in this child. It was quite possibly the latter, since Mary was not one to hide true grief. When her sister suddenly passed years later, Bethell lamented lengthily: "What a mysterious providence, it was such a shock to my feelings, my health suffered from it, and two weeks after I was taken sick with a hemorage from the womb, was confined to my bed two weeks, and a month to the house." In contrast to her rationalization for Phereba's death, there was no resignation to God's will here, but rather puzzlement over His purpose. Otherwise, God is absent from Bethell's written thoughts as she contemplated her sister's death and the miscarriage. But notably, while her sister's death drew a dramatic reaction, the loss of yet another, albeit unborn, child elicited no emotional outpouring. Following Phereba's tragedy in 1852, Mary Bethell seemingly went numb to her children's deaths and, quite possibly, lives. She had loved Phereba too much and angered her God, and it appears that she limited her love for future children out of fear of losing them.[14]

Bethell's lack of reaction may represent much more than simple emotional detachment, however. Her story evidences a powerful example and an equally powerful exception to what historian Ann Douglas has labeled the "domestication of death." First, the exception: in the mid-nineteenth century, women and evangelical ministers expanded power in "the free-for-all, intensely competitive democracy of American culture" by proving the insignificant (among whom children were the most evident) were indeed significant . . . that "the dead could live" . . . that "the last shall be first." Yet, nowhere in Bethell's diary is there any hint that she expected her children to live on, waiting to redeem her and usher her to salvation. Despite her strong religious sentiments, Bethell did not, indeed probably dared not, glorify her children: they did not await her in an afterlife; she let them fade into memory. Yet, that Bethell did not recognize the ecstatic redemption of childhood death is made more exceptional by the manner in which the rest of her story *exemplifies* the domestication of death. Her home was a household clearly divided into separate spheres; in fact, her husband is not found in these episodes of childhood death. Mary Bethell shouldered the grief and pain of mourning. The Victorian rationalization for burdening mothers with mourning emanated from a belief that they would most benefit from the resulting spiritual challenges. Bethell's diary demonstrates well the spiritual journey that childhood death precipitated in her life.[15]

Contrary to Victorian desires for the gendered construction of mourning, however, grief most certainly affected fathers. Lunsford Yandell, a professor of chemistry at Transylvania University in Kentucky, wrote a series of diary entries in 1836 relating his struggle with the illness and death of his young son, Wilson:

June 12th . . . My alarm and anxiety are agonizing. . . . His death, in less than 24 hours, would not surprise me! What can I say? The thought overwhelms me. . . .

June 13th . . . The trial to us is, indeed, awful. Our hearts are bound up in the lovely boy. Half the charm of our existence goes with him. Our house is filled with weeping, and henceforward will wear the air of desolation. All about it is gloom. . . . P.S. It is all over. Even while writing the lines within, he began to gasp for his last breath. He died at half past 8 in the morning—being 5 years, 11 months, & one day old. What a loss to us! I am unfit to add more.

June 15th . . . it is an overwhelming sorrow—burying beneath it our dearest hopes & brightest earthly prospects. I have not yet derived that consolation from Religion, which it is the privilege of the Son of God to enjoy. No doubt it is because I have not done my duty in times past—because I have been worldly, & not spiritually-minded—because I have followed eagerly after earthly pleasures—fame, riches, and the approbation of men, & have not held that close communion with my Maker that I ought. I am bowed down greatly. I reproach myself bitterly for having been so lukewarm a Christian—for having given out to the world *so dim* a light, and I sometimes even fancy that my sins have caused this blow to fall upon our lovely child, who is thus torn from us to show me how wicked I have been, and to drive me, by the terrible chastisement, to a closer walk with God.

For Yandell, the pursuit of manhood cost him and his family dearly. There is a touch of pragmatism in the diary, including trying to rationalize death itself, but Yandell mourned as deeply as his wife in the days following Wilson's passing. Trying to reason whether his son was truly in heaven or simply buried in the ground, Yandell admitted "that a shade of doubt" remained but that humans would always have that doubt "because we cannot feel all this as forcibly as we ought—how *thoroughly* persuaded of its truth—that death and separation have such terrors for us."[16]

The differences between Bethell's and Yandell's remembrances are striking. Bethell, a member of a New Light Methodist congregation, quite clearly concluded that God punished her for loving Phereba too much, possibly forcing her as a mother to love her later children less so as not to ire her vengeful God. Within New Light theology, open recognition of one's sins was requisite to conversion and salvation. There was also an implied connection between female faith and motherly capabilities: God favored women who acted as pious and humble mothers, rewarding them with robust and healthy children. In Bethell's world, God warned her of her spiritual weakness through Phereba's death and rewarded her faithfulness, if only briefly, with John.[17]

Yandell also attributed his child's death to God's effort to draw him toward salvation, but it was not central to his conceptualization of his son's death. "I sometimes even fancy . . .": indeed, the wording is curious, suggesting Yandell's own ambivalence toward the thought when he did consider it. Self-condemnation appears almost an afterthought to a more central concern—his inability to find solace. Yandell was not a New Light; in fact, untouched by the evangelical impulse, he was "*so dim* a light" that we might be a bit surprised by his connection of childhood death to parental sinfulness. Nineteenth-century expectations as to mourning, however, made Yandell particularly sensitive to his anguish over Wilson's death. Fathers and husbands were not supposed to mourn excessively. Even as American culture turned more toward ostentatious mourning rituals, the burden of mourning fell not to men but to women. Grief became feminized, rules emerged as to appropriate clothing, and mourning periods became codified: widows mourned for two years; mothers were to grieve for one year. Fathers, however, were to resume their normal routines shortly after their children's funerals. Yandell's eagerness to overcome his sorrow (and his frustration at being unable to do so), then, makes sense given societal expectations for his gendered role.[18]

In contrast to Bethell's waning investment in her children's deaths and Yandell's male-gendered construction of mourning stands the experience of Mary

Henderson, a resident of Salisbury, North Carolina. Henderson sent her young sons off to school on December 21, 1854, knowing that whooping cough was circulating among the town's children, "but either from thoughtlessness or I know not what did not take them from school—I now so acutely feel this was my terrible and fatal error, they were old enough to stand the disease but my little babe was only two weeks old for her sake." The boys did indeed bring the disease home, and their infant sister became ill. Mary treated her with calomel and belladonna, inducing violent vomiting and consequently damaging the child's gastrointestinal tract and killing her. In the meantime, another very young child, Edward, developed the whooping cough. The doctor came and employed the same medical techniques, with the same consequences: "I never can excuse myself for not seeing that the emetic was urged too far, I ought my own judgment should have told me that *no child* especially one coughing for three months with whooping cough could stand so much vomiting." No sooner was Edward buried than his older brother Baldy became ill and died, followed by another.[19]

Four children expired in eighteen months (a fifth had died prior to this epidemic), and Henderson's diary became a tome of regrets and almost abusive introspection: "The *Dr did it all*, he gave me the medicine and stood by and saw it operate, *he* did it not I but I ought to have known he was urging it too far"; "'don't whip me mommy, me be good boy' how often that rings in my ears it was almost the last sentence I heard my darling little boy speak in health"; "I fear I sometimes in trying to estrange and separate him from the little negro child that I said things to hurt his tender feelings for he had a warm affectionate heart"; "my house and home seem desolate and deserted but two of our seven children left, often have I longed for quiet when our children have been noisy and up-roarious, now it is *painfully quiet*"; "I feel so unhappy too about the two remaining ones thinking it may be God's good pleasure to recall them and shuddering at the bare idea—how sad, so very sad my home is." Henderson's pain and grief poured into the diary.

Her words also relate her conviction that the children's deaths had been avoidable. Had she not sent the two boys to school and had she not administered the doctor's remedy, all of her children might still have been alive. It was a particularly bitter tonic to swallow, since Henderson worked ceaselessly to save her children once they became ill. When her slave Polly first detected something wrong with Edward, Mary immediately took charge as the family's primary health-care provider. Southern mothers used health-care books like William Buchan's *Domestic Medicine* to guide their preventative measures. Despite, or perhaps because of, her access to such professional advice, the panic of discovering yet another stricken child demoralized Henderson. She placed her "hand upon his forehead and found it burning hot. . . . I told Sister he had a fever and really was so shocked I became appalled, lost all presence of mind. . . . I became unnerved and beside myself—we had water put on, a tub brought in, mustard and everything preparatory but Sister begged me to send for a doctor." Yet Henderson seems to have been already rattled by the first child's death, since it was not her own motherly intuition but Polly's diagnosis and her sister's interference that inspired her to act upon Edward's illness.[20] In fact, as each child became ill, Mary Henderson expressed surprise at the disease's progression through her family.

As Henderson sought an explanation for her children's deaths, she was not as ready as either Bethell or Yandell to attribute it to a wrathful God. Her first complaint arose against the doctor who had entered her home only through her sister's urging. Once arrived, he took charge, administering doses of calomel and belladonna with little positive effect. We know nothing more about this doctor, but Henderson's acquiescence to his authority is important. Male physicians had been making inroads into home practice since the late eighteenth century. What had once been a woman's sphere of domestic health care gradually gave way to the professionalized medical community of college-trained doctors. But with authority came responsibility. Mary Henderson directly blamed him for Edward's death: " . . . *he* did it not I." This may be the reason that when the fourth child became ill, Henderson refused to send for the doctor but instead relied on her slave nurse who, "old and experienced but selfish and lazy," "neglected my precious little lamb . . . and overfed her I fear with tea and bread *too much sweetened*," which Mary claimed led to poorer health and eventual death.[21]

What is particularly moving when reading Henderson's diary is the line that concludes, "how sad, so very sad my home is." Childhood death challenged the perpetuation of the family; instead of seven children in whom the future would be invested, only two remained in the Henderson home. Additionally, when she wrote the words, Henderson was in the midst of a three-year mourning period over the deaths of the four children, a period sufficient to emotionally if not physically isolate her from society. As one scholar explained, "Far from turning their backs on the dead, Romantic mourners were asked to turn their backs on the living." Forced to retreat further into her saddened home, Henderson became overly protective of her remaining children, even chiding God for instilling fear into them.[22]

Societal rules for parental mourning, then, had the potential to disrupt families beyond the tragedy of death. To ensure that people like Henderson did not lose faith in God or security in their homes, at times of childhood death and other spiritual trials, intimate families became targets of Christian evaluation. In the 1850s, the *Presbyterian Banner* reproached mourning parents who thought of their deceased child as "resting away yonder in the lonely grave, and whilst his brothers and sisters are sleeping sweetly at home that dear one is in his grave." Situating the deceased in this world or forgetting them altogether exposed a lack of faith. Christian parents were expected to mourn differently. As E. Lively expressed in consoling a friend upon the death of her child, "you have now another tie in Heaven and remember as your ties are increasing there you have more and stronger calls to lead you to the bleeding side of Jesus his grace is sufficient for use under all circumstances and he will not lay upon us burdens we are not able to bear but on the contrary he in his wisdom devises such means and ways to bring us into submission to his will as at first seems grievous and hard for us to bear but in after years may result in our benefit both temporal and spiritual."[23]

Not surprisingly, it was very much the same logic that underlay patriarchy—whether the father, the doctor, or God, the patriarchal authority demanded much in his wisdom, but nothing that should not ultimately benefit dependents. Women like Bethell, already stripped of independence and deeply enmeshed in patriarchal power relations, adjusted to God's patriarchal demands and forsook their children. Other women like Henderson recognized but resented the patriarchal power—both supernatural and medical—that robbed them of their joys and made them weary with grief. "I am wretched miserable cannot even pray," Henderson protested. "This consuming guilt stupefies and unfits me for every duty." Still other women, like Lunsford Yandell's wife, Susan, fully accepted God as Patriarch and immediately situated their deceased children in Heaven. Yandell's grief began in June 1856 with the death of her son, and four months later, she was just as deeply grief-stricken: her "wounded heart is not at all healed." She kept the boy's chair by her bed, imagining that he "is now a guardian angel watching over his dear mother, while she is here alone, and wondering why she weeps." In visualizing the child's return as an angel, Yandell reconstituted a whole family here on earth and reinforced notions of familial reunion in the afterlife. "God sends guardian angels, and why not send those who love us most?" she contemplated.[24]

Still, women were not expected to mourn to the point of melancholia. When the mother's mourning period ended a year or, as in Henderson's situation, several years later, she was to return to the business of domestic life. It was often painful. "The world knows little of the secret sorrows that rend the bosoms of many of those who are gayest in company," lamented Susan Yandell upon having to socialize with others. "That is not the place for grief, they do not sympathize with one. I find that constant occupation, books, or company absolutely necessary for me." But then the entry returns to the despair of grieving parent: "I ought not to trust my self alone an hour in the day, much less at night." Anne Swann, too, ached with the weariness of mourning: "*Three* months has lapsed by, and yet my selfish heart daily & hourly mourns for my departed Idol; and every returning *Sabbath* (at the ringing of the Church Bell) am I reminded that at that time, was the last struggles of my beloved Child." Church bells had long been tolled to spread news of individuals' deaths, usually ringing out the age of the deceased. Few southerners, however, could claim a weekly communal reminder of their child's death like the tolling of the church bell. Certainly, as the bell tolled beyond her son's age, it reminded Swann of the lost years of his life.[25]

It is not surprising that, while the deep and prolonged grief of mothers is unavoidable in the sources, reference to fathers' grief is rare. Southerners just were not accustomed to acknowledging male emotions and bereavement because open expression of either reeked of femininity. Men could mourn, but privately and limitedly. When the father's mourning period ended in a few days after the funeral, he was expected to return to the business of providing for family and contributing to community. Upon the death of their first daughter, Mary Henderson's husband suffered "so much I feared he would soon follow, but he got better and instead of struggling at home against my grief . . . I must think needs a change." While she anticipated prolonged grief on her part, she assumed her husband's ability to recover more quickly, possibly with just a change of scenery. When men mourned publicly, they were often emasculated. For example, as a preface to the poem about the "elder Shepherd" partially quoted earlier in this essay, an editor wrote, "There is a feeling in these words, the power of which parents alone can know. A mother must have written them, or if a father, he had a mother's heart." Within southern Victorian culture, men could not embrace feeling or emotion without risking their masculine image.[26]

Childhood death, then, challenged men who had already achieved household status and manly mastery by forcing them to confront their own masculinity. Being asked to submit to the will of the Patriarch undermined their vaunted independence. For example, Yandell initially interpreted God's purpose as counter to his own pursuit of manhood. Submission to God's will was a threatening proposition to many southern men, since it either forced them to share patriarchal authority (with God and his representative ministers) or it weakened their sense of masculinity by promoting a more dependent and, consequently, emotional and "feminized" character. Even as men became overwhelmed with grief in the privacy of the home, achieving and maintaining manliness required displays of composure in the homosocial public realm in which men moved.[27]

Lack of public emotions, however, does not mean that fathers mourned less than mothers, only differently and more privately. Given the opportunity to express themselves in private diaries, men were often more tender and as grief-stricken as their wives. Lunsford Yandell's pain is obvious in his entries. For more religious men, a child's death translated into opportunity to embrace the emotional connection to family and God and reject the corporeal world. Between May 31 and June 4, 1854, James H. Greenlee of Burke County, North Carolina, began every entry with a report on his baby's illness, always following with a lengthy supplication to God to have mercy on the family and "grant grace to submit." When the infant died on June 4, Greenlee pleaded with God to "sanctify this bereavement to us as Parents & Children[,] wean us from the world[,] show us its *vanity* and nothingness."[28]

While white fathers grieved deeply over their own children's deaths, as household patriarchs, their attitudes toward the deaths of slave children seemed almost callous. "I had ahold of her hand as the last gasp was taken," remembered Everard Green Baker about a seven-year-old slave girl on his plantation in Jefferson County, Mississippi; "her skin was moist & warm when she died & for several hours, she was opened & a large wad of worms found in the smaller bowels,—which caused her death—weather warm very."[29]

That the child was African American makes this brief episode quite important in revising Stowe's version of the southern childhood deathbed scene. This was the antithesis to Little Eva's death: Eva was white, comfortably situated in her private room, surrounded by her white intimate family and her black household family, accorded a lengthy monologue assuring us all that she was heavenbound, and allowed to "sleep." The black slave girl, lying in a bed and cabin that did not belong to her family and gasping for air in her final moments, left no monologue and was held by a man who, even if he may have been her father, was not her parent. Her recorded fate was dissection rather than heaven, and her eulogy was a clinically written statement which ended with a weather report. With the white patriarch remaining in the room, grasping her hand, one cannot help but wonder: Where were the parents? Had the patriarch displaced them as the parental figure at childhood death? Was there any proclamation of Christian acceptance of the inevitable? Was there absolution for the observers? The answers are beyond our reach, but Baker's clinical language to describe the girl's last gasp dramatically counters the eloquence with which Stowe portrayed Little Eva's last breath.

South Carolina planter David Gavin was even less interested in the humanity of the child who died on his plantation in June 1859: "Celia's child died about four months old. . . . This is two Negroes and three horses I have lost this year." In his report on plantation management, Thomas Affleck of Mississippi wrote of expectations for natural increase of slavery: "Of those born, one half die under one year." In his 1854 assessment of plantation capital, John Horlbeck of Charleston, South Carolina, recorded sixty-six slave deaths, including eleven infants, three of which also cost the mothers' lives. His list included:

Names	age	how acquired	Remarks	
Infant			(Dead 1844)	25
Molly	12	increase	(Dead 1854)	
Infant		d[itt]o	Dead	
Harry	17	d[itt]o	(Dead 1854)	800
Infant		d[itt]o	Dead	25
Paul	4	increase	(Dead 1854)	

To the white patriarch, the death of a slave child was foremost an economic loss: the figures in Horlbeck's unlabeled fifth column, for example, indicated value. Yet, before we dismiss these planters as callous and indifferent, it is important to realize that the patriarchal conceptualization of loss actually bound slave children's deaths to those of white children.[30]

The commodification of the black child's body would lead us to believe that the death of the slave child was considered a loss of income while the death of a white child elicited more heartfelt mourning. But many white southern parents objectified their own children's deaths as a squandering of future potential rather than the loss of an emotionally attached child. Recall Lunsford Yandell's pain at burying "our dearest hopes & brightest earthly prospects." A popular poetess of mortuary verse, Lydia Sigourney, related how "innumerable tender sympathies are cut away; the glowing expectations, nurtured for many years, are destroyed & the *cold urn* left in its place." It was not her son but expectations for his future which had been cultivated for years and then smashed just as he "arrived to the age of manhood." A poem entitled "The Little Grave" related it more lyrically:

'Tis a little grave, but oh! Beware!
For world-wide hopes are buried there,
And ye, perhaps, in coming years,
May see, like her, through blinding tears,
How much of light, how much of joy,
Is buried up with an only boy.[31]

Southerners associated such rhetoric more often with the deaths of boys, and by no means did white parents perceive the economic loss of a slave child as synonymous to the lost potential of their sons. Ultimately, the slave child could be replaced; the white child could not.

Still, as plantation patriarchs, slave owners expected "our family" to continue into the afterlife. In a southern apologist response to *Uncle Tom's Cabin*, the author of *Aunt Phillis's Cabin* (1852) assured readers that deceased slaves would continue as dependents. "Kind master, weep not," the deathbed scene of Aunt Phillis began. "She will bear, even at the throne of God, witness to thy faithfulness. Through thee she learned the way to heaven, and it may be soon she will stand by thee again, though thou see her not. She may be one of those who will guide thee to the Celestial City; to the company of the redeemed, where will be joy forever." Like the death of a white child, the death of a black child (or adult) translated into how it spiritually benefited white adults.[32]

Of course, from the black parents' perspective, the loss of a child was fraught with emotion. Fannie Moore, a South Carolina slave, remembered her younger brother's death. Her mother was a fieldhand and returned one evening to discover the boy had died. She knelt "by de bed and cry her heart out." Moore's mother returned to the fields the next day as the boy's uncle carried him in a small pine box to the plantation's burying ground. Fannie watched her mother "just plow and cry as she watch 'em put George in de ground." The episode relates a great deal about the contrasts between white and black families in mourning. White women were expected to assume the *task* of mourning, but the rigor of plantation work did not allow black women the *luxury* of mourning. In white remembrances of childhood death, fathers are absent because of cultural expectations about masculine mourning: men were not to be seen as weak or emotional. In this black remembrance, as in others, fathers were just absent—either on another plantation or sold away—forcing maternal relatives like Fannie's uncle to perform burials and provide emotional support.[33]

As parents, black southerners felt the same parental losses as white southerners, but they could never really affirm that loss as completely their own. As slave owner, the planter claimed not only their time but, as evidenced in Horlbeck's inventory, their children as well. In the summer of 1855, a slave girl fell into a well on James M. Tolbert's Alabama plantation and drowned. "She was four years three months and 3 days old Anthony Come to the plantation after Me," Tolbert remembered. "I Come home Made a Coffin and buried My little negro I am Sorry my little negro is dead, but I Cant help it." Tolbert clearly understood the girl as his; whether as property or out of an emotional attachment may be beside the point—he laid claim to her. But Tolbert also absolved himself of any responsibility. We do not know how the girl's parents responded or even if they lived on the same plantation, but most certainly they would have interpreted her death as their loss, not Tolbert's.[34]

Like white parents who viewed the death of a child as more than solely a loss of life, investing childhood death with issues of divine disfavor or lost future potential, black parents interpreted more into their children's deaths than the loss of a child. Harriet Jacobs recalled her son's illness: "I loved to watch his infant slumbers; but always there was a dark cloud over my enjoyment. I could never forget that he was a slave. Sometimes I wished that he might die in infancy. God tried me. My darling became very ill. The bright eyes grew dull, and the little feet and hands were so icy cold that I thought death had already touched them. I had prayed for his death, but never so earnestly as I now prayed for his life; and my prayer was heard. Alas, what mockery it is for a slave mother to try to pray back her dying child to life! Death is better than slavery."[35] Imagine Mary Henderson, mother to four children stricken down by the whooping cough, finding mockery in her efforts to save her children!

From the perspective of the slave quarters, what made black slave children's deaths distinct from white children's deaths was that African American parents took solace and even joy in childhood death as redemption from enslavement. Without socially defined periods of mourning, black southerners could blend grief with their prolonged desires for freedom. One of the few funeral hymns to relate this notion to children was "Little Baby Gone Home":

> De little baby gone home,
> De little baby gone home,
> De little baby gone along,
> For to climb up Jacob's ladder.
> And I wish I'd been dar,
> I wish I'd been dar,
> I wish I'd been dar, my Lord,
> For to climb up Jacob's ladder.

Any student of southern history is familiar with slaves' association of dying with freedom. "I Want to Go Home," "One More River," "The Coming Day," "Crossing the River Jordon": slave spirituals were filled with references to escaping slavery through death, although the typical assumption was that such lyrics pertained to adults. Sung sorrowfully and repeatedly, like a rumbling dirge, "Little Baby Gone Home" emphasized escape as the theme of black childhood death.[36]

Yet, even as black southerners' attitudes toward childhood death seem strikingly different from those of white southerners, there was common ground in ideas of the role of patriarchy and the hope of family reconstitution. African folkways had long taught that on the way "home," the deceased met ancestors who accompanied him or her on the journey. As former slave Charles Ball remembered, one slave father buried his young son with "a small bow and several arrows; a little bag of parched meal; a miniature canoe, about a foot long, and a little paddle (with which he said it would cross the ocean to his own country), a small stick, with an iron nail, sharpened, and fastened into one end of it; and a piece of white muslin, with several curious and strange figures painted on it in blue and red, by which, he said, his relations and countrymen would know the infant to be his son, and would receive it accordingly, on its arrival amongst them." Ancestors would receive the child among them and incorporate him into the reconstructed family of the spirit realm.[37]

Like whites, then, blacks conceptualized the long-dead welcoming the recently deceased. Despite the shared culture trope, however, reconciliation with African ancestors did not fulfill the "Christian" requisites for the proper Victorian deathbed scene. Three years after *Uncle Tom's Cabin* appeared, a response was published as *Cassy; or, Early Trials* (1855). This was not the Cassy from Stowe's book but a comparable character: a young girl whose mother failed in running away from slavery and, in desperation, sold Cassy to a white woman returning to Ohio from Mississippi. In a scene remarkably similar to Little Eva's deathbed, Cassy lay dying as her adopted mother drew clear distinctions between the African American worldview and the white Victorian version of afterlife:

> "If I were to say," said Mrs. Hall, "that I was going to take you to Africa, to the home of your mother, and that you would see her there, and birds and flowers more beautiful than any you have ever seen, you would be very happy. I know you would! Well, Cassy, you are going to a home more beautiful than Africa. In Africa you would feel heat, and thirst, and pain; but in heaven there is no pain, nor sorrow, nor sighing. The Bible tells us that God sits there on a white throne, surrounded by glorious angels, who, with harps in their hands, sing beautiful songs about God. You like singing, Cassy. In heaven you will hear sweeter singing than you ever did on earth!"

In describing Africa much as Victorians would have described Hell—heat, thirst, pain, sorrow, sighing—Cassy's "mother" forced her to choose between Heaven

"Carlo looked at her and gave a low whine."

Fig. 3. *Cassy; or, Early Trials* (Boston: John P. Jewett, 1855), 31. Courtesy of Harriet Beecher Stowe Center, Hartford, Conn.

and Africa, fulfilling the Victorian deathbed scene requirement of conversion and salvation.[38]

Ironically, the illustrations used in *Cassy* were left over from *Uncle Tom's Cabin*, making the comparative deathbed scenes more revealing. In contrast to Little Eva, neither an extended family nor an intimate family surrounded Cassy's deathbed; her only companion was her dog. Without an audience, Cassy's final moments were not spent in a comforting and exalting monologue. Instead, the author portrayed the girl as panicked, asking her adopted mother, "Am I going to die?" and receiving assurance that God would either cure her or take her to Heaven.

Fig. 4. *Cassy; or Early Trials* (Boston: John P. Jewett, 1855), 32. Courtesy of Harriet Beecher Stowe Center, Hartford, Conn.

And thus race mattered a great deal in conceptualizing southern children's deathbed scenes. In a strange twist, the final illustration meant to portray Cassy's arrival in Heaven had originally been drawn as Eva's arrival in Heaven. For readers of *Cassy*, then, the image inverted the heroine's race, making her white as she reached out to white angels. The accompanying text concluded, "The little black girl, the despised negro, was consigned to the grave; but her soul had taken flight, to dwell for countless ages, through all eternity, in the mansions of the blessed!" In selecting Heaven over Africa, Cassy chose the white ideal of the afterlife, made even more ironic by the physiological truism that, when African Americans die, their skin tones darken, emphasizing postmortem the uniqueness of their pigmentation. It was the ultimate Victorian deathbed conversion: she abandoned her blackening body to the grave as her purified, whitening soul departed for the elegant "big house" of Heaven.[39]

Cassy's family ties were negligible at best. Taken to Ohio by her adopted mother, a white widow, she was free from the patriarchal and racial constraints of southern family life, white and black. Her decision to sacrifice reunion with her mother in Africa for eternal heavenly life evinced that freedom. Reconstitution of family in Heaven was a central component of Victorian deathways, but it was most relevant when family had shaped earthly life. For antebellum southern whites, as represented by Little Eva, reunion included "our family" and re-created the patriarchal structures of family and household so familiar in earthly life. For antebellum southern blacks, familial reconstruction included centuries of ancestors, binding the deceased to their African heritage, liberating the soul from the bonds of slavery, and rejecting the biracial extended family created during enslavement. "Our family, white and black"—white southerners employed the phrase not only to suggest the biracial nature of their households but also to intimate the affective bonds between blacks and whites. When it came to the most difficult moments in family lives, however, when children died and parents mourned, the lie of "our family, white and black" was exposed.

Notes

1. Harriet Beecher Stowe, *Uncle Tom's Cabin; or, Life among the Lowly* (Boston: John P. Jewett, 1852), chap. 26, quotations on 418, 428; Stowe, *Pictures and Stories from Uncle Tom's Cabin* (Boston: John P. Jewett, 1853), 28–29.

2. Philippe Ariès, *The Hour of Our Death*, trans. Helen Weaver (New York: Vintage, 1982), 470–74, quotations on 473; Ann Douglas, *The Feminization of American Culture* (New York: Alfred A. Knopf, 1977), 245; James J. Farrell, *Inventing the American Way of Death, 1830–1929* (Philadelphia: Temple University Press, 1980), 40; Gary Laderman, *The Sacred Remains: American Attitudes towards Death, 1799–1886* (New Haven: Yale University Press, 1996), 56; Mary Louise Kett, *Sentimental Collaborations: Mourning and Middle-Class Identity in Nineteenth-Century America* (Durham, N.C.: Duke University Press, 2000), 57–58; Franny Nudelman, *John Brown's Body: Slavery, Violence, and the Culture of War* (Chapel Hill: University of North Carolina Press, 2004), 19–23.

3. Sylvia D. Hoffert, "'A Very Peculiar Sorrow': Attitudes toward Infant Death in the Urban Northeast, 1800–1860," *American Quarterly* 39 (winter 1987): 601–16, quotation on 602; Laderman, *The Sacred Remains*, 56; Douglas, *The Feminization of American Culture*, 240–72; Farrell, *Inventing the American Way of Death*, 30–43; Sandra M. Gilbert, *Death's Door: Modern Dying and the Ways We Grieve* (New York: W. W. Norton, 2006), 332–65.

4. James Marten, "Fatherhood in the Confederacy: Southern Soldiers and Their Children," *Journal of Southern History* 63 (May 1997): 269–92.

5. The death rate per 1,000 births for white infants in the United States was 216 in 1850, 181 in 1860, and 214 in 1880. It is more difficult to determine black infant death rates, although for 1850, the rate has been measured at 340, placing the average rate for *all* American children in

that year at 278. In Victorian England, the rates were notably lower: 143 in 1840, 148 in 1860, and 153 in 1880. See Samuel H. Preston and Michael R. Haines, *Fatal Years: Child Mortality in Late Nineteenth-Century America* (Princeton: Princeton University Press, 1991), table 2.5; Richard H. Steckel, "A Dreadful Childhood: The Excess Mortality of American Slaves," *Social Science History* 10 (Winter 1986): 427–65; Michael R. Haines, "Estimated Life Tables for the United States, 1850–1900," *Historical Methods* 31 (Fall 1998): 149–69; Pat Jalland, *Death in the Victorian Family* (New York: Oxford University Press, 1996), 120.

6. Lawrence Stone, *The Family, Sex, and Marriage in England, 1500–1800* (New York: Harper and Row, 1977), 651–52; Jane Turner Censer, *North Carolina Planters and Their Children, 1800–1860* (Baton Rouge: Louisiana State University Press, 1984), 16–17.

7. Stowe, *Pictures and Stories from Uncle Tom's Cabin*, 27.

8. Kett, *Sentimental Collaborations*, 57, 80–84, 87–88; Jane P. Tompkins, "Sentimental Power: Uncle Tom's Cabin and the Politics of Literary History," in *Uncle Tom's Cabin*, ed. Elizabeth Ammons (New York: W. W. Norton, 1994), 506–7; Veronica Margrave, "Rethinking Contemporary Criticism of *Uncle Tom's Cabin*: Unraveling the Myth of Transparency," www.cortland.edu/COWRC/WritingContest/2002/margrave.pdf; Farrell, *Inventing the American Way of Death*, 34. On the metaphorical intersection between family and national identity, see Amy Murrell Taylor, *The Divided Family in Civil War America* (Chapel Hill: University of North Carolina Press, 2006), 7–10.

9. Julia A. Paisley Gilmer Scrapbook, ca. 1858–70, Addison Gorgas Brenizer Collection, 1858–70, Southern Historical Collection, Wilson Library, University of North Carolina at Chapel Hill; Hoffert, "A Very Peculiar Sorrow," 601–2; Douglas, *The Feminization of American Culture*, 240–72; Jan Lewis, *In Pursuit of Happiness: Family Values in Jefferson's Virginia* (New York: Cambridge University Press, 1983).

10. Untitled poem, Gilmer Scrapbook; Stephanie McCurry, *Masters of Small Worlds: Yeoman Households, Gender Relations, and the Political Culture of the Antebellum South Carolina Low County* (New York: Oxford University Press, 1995), 171–72; Christine Leigh Heyrman, *Southern Cross: The Beginnings of the Bible Belt* (New York: Alfred A. Knopf, 1997), 189.

11. Anne S. Swann Diary, 27 October 1835, Swann Family Papers, Southern Historical Collection; Elizabeth Fox-Genovese, *Within the Plantation Household: Black and White Women of the Old South* (Chapel Hill: University of North Carolina Press, 1988), 38–39, 42–44, 60–64; Jean E. Friedman, *The Enclosed Garden: Women and Community in the Evangelical South, 1830–1900* (Chapel Hill: University of North Carolina Press, 1985), xi; Brenda W. Stevenson, *Life in Black and White: Family and Community in the Slave South* (New York: Oxford University Press, 1996), 115–16, 323; Bertram Wyatt-Brown, *Southern Honor: Ethics and Behavior in the Old South* (New York: Oxford University Press, 1982), 50–51.

12. Laderman, *The Sacred Remains*, 54; Heyrman, *Southern Cross*, 4–5; Donald Mathews, *Religion in the Old South* (Chicago: University of Chicago Press, 1977), 62; Wyatt-Brown, *Southern Honor*, 35; Wyatt-Brown, *The Shaping of Southern Culture: Honor, Grace, and War, 1760s–1880s* (Chapel Hill: University of North Carolina Press, 2001), chap. 4; Fox-Genovese, *Within the Plantation Household*, 31–32; McCurry, *Masters of Small Worlds*, 6–7.

13. Mary Bethell Diary, 1 January 1853, Southern Historical Collection, emphasis added. On southern women and their conceptualization of a vengeful God, see Friedman, *The Enclosed*

Garden, 35; Heyrman, *Southern Cross*, 34; Sally G. McMillen, *Motherhood in the Old South: Pregnancy, Childbirth, and Infant Rearing* (Baton Rouge: Louisiana State University Press, 1990), 173–75. I am particularly grateful to Jennifer Baker, who introduced me to Mary Bethell and Mary Henderson through her own research; see "Faith Tempered by Tragedy: Antebellum Women in North Carolina," presented at North Carolina Graduate Student History Conference, Raleigh, 24 February 2007, copy in possession of the author.

14. Bethell Diary, 10 October 1853, 11 April 1854, 7 September 1859; Martha V. Pike and Janice Gray Armstrong, eds., *A Time to Mourn: Expressions of Grief in Nineteenth-Century America* (New York: Museums at Stony Brook, 1980), 17.

15. Douglas, *Feminization of American Culture*, 202.

16. Lunsford Yandell to unknown, 15 June 1836, Yandell Family Papers, Filson Historical Society, Louisville, Ky.

17. Heyrman, *Southern Cross*, 202–4; Marcus J. Borg, *The God We Never Knew: Beyond Dogmatic Religion to a More Authentic Contemporary Faith* (New York: HarperCollins, 1997), chap. 2.

18. Ferrell, *Inventing the American Way of Death*, 34; Philippe Ariès, *Western Attitudes toward Death from the Middle Ages to the Present* (Baltimore: Johns Hopkins University Press, 1974), 66–68; Margaret J. Coffin, *Death in Early America: The History and Folklore of Customs and Superstitions of Early Medicine, Funerals, Burials, and Mourning* (Nashville: Thomas Nelson, 1976), 197–99; Lawrence Taylor, "Symbolic Death: An Anthropological View of Mourning Ritual in the Nineteenth Century," in Pike and Armstrong, eds., *A Time to Mourn*, 40–43.

19. Mary Henderson Diary, 21 December 1854, 30 June 1855, James S. Henderson Papers, Southern Historical Collection; McMillen, *Motherhood in the Old South*, chap. 6.

20. Henderson Diary, 21 December 1854; McMillen, *Motherhood in the Old South*, chap. 6; Steven Stowe, *Doctoring the South: Southern Physicians and Everyday Medicine in the Mid-Nineteenth Century* (Chapel Hill: University of North Carolina Press, 2004), 133–34; William Buchan, *Domestic Medicine* (1769; reprint, Boston: Otis Brothers, 1848).

21. Henderson Diary, 8 July 1855; Paul Starr, *The Social Transformation of American Medicine* (New York: Basic Books, 1982), 81–88. The gendered tension between women as healthcare providers and male physicians has been explored particularly as it related to midwifery; see Laurel Thatcher Ulrich, *A Midwife's Tale: The Life of Martha Ballard, Based on Her Diary, 1785–1812* (New York: Knopf, 1990), 254–55; Judith Walzer Leavitt, *Brought to Bed: Child-Bearing in America, 1750–1950* (New York: Oxford University Press, 1986), 100–101.

There is some evidence that, even as male physicians encroached on the women's traditional role as family health-care providers, patriarchs retained their roles as health-care providers for the slaves. See, for example, Drew Gilpin Faust, *James Henry Hammond and the Old South: Design for Mastery* (Baton Rouge: Louisiana State University Press, 1982), 75–76.

22. Taylor, "Symbolic Death," 40–43.

23. "The Child Is Not, and I, Whither Shall I Go"—Gen. xxxvii: 30, *Presbyterian Banner*, n.d., in Gilmer Scrapbook; E. Lively to Matilda Miller, 15 February 1857, Rare Book, Manuscript, and Special Collections Library, Duke University, Durham, N.C.

24. Henderson Diary, 28 October 1855; Susan Yandell to Martha, 18 October 1836, Yandell Family Papers, 1823–87, Filson Historical Society; Elizabeth Reis, "Immortal Messengers: An-

gels, Gender, and Power in Early America," in *Mortal Remains: Death in Early America*, ed. Nancy Isenberg and Andrew Burstein (Philadelphia: University of Pennsylvania Press, 2003), 163–75.

25. Yandell to Martha, 18 October 1836; Swann Diary, 18 October 1835; Coffin, *Death in Early America*, 72.

26. Heyrman, *Southern Cross*, 189; Henderson Diary, 17 February 1854; McCurry, *Masters of Small Worlds*, 81, 84–85.

27. Stephen Garton, "The Scale of Suffering: Love, Death, and Victorian Masculinity," *Social History* 27 (January 2002): 41.

28. James H. Greenlee Diary, Southern Historical Collection.

29. Everard Green Baker Diaries, 22 August 1850, Southern Historical Collection.

30. David Gavin Diary, 18 December 1859, Southern Historical Collection; T. Affleck, "On the Hygiene of Cotton Plantations and the Management of Negro Slaves," *Southern Medical Reports* 2 (1850): 429–36, quote 435; Horlbeck Family Book, Southern Historical Collection.

31. L. H. Sigourney to unknown, 30 November 1851, Lydia Howard Sigourney Papers, 1791–1865, Rare Book, Manuscript, and Special Collections Library; "The Little Grave," Gilmer Scrapbook; Gilbert, *Death's Door*, 337; Lorri Glover, *Southern Sons: Becoming Men in the New South* (Baltimore: Johns Hopkins University Press, 2007). On parents' conceptualization of children not only as labor but as "social capital," see Steven Mintz, *Huck's Raft: A History of American Childhood* (Cambridge, Mass.: Belknap Press, 2004), 77–78.

32. Mary H. Eastman, *Aunt Phillis's Cabin; or, Southern Life as It Is* (Philadelphia: Lippincott, Grambo, 1852), 263.

33. Norman R. Yetman, *Life under the "Peculiar Institution": Selections from the Slave Narrative Collection* (New York: Holt, Rinehart and Winston, 1970), 228; Wilma King, *Stolen Childhood: Slave Youth in Nineteenth-Century America* (Bloomington: Indiana University Press, 1997), 9–12.

34. James M. Tolbert Diary, Alabama Department of Archives and History, Montgomery.

35. Harriet Jacobs, *Incidents in the Life of a Slave Girl, Written by Herself*, ed. L. Maria Child (Boston: privately published, 1861), 96.

36. Eugene Genovese, *Roll, Jordan, Roll: The World the Slaves Made* (New York: Vintage Press, 1972), 196–202; Thomas Wentworth Higginson, "Negro Spirituals," *Atlantic Monthly*, June 1867, 685–94; Regina Dolan, "Negro Spirituals and American Culture," *Interracial Review*, April 1958, available at www.nathanielturner.com/negrospirituals.htm.

37. Charles Ball, *Fifty Years in Chains; or, The Life of an American Slave* (New York: H. Dayton, 1859), 197–98; Sylvia R. Frey and Betty Wood, *Come Shouting to Zion: African American Protestantism in the American South and British Caribbean to 1830* (Chapel Hill: University of North Carolina Press, 1998), 51–56; Karla FC Holloway, *Passed On: African American Mourning Stories* (Durham, N.C.: Duke University Press, 2003), 4–5; Mechel Sobel, *The World We Made Together: Black and White Values in Eighteenth-Century Virginia* (Princeton: Princeton University Press, 1987), 171–77, 214–25.

38. *Cassy; or, Early Trials* (Boston: John P. Jewett, 1855), 31–32.

39. Holloway, *Passed On*, 26–27.

4

Female Families

Same-Sex Love in the Victorian South

ANYA JABOUR

∼

In 1872, Lizzie Grove wrote to her dear friend and cousin, Laura Brumback, about her studies, women's fashions, and neighborhood news, including gossip about the two young women's supposedly impending marriages. "People must be afraid you and I won[']t get married it seems to work on their minds considerably," she commented wryly. The local gossipmongers might have been still more concerned had they known how Lizzie addressed Laura in the women's private correspondence, calling her "my *dearest Husband*" and "my Dear dear Husband" and signing her letters not Lizzie Grove but Lizzie G. Laura. Although physically separated—Lizzie resided in Missouri, and Laura was the daughter of Virginia migrants to Illinois—the two women remained "faithful" to one another, sharing dress patterns, their hopes for the future, and their doubts about men, marriage, and motherhood with each other. Six years after Lizzie commented on rumors of the women's engagements, both women were still unmarried. Writing to Laura about weddings in her neighborhood in 1878, Lizzie commented with disgust about one new bride, "that old dumb thing what did she want with a *man*."[1]

The intimate and enduring relationship between these two women and their distaste for men, marriage, and motherhood suggest that same-sex relationships offered young women in the nineteenth-century South an attractive alternative to "traditional" family life, defined by the southern family values of male dominance and compulsory heterosexuality. Despite the consternation of the young women's neighbors, the relationship that Lizzie and her "dearest Husband" enjoyed was not an isolated occurrence in the Victorian South. Rather, research in southern women's personal correspondence between 1840 and 1900 indicates that many young women cherished same-sex relationships and regarded what might be called "female families" as desirable, even if not fully viable, options.[2]

While women's historians have long been aware that northern nineteenth-century women enjoyed close and mutually supportive "bonds of womanhood" within what Carroll Smith-Rosenberg, in her classic essay on women's relationships, called a "female world of love and ritual," less attention has been paid to southern women's intimate relationships with each other. Although several scholars have remarked upon the importance of southern women's friendships, most have emphasized that, for southern women, friendship and kinship were closely connected and have posited that female friendships served as preparation for, rather than offering an alternative to, conventional marriage.[3]

Discussion of southern women's same-sex relationships is complicated by the difficulty of defining women's sexuality. In nineteenth-century America, definitions of female sexuality were in transition. For most of the nineteenth century, women—at least well-to-do white women—were presumed to be "passionless." As a result, most people considered female friendships to be innocent of sexual overtones, even when to modern eyes such friendships appear clearly erotic. Because the presumed asexuality of women's relationships with one another reinforced popular definitions of ideal femininity, and perhaps because women's romances did not appear to challenge either compulsory heterosexuality or male dominance, such relationships were generally accepted and often encouraged. Toward the end of the nineteenth century, at the same time that a generation of "New Women" began to reject what Jane Addams called "the family claim" in favor of community service and professional careers, a group of scientific, psychological, and medical professionals on both sides of the Atlantic, known collectively as "sexologists," gained an American audience. The sexologists recognized relationships between women as sexually active and stigmatized them as socially deviant. Thus, by the turn of the century, American women became "increasingly self-conscious" about their affection for other women. However, well into the twentieth century, many women ignored the implications of the sexologists' concerns and continued to conceptualize their relationships with other women as "romantic friendship."[4]

Contemporary scholars, no less than Victorian Americans, disagree on the best way to define lesbian sexuality. While some historians argue for a continuum of homoerotic feeling, which appears often in nineteenth-century manuscripts, others insist on the importance of sexual activity, which is more difficult to document or define. As Blanche Wiesen Cook has pointed out in her critique of what she terms "the historical denial of lesbianism," historians routinely apply a higher standard of physical evidence to determine homosexuality (which most scholars tend to deny) than heterosexuality (which most scholars tend to assume). In researching the nineteenth century when few historical subjects openly discussed sexuality of any kind, requiring positive proof of homosexual activity equates to denying homosexuality's very existence.[5]

If documenting lesbian sexuality is difficult, defining lesbianism is nearly impossible. The critical issue here is whether to define women's relationships as they themselves did—in a context in which most well-to-do white women either, quite simply, would not have recognized themselves as the "mannish lesbians" beginning to gain negative attention or, equally sensibly, would have rejected a label associated with perversion, promiscuity, and prostitution—or in terms of contemporary identity politics. If, as Wiesen Cook suggests, "the legal and social manifestations of bigotry and repression are reinforced and validated by the historical denial of lesbianism," then it becomes important to "insist on the word lesbian" to describe women's intimate relationships with one another, even if they did not use the word themselves. Thus, as Leila J. Rupp has pointed out, "we are faced with a choice between labeling women lesbians who might have violently rejected the notion or glossing over the significance of women's relationships by considering them asexual."[6]

In their efforts to reclaim the gay and lesbian past, some historians have experimented with definitions of lesbianism that do not depend on evidence of either sexual contact or self-identity. In 1979, Wiesen Cook averred, "Women who love women, who choose women to nurture and support and to form a living environment in which to work creatively and independently are lesbians." Two decades later, Lillian Faderman proposed a definition for lesbianism that harks back to Wiesen Cook's definition: "What all these people had in common," she remarks in her study of women reformers in Progressive-era America, "was that beloved women were centrally implicated in their emotional lives, and . . . their intimate relationships with other women helped enable their achievements" by liberating them from domestic responsibilities.[7]

While both American and British scholars have attributed lesbianism to their nineteenth-century subjects, historians of the American South have been reluctant to follow their lead.[8] In part, this may be because feminist consciousness and lesbian identity are often linked in extant scholarship, and feminism's inroads into the American South were both limited and late. In her study of southern women's higher education, Christie Anne Farnham argues that even though schoolgirls in the Old South mimicked heterosexual courtship in their relationships with each other, "romantic friendships did not impede future marriages," and "romantic friendships in Southern schools do not seem to have been productive of lesbian communities" that freed women from service to their families and from the patriarchal mandate to serve a husband and children. Thus Farnham does not define southern schoolgirls' same-sex relationships, however intimate, as lesbian.[9]

Allowing for differences in interpretation, both Farnham and Faderman suggest that a fruitful way to discuss women's relationships with each other is to examine whether same-sex relationships offered women freedom from male dominance, domestic drudgery, and unceasing childbearing. In the case of nineteenth-century southern women, the answer is clearly and resoundingly "yes." Whether that leads to defining such relationships as "lesbian" is another question, with the answer depending on the women's self-definition and their sexual activity. Since definitions of female sexuality were in flux, and extant sources are often ambiguous regarding sexual activity, the answer to this question can be only "maybe."

I contend, however, that the first question remains an important one. Moreover, it leads to a new question: Did same-sex love (whether defined as "lesbian" or not) offer women a potential alternative to heterosexual family life? This essay offers an affirmative, if qualified, response to this question. Same-sex relationships offered women in the Victorian South an escape from patriarchal power, household responsibilities, and constant childbearing. But such relationships were potentially more than a refuge from heterosexual family life; they represented an alternative form of family life: all-female family units.

By focusing on "female families," this essay casts southern women's intimate relationships with each other in the context of women's and family history rather than from the standpoint of the history of lesbianism or sexuality studies. It thus responds to Sharon Marcus's assertion that "lesbian lives are best studied as part of the general history of women and the family, and that heterosexual women's lives can only be fully understood if we attend to their friendships with women." Looking at female-to-female relationships within this context reveals what we can know about women's relationships, rather than what we cannot know. It also sheds new light on southern family history, particularly on what Marcus calls "the play of the system" and on its limits. When we juxtapose the wishes and experiences of women in the Victorian South against those of their counterparts in the American Northeast and Great Britain, it becomes clear that while at least some southern women regarded female families as a desirable variant on the family form, southern women's ability to sustain same-sex relationships was severely circumscribed.[10]

While the women discussed in this essay imaginatively evaded the bounds of patriarchal society to create self-defined, all-female family units, they were unable to sustain these alternative forms of family life in the context of southern family values of male dominance and heterosexual marriage. Rather, the evidence presented here suggests that although southern women may have dreamed of and briefly attained female-to-female relationships defined in familial terms, they were unable to translate those relationships into lifelong lesbian partnerships. Women may have found temporary refuge from southern family values in female families, but ultimately they found it impossible to translate their desire for and enjoyment of same-sex intimacy into a viable alternative to southern patriarchy. Southern family values effectively prevented women from sustaining female families in the nineteenth-century South.

What characterized female families in the Victorian South? Broadly speaking, women who formed or hoped to form female families had serious doubts about heterosexual activity, patriarchal prerogatives, and uncontrolled reproduction—or, as they expressed these concerns, about men, marriage, and motherhood. Repelled by these central aspects of conventional families, these women also found comfort in close ties with other women. They flourished in relationships that offered emotional intimacy, provided support for intellectual development and professional careers, and allowed women to enjoy physical closeness without risk of pregnancy.

Concerns about conventional family life and attractions to female friendship were widespread in the nineteenth-century South. What set the members of female families apart from their peers was that they framed their relationships with other women in terms of love, marriage, and family, much as female couples in the American Northeast and Victorian England did. Against the backdrop of anxieties about men, marriage, and motherhood, and acknowledging the attractions of emotionally, intellectually, and physically fulfilling relationships with other women, some southern women in the Victorian era cast their romantic friends as lovers, children, spouses, and parents—creating female families bound by same-sex love.[11]

As other scholars have observed, women in the Victorian South often expressed anxiety about men and motherhood. Some of women's worries about men concerned sexual activity. Shortly before her own belated wedding, in 1878, Lizzie Grove pondered: "Just think two more nights and then—why then I surely will have to go to bed with a—man. How odd it will seem."[12] Like other nineteenth-century women, Lizzie would have regularly shared a bed with other women—female relatives, school roommates, and romantic friends. The reason for her consternation, then, was not mere physical intimacy but heterosexual activity.

Concerns about sexual intercourse were common among women in the Victorian South. One reason for women's anxiety about heterosexual activity was the potential for pregnancy; in nineteenth-century America, there was simply no safe, effective, and reliable way for a heterosexually active woman to control her own reproduction. Moreover, in the absence of laws against marital rape, there was also no legal way for a married woman to control her own sexuality. Small wonder, then, that Anne Firor Scott has concluded that mid-nineteenth-century women's dissatisfaction with the southern patriarchy "centered on women's lack of control over many aspects of their own sexual lives and the sexual lives of their husbands."[13] Indeed, shortly after her own marriage, Lizzie Grove commented nervously on an acquaintance's childbirth: "I do think women are haveing [*sic*] fearful times this fall I'm so glad I'm not so."[14] Men and motherhood were both closely linked and equally worrisome.

Many southern women also indicated grave doubts about men and marriage. As Joan Cashin noted in an article on the Dogan sisters of South Carolina, southern women expressed concern that husbands might prove unloving or unfaithful and worried that uncaring husbands would abuse their power in the marriage relationship.[15] In the 1840s and 1850s, Virginian Frances Bernard received a series of letters from a circle of friends comparing marriage to a man to friendship with a woman, with marriage invariably coming out the loser. One friend, Elise, expressed skepticism about marital happiness and begged Frances to join her in her resolve to remain single. "Let me live and die in single blessedness," she vowed, rather than make an unhappy match. "I can imagine no state more miserable than to be joined for life to one who has not affection & confidence." Another friend commented on the "beaux" in her area, but sighed with relief, "As for myself I am not trouble[d] with that sex [i.e., men]." For Frances Bernard and her friends—as for many other young women in the Old South— female friendship was clearly superior to heterosexual marriage. As Bernard's friend Elise expressed it, "maiden liberty" was preferable to "a [man's] name."[16]

Wary of heterosexual activity, male dominance, and unceasing childbearing, many women in the nineteenth-century South found comfort and solace in same-sex relationships. Southern women often commented on the emotional intimacy and mutual support they found in such relationships. Frances Bernard's friend Elise, who worried that marriage to a man might prove "miserable," was much more optimistic about her relationship with Frances. "You expressed an idea in your last letter which pleased me so much," she wrote, "and which I believe, as I feel the same. You say that any enjoyment loses half its pleasure in which I cannot share it with you. Well really I beleive [*sic*] our attachment is so very strong that any scene of rapture shared together would be greatly heightened or any pang of sorrow softened by mutual sympathy."[17] Within the context of same-sex relationships, if not in conventional marriage, it was possible to combine "maiden liberty" with "mutual sympathy."

Many southern women sought emotional support and sisterly understanding in female friendship. Some women also indicated that they found their female friends to be supportive of their intellectual development and, in some cases, their ambitions for professional careers. This was an important and unique aspect of women's same-sex relationships in the Victorian South. While married women were expected to set aside their own ambitions and replace them with ambitions for their husbands' success, women's same-sex friendships could provide both emotional and practical support for female ambition.

Elizabeth Scott Neblett's midcentury diary offers insights into southern wives' displaced ambitions. Neblett commented frequently on the mismatch between southern femininity and female ambition. "Ambition!" she declared in one entry. "Who is there that have not had dreams of ambition? What hearts have remained dull and sluggish, always pulsating with the same even slow throbs? Every heart it seems to me, must have some kind of ambition." Yet for Neblett, as for other southern women, ambition proved incompatible with marriage. On the eve of her own marriage, Neblett reflected on the relative importance of female ambition and heterosexual marriage: "[Ambition] has been the ruling passion of my life, in all things save love. There a weakness is every manifest, and ambition is drowned in the play of stronger, and opposite passions." Once committed to marriage, Neblett "drowned" her own ambition and submerged it into her husband's: "When my heart is enlisted, I am ambitious for *him*, to a painful degree." Neblett regarded ambition as inappropriate for a woman. "Heaven in her wisdom has placed insurmountable barriers between me and my individual ambition," she mused. "I can never gain worldly honors. Fame can never be mine. I am a *woman!*" But Neblett was not simply a woman, but a married woman. As a proper southern wife, Neblett resolved to replace her own ambitions with those of her husband. "Being a woman I can never arrive at any greatness & fame; all the ambition of my soul is centered upon him."[18]

As Lillian Faderman has observed in her study of women reformers in Progressive-era America, however, women who formed lifelong partnerships, or "Boston marriages," with other women found that such relationships actually fostered female ambition and achievement.[19] In her study of Victorian England,

Sharon Marcus has suggested that "female marriages" not only granted their participants the ability to be in a truly egalitarian relationship but also served as a model for bringing heterosexual marriages into line with the companionate ideals of reciprocity and equality within marriage.[20] In the American South, at least a few women envisioned finding the same sort of egalitarian partnership and mutual support that these scholars have identified elsewhere within the context of female families. While conventional marriage was a barrier to female ambition, same-sex love might instead be an avenue to female achievement.

For many southern women, as for women in the Northeast and in Victorian England, the female academy was an important introduction to a world in which female friendship and academic achievement were closely connected. The correspondence of the Faison family, a multigenerational group of female students in North Carolina, indicates the importance of school relationships. Martha Faison urged her daughter, Winifred, to make the most of her time at the female academy, calling attention to the different members of the school community. "Be consciencious [*sic*] in the discharge of all your duties, be always respectful to teachers, kind, polite and considerate to your companions, hope you have pleasant roommates, as you will be thrown more intimately with them," she remarked. Mollie Faison, a graduate of the Charlotte Female Institute, told Winifred to expect to form close ties while at school. "I know you will become so attached to Teachers and girls you will hate to leave," she predicted. "It is the nicest place in the world for girls so many pleasant and congenial companions, and things." Aunt "Em," writing to Winifred in 1889, summed up the importance of society in the academy: "There is a little world in a Boarding school."[21]

The "little world" of the academy was a female community: a space inhabited and directed by women. In the female academy, what Gerda Lerner has termed "clusters of learned women" and "affinitive clusters" of female friendship overlapped. Southern schoolgirls found both affection and intellectual challenges when they left home for school. This was an important precondition for an identity separate from the natal-family circle; it was also one route to an alternative definition of family life. As scholars of women's colleges in the North and in England have pointed out, "Formal institutions were alternatives to the nuclear family." In the context of such "woman-controlled spaces" as the female academy, young women forged loyalties to each other and to the values of the school that cut across—and sometimes superseded—their traditional loyalties to their families, kin, and neighborhoods. In the nineteenth-century South as well, female academies offered a "social space . . . outside the family" where women-in-the-making could lead "women-focused lives."[22]

Students at female academies formed close relationships with female faculty. Mary Frances Gray, a student at Wesleyan Female College in Murfreesboro, North Carolina, in the 1870s, reveled in her friendships with her teachers. "My teachers all seem to love me," she wrote to a friend from home. "The matron says she loves me better than any girl in school."[23]

Students' relationships with their teachers could have a lasting impact on their futures. In both the Northeast and in England, female educators inspired schoolgirls to pursue careers rather than husbands. As Martha Vicinus points out in her study of higher education in Victorian England, "An emotional relation between a student and teacher was frequently the impetus for a career of dedicated service, rather than a preamble to marriage."[24] This was no less true for southern students in nineteenth-century America. Josephine Simrall, a native southerner who attended Wellesley in the early 1890s, idolized her Bible teacher, Miss Scudder. "She is such a wonderful woman, and a fine literary scholar," she praised the teacher in a letter to her mother. Miss Scudder proved to be a major role model for Simrall, inspiring her to consider a future as a settlement house worker.[25]

Female educators were role models in other ways as well, demonstrating in their daily lives that a professional career did not require sacrificing a personal life. At women's colleges in New England, female faculty frequently formed long-term relationships with each other. This pattern was so common, in fact, that in her study of Wellesley College, Patricia Palmieri described the school as an "Adamless Eden." A similar pattern characterized late nineteenth-century southern campuses, where so-called spinster schoolmarms often paired off together. At Warrenton Female College in North Carolina in the 1870s, Bettie Joyner and Maria Duty taught and lived together. The couple's commitment to one another and to their careers was common knowledge. "For two days on the blackboard in the Chapel has been written 'Miss Duty and Miss Bettie Joyner, darlings forever," Maria informed Bettie, adding, "I know not who wrote it but it was put there by some one who knows very well the feelings of my heart."[26]

Romantic relationships between professional women permitted American and British women to pursue both financial independence and emotional fulfillment. They offered similar prospects to southern women. Lizzie Grove and Laura Brumback recognized this possibility when they planned to become teachers together. "I know I would like teaching splendid," Lizzie wrote to her *"dearest Husband."* Part of Lizzie's eager anticipation of a teaching career was her expectation that the two women would enjoy a shared future in Virginia: "If I could teach next summer we would go to Virginia next fall if you would wait that long." Expressing longing for her partner's company—"I am enjoying the plea-sures of life as well as could be expected being away from those I *love*," she wrote meaningfully—Lizzie saw an opportunity for both financial independence and emotional interdependence if she and her companion lived and taught together. In such a situation, rather than pursuing her studies "all by my self" and "*weep-ing* and *pining*" for her friend's company, Lizzie would be able to enjoy "a good long *talk* with" her closest companion.[27]

Other southern women involved in intense female friendships likewise pur-sued careers as teachers, one of the few respectable options for self-support available to nineteenth-century southern women. For instance, several of the Southgate women's correspondents, discussed below, supported themselves by teaching.[28] At least some southern women aspired to, and sometimes imitated, a pattern common in northern women's colleges, in which female faculty cre-ated both a professional network and a supportive community based on female friendship.[29]

Students at female academies also enjoyed physically fulfilling and sexu-ally unthreatening relationships with one another. As Christie Anne Farnham has observed, students in the South's female academies frequently shared beds. While it is difficult if not impossible to know if girlish displays of affection such as hand-holding, hugging, and kissing extended to sexual intimacy, it is clear that female students prized the night hours as a time to share confidences—and perhaps caresses as well.[30]

A rare description of one southern schoolgirl's sleeping arrangements was contained in one of Wellesley junior Josephine Simrall's letters home in 1892, describing a night spent with a classmate named Elizabeth:

> Yesterday evening we spent lying on the floor in the firelight, listening to music and telling stories—the weirdest, most ghostly stories you ever heard, then after we went to bed Elisabeth & I staid awake until almost twelve o['] clock, absorbed in a deep theological discussion—so that we were entirely too sleepy to get up to breakfast this morning & I had to beguile the cook into giving us a cozy little meal by ourselves.[31]

While it is impossible from this account to determine that the girls' sleepover involved sexual contact, it is equally impossible to determine that it did not. As William Benemann has argued with reference to men's relationships, "Although it would be unwise to assume that a deep and abiding affection between two men [or in this case, two women] necessarily implied a sexual relationship, it would be equally wrong to assume that such a relationship *never* included a sexual component."[32]

Certainly some nineteenth-century southern women's comments on sharing beds with female friends suggest that something other than sleep occurred on such occasions. Simrall's description of her slumber parties with classmates, while set at a northern school, differed from those describing southern schools more in length than in content; southern students frequently wrote about their shared sleeping arrangements, sometimes in suggestive ways. Kate Sanborn wrote to her old school friend Lessie Southgate to communicate that she found it impossible to "keep from smiling" when she thought back to the time they spent together in "my room *in the dark*," while Lessie wrote about another female friend who "sat up with me enjoying a delightful—snooze all night."[33] Lacking either a conceptual framework or an established vocabulary for lesbian sexuality, such coy references might best be understood as descriptions of female-to-female sexual contact. Even if this were not the case, however, such comments make it clear that women involved in same-sex intimacy found pleasure in each other's company in bed together.

Other accounts make it clear that sharing a bed was a public statement of an important, and often exclusive, relationship. Aunt Em, a graduate of a female academy herself, wrote to her niece Winifred Faison at the Augusta Female Seminary in Staunton, Virginia, in the 1880s to inquire, "*Who is your bed-mate?*" Upon learning that Laura Brumback's absence would be prolonged, Lizzie Grove playfully threatened: "I see I will have to get me another 'honey Pet' one that will stay with me of nights as *you* have gone back on me." Pet names were often closely linked to sharing a bed, as when Mattie Southgate called one of her schoolmates her "Bed Bug."[34]

Carroll Smith-Rosenberg's study of northern women suggests that even after marriage, women continued to share their beds with female friends, sometimes even ejecting their husbands from the bedroom to obtain privacy. More research needs to be done on the South to determine if southern schoolgirls continued to enjoy "long, comfortable bed-time talk[s]" with their female friends after reaching adulthood. Certainly some wished to. Two years after their respective marriages, Lizzie wrote to Laura: "How much I would love to see you tonight. I know we would not sleep one *wink*."[35]

Whatever physical contact female bedmates did or did not have, sleeping with other women offered a benefit that sleeping with men could not: sharing a bed with a woman could not result in an unwanted pregnancy. In an era before reliable birth control was readily available, this was no small matter. As Elizabeth

Scott Neblett wrote to her husband in the 1860s, "This constant and never ceasing horror I have of childbearing constantly obtrudes itself between me & my desire & longing to see & clasp you round the neck once more." As a result of her fears of pregnancy, Neblett concluded, "my longing wears a curb."[36] In same-sex relationships, however, fear of pregnancy did not interfere with physical pleasure.

Southern women occasionally made comments indicating that they were well aware of this advantage of same-sex intimacy. Abandoned by her female partner, who left school to marry a male suitor, southern schoolteacher Maria Duty remained committed to both her former roommate and to female friendship. "Connie Leggett saw Mrs. A. in vacation," she remarked in one of her letters to Bettie Joyner; "she has another little babe. Pitty [*sic*] on the people! where do so many babies come from?" Maria, of course, knew the answer to her question, and she also knew the solution to her dilemma, which was to surround herself with other women rather than form an attachment to a man. After Bettie's departure, she wrote: "Geneva rooms with me. . . . Take all my walks with Mrs. Hahr and Miss Lizie. I find [Geneva] very pleasant, and I love her, but will not give her *your* place in my affections."[37] In female friendship, southern women could find pleasant and affectionate company—and perhaps also physical intimacy—without the risks of pregnancy and childbirth that accompanied heterosexual relationships.

Wary of heterosexual relationships and drawn to same-sex romances, some women in the Victorian South regarded female friendship not as a prelude to conventional family life but as an alternative form of family life. Women in the nineteenth-century South did not use the new terminology developed by sexologists to describe their relationships; that is, they did not refer to themselves as sexual inverts, perverted homosexuals, or mannish lesbians. Rather, much like their counterparts in England, they used the familiar language of familial ties to describe their relationships with other women, creating what Martha Vicinus describes as "metaphoric versions of the heterosexual nuclear family." Referring to one another as lovers, spouses, parents, and children, southern women involved in same-sex relationships avoided drawing negative attention to themselves at the same time that they engaged in the radical project of creating an alternative form of family life in the American South.[38]

Perhaps the most common way for southern women to describe their intimate relationships with other women was in terms of romantic love and heterosexual courtship. When a young woman who signed herself Elise spoke of the strong "attachment" she shared with Frances Bernard, she used the language of romantic love, in which self-revelation and emotional identification were of vital significance. "I feel we are one," she pronounced. But Elise went further; she defined her relationship with Frances as an exclusive one, writing: "I have positively concluded My Fan: that the friendship I have formed for you is the warmest I have ever had with any girl." Given the romantic and exclusive nature of this relationship, it is not surprising that Elise explicitly compared her feelings for Frances to those of a male suitor's feelings for a female lover. "Were I a gentleman," Elise concluded, "it would only be for you to say 'yes' to make us one for life & to know no separation."[39]

Elise and Frances corresponded in the mid-nineteenth century, before a gender-neutral vocabulary existed to describe women's romantic attachments. By the late nineteenth century, women had new words for such intense same-sex attachments. Writing from North Carolina's St. Mary's School in the 1890s, a friend confided to Harriet Bowen: "There are lots of new mashes. Fanny Sams [?] is *silly* over Miss Brattle, and Lisa is pretty badly struck." As Lillian Faderman has suggested, when Victorian women discussed "mashes," "smashing," or "spooning," they responded to the heightened awareness of same-sex love by creating a new vocabulary to describe women's intimate relationships that did not carry the weight of the sexologists' revulsion at sexual perversion (at one end of the scale) or their condescending pity for sexual inversion (at the other, most sympathetic, end of the scale).[40]

Other women in the late nineteenth-century South continued to describe their passionate feelings for other women in more traditional language. Perhaps because the gender-neutral language of "smashing" evoked the morally questionable category of homosexuality, comparisons to courting couples remained common throughout the nineteenth century. In the 1890s, Eloise Whitaker, a student at the North Carolina State Normal and Industrial School, confided to her friend Liz about her feelings for her teachers:

> I love Miss Perry so good now that maybe I'll learn to love Latin. I'm loving Miss Bruere to kill too. . . . I sit at the table and peep up to Miss Kirkland's table at Miss Bruere and dote on her. I was going to give her some . . . flowers but she was so much sweeter than the flowers that I couldn't make up my mind to give them to her. . . . I reckon you think I'm cracked talking so much about love but you are having a time with the boys & why not I love women?[41]

By comparing her love for women with her friend's flirtations with "the boys," Whitaker suggested that her crushes on her teachers went beyond a platonic, or even a romantic, attachment. Yet, while aware that some might think her "cracked," she defended her choice of love object(s) as at least as valid as her friend's "time" with young men.

Similarly, in the 1880s, North Carolinian Mattie Southgate carried on a passionate correspondence with a female friend known variously as "Wilbur," "Willie," and "Will." Willie's masculine nom de plume coincided with the role she played in this relationship. Like Elise, Willie described herself as the pursuer, comparing herself to a male suitor. "I don't care how many University chaps fall in love with you," Willie wrote in one passionate letter to her inamorata; "they cannot get you—my claim comes first, I have always claimed you as my sweetheart. . . . I shall always claim you as my sweetheart whether you like it or not." Like other same-sex couples in the Victorian South and elsewhere, Mattie and Willie appear to have been both romantic and exclusive. Although the details are unclear, their relationship clearly was characterized by a great deal of jealousy and possessiveness on both sides. Mattie, hearing rumors that Willie had formed an attachment to a "Miss. M.," wrote to demand full disclosure. Willie defended herself against the charge of inconstancy, saying that "Miss. M. I hope is as true a friend to me now as she was during my stay in D. [Durham] nothing more. Please tell me why you thought she was any-thing more than a friend? . . . There is not one in D. who knew, who made my heart beat with the warmest affec[tion] but *you & you know it.*" By distinguishing between "a true . . . friend" and "more than a friend," these women indicated that they did not consider their relationship platonic. Moreover, by insisting that Mattie would "always" be her "sweetheart," Willie raised the possibility that the pair's connection was not only romantic and exclusive but also permanent.[42]

Like the women featured in Marcus's study of Victorian England, some southern women drew a distinction between romantic, erotically charged, and exclusive relationships and less significant ones—between "friends and 'friends,'" between "female friends," "female lovers," and "female couples." Moreover, allusions to permanent relationships linked references to lovers, "sweethearts," or "darlings," evoking courtship, to references to spouses, "husbands," and "wives," suggesting marriage. As Marcus contends, "the rhetoric of female marriage" used the most powerful "language of the day" to announce, acknowledge, and authorize same-sex relationships.[43]

There was no southern equivalent to the term "Boston marriage." Women's same-sex relationships never became common enough in the Victorian South to warrant the coining of a new and widely used expression to describe women's committed relationships and shared households. Nonetheless, in their personal correspondence, southern women sometimes compared their intimate relationships to marriages. Some women hinted at the marital quality of their relationships by celebrating their "anniversaries." One of Mattie Southgate's friends, Kate Christian, who apparently came on the scene after the jealous Willie departed, expressed dismay at the prospect of Mattie's marriage. "If you get a house of your own," she demanded, "how are you going to keep mine?" Comments like these suggested that at least some southern women hoped that their female "spouses" would provide them with a domestic partnership, as well as with emotional support. These southern women's writings thus indicated that, like the northern women featured in Faderman's study of lesbian reformers, southern women involved in same-sex relationships saw distinct advantages to "lesbian domesticity" when compared with heterosexual marriage.[44]

Lizzie Grove and Laura Brumback made the most explicit comparisons to marriage. Lizzie called Laura her "Own Dear Husbing" and referred to herself as Laura's "dear wife." Like women in Victorian England, this couple used not only marital but also gendered language to describe their relationship. This may be particularly significant in light of Martha Vicinus's observation that "gender inversion was the most important signifier of same-sex desire" in Victorian England. Even when these two women decided to marry men, they continued to use this terminology, perhaps suggesting some familiarity with the Mormon practice of plural marriage. "You shall be my first husband," Lizzie assured Laura on the eve of her wedding, in 1878, "he my second. as you have been so faithful I will not go back on you now. you shall still be mine."[45]

While Lizzie and Laura formed a "couple" of "husband" and "wife," North Carolinian Mattie Southgate and a group of her friends formed an entire family. The youngest daughter of a Durham family, Mattie attended Wesleyan Female Institute in Staunton in the early 1880s. Prior to her marriage in 1884, she received numerous letters from former schoolmates. Many of these revolved around the pact that she and three of her schoolmates had made to remain single and to bind each other in a "family" of father, mother, and sons. Each of the young women assumed a new name to mark this relationship, which was linked to a solemn covenant to remain single. The new names reflected the women's masculine and feminine roles within their group. "Sammie Eddie" and "Mary Eddie" were "father" and "mother." The "sons" were Mattie, known as "Tom," and another girl, who took the name of "Dean."[46] By adopting new names and assuming familial roles, Mattie Southgate and her friends consciously created an all-female family.

In many of the preceding examples, the participants in these dyads and groupings of women chose not only familial terms for one another but also gendered ones. In romantic dyads, one partner often played the suitor or "husband," while the other partner played the love object or "wife." In the Mattie Southgate family group, only one of the four women involved played a feminine role as "mother"; there were no daughters in this self-defined family unit. However, the gender identities were not fixed. Like women in Victorian England, women in the nineteenth-century South assumed both masculine and feminine identities within the context of same-sex relationships. Thus, while Mattie Southgate was a juvenile male, "Tom," within her four-person family grouping, her other correspondents never referred to her as Tom. Rather, her lover "Willie" quite explicitly cast herself as a male suitor and Mattie as the female recipient of Willie's affections, while Mattie's other suitor, Kate, expected Mattie to keep house for her, as a wife would do. Mattie thus was simultaneously a male "son" and a female "sweetheart" and "housekeeper." At least in the world of female friendship, it was possible for an individual to play either a male or female role, or even both, if she chose.[47]

Yet it was not necessary for women to play a role at all. Bettie Joyner and Maria Duty were "darlings forever," but their correspondence does not indicate that either partner took (or wished to take) the part of a man. Instead, these two women referred to each other in the language of female friendship, even as they demonstrated the emotional connection associated with romantic love. "Friend, I knew not how happy we were or how much I loved you until you were gone," Maria wrote to Bettie in 1873. "I believe I love you more ardently than any other person living." By using the term "friend" to refer to her "darling" while also insisting on her "ardent" love for her, Maria, like lesbians in Victorian England, may have been claiming both "the right to privacy associated with marriage and the public privileges accorded to female friendship." For, as Sharon Marcus suggests, "to call one woman another's superlative friend was not to disavow their marital relationship but to proclaim it in the language of the day."[48]

Further research is necessary to learn more about the extent of physical intimacy, the significance of role-playing, and the use of language within southern women's same-sex relationships. Perhaps most significantly, we need to know how much opportunity women in the Victorian South had to realize their dreams of creating female families. In this study, all of the women who could be identified eventually married men. Thus, while they seem to have regarded same-sex relationships as desirable alternatives to heterosexual family life, they also seem to have been unable to create lasting partnerships with their female lovers.[49]

The same is true of Rebecca Alice Baldy, whose letters to Narcissa Josephine Varner form the basis of one of the only published essays on lesbianism in the nineteenth-century South. Baldy was a schoolteacher who lived with and supported her widowed and ailing mother and sickly siblings in rural Georgia. In her essay on the one-sided Baldy-Varner correspondence, which dated from 1870 and 1871, Elizabeth Knowlton defines Baldy as a lesbian. Baldy's life exhibits many parallels to the women in this study. Baldy used the language of courtship and domesticity to describe the relationship she wished to create with Varner, whom she had met nearly two decades earlier when both were students at LaGrange College. In her mid-thirties, Baldy dreamed of founding a school with Varner, which would allow Baldy to continue to support her mother and siblings while also maintaining an intimate relationship with Varner. Her detailed plans for a shared future included building a private "cottage" as the couple's residence, where the two could enjoy what Lillian Faderman describes as "lesbian domesticity."[50]

Baldy's lengthy description of the relationship she envisioned is replete with what Sharon Marcus calls the "rhetoric of female marriage":

> I will 'please to say' that I can never love [a] human being more than I do you—that I want you every day, to sew, & read, & talk with me—that every night I want you with me that you may take me in your arms & and let me kiss you to sleep—that every morning I want you with me that I may wake you with a kiss—that I wish I could always make you happy & that you would always love me. Will you love me always Josie, even when I am old?[51]

Baldy wanted to create a female family in which she would support both her female kin and Varner, whom she described as "somebody to be loved & petted and kissed & cared for, & taken care of." Baldy perceived a female family as one in which she could be both a successful professional and a "devoted, sincere & constant lover." Yet Baldy never attained her desire to share her daily life with her "Dear Josie," and their extant correspondence spanned only a single year.[52]

Why were southern women's same-sex relationships temporary? In the case of the Baldy-Knowlton relationship, Knowlton interprets the one-sided correspondence as indicative of a lack of reciprocity and attributes the end of the relationship to Varner's lack of interest. "Miss Joe did not love Alice Baldy the way Alice loved her," she concludes. Another explanation, more consonant with scholarship on nineteenth-century southern women's history, is that very few women in the nineteenth-century South were able to avoid marriage. As Christine Jacobson Carter has indicated in her work on single women in the antebellum South, unwed women validated their choice and gained financial support by serving their families of birth as "maiden aunts." Thus, although unwed women in the Victorian South might depend on other women for emotional support, they were unable to evade the demands of their natal families to create female families. Instead, like Mary Telfair, who maintained a forty-year correspondence with her school friend Mary Few and frequently visited her in Philadelphia, but maintained her residence near her kin in Savannah, unmarried women in the nineteenth-century South found that the demands of the families into which they were born precluded their participation in female families of their own choice. Although at least some southern women regarded same-sex love as a solid basis for an alternative definition of "family," then, southern family values inhibited the formation of female families in the Victorian South.[53]

Since none of the women in this study were successful in their aim to redefine the southern family, what significance should scholars attach to them? This essay is based on the correspondence of a select set of nineteenth-century southern women who created, or hoped to create, female family units and thereby avoid heterosexual marriage and male dominance. While extant scholarship suggests that such women were few in number, it likewise suggests that many more southern women shared many of these women's attitudes, such as the women in Carter's recent study of "southern single blessedness," or the adolescent girls in Drew Gilpin Faust's book on women in the Civil War South who eagerly read Augusta Jane Evans's blockbuster novel *Macaria* and identified with its unmarried protagonist. Given psychological research that emphasizes the "plasticity" of women's sexuality (i.e., the degree to which economic and social forces shape women's sexual activity and sexual identity), the fact that any women in the Victorian South envisioned the possibility of creating a lesbian subculture is remarkable. As Catherine Clinton has observed, women without men existed "on the fringe of southern society," and those who dared to remain single by choice were both "rare" and "aberrant." By borrowing from the revered trope of family ties at the same time that they rejected southern family values, the women featured here engaged in what Glenda Riley has elsewhere described as a "subtle subversion" of southern culture. Their inability to form lasting female families speaks to the power of the southern family values of male dominance and compulsory heterosexuality at the same time that their desire to form female families testifies to the women's determination and creativity. Both women's imaginative liberty and their limited options are essential to a full understanding of family life in the Victorian South.[54]

Notes

1. Lizzie Grove to Laura Brumback, 18 May 1872, 23 October 1873, 15 October 1878, 5 and 18 November 1878, Grove Family Papers, Virginia Historical Society (VHS).

2. The phrase "compulsory heterosexuality" comes from Adrienne Rich, "Compulsory Heterosexuality and Lesbian Existence," *Signs* 5 (Summer 1980): 631–60. For an introduction to the importance of patriarchy in the Old South, see Joan Cashin, *A Family Venture: Men and Women on the Southern Frontier* (New York: Oxford University Press, 1991); Catherine Clinton, *The Plantation Mistress: Woman's World in the Old South* (New York: Pantheon Books, 1982); Jean E. Friedman, *The Enclosed Garden: Women and Community in the Evangelical South, 1830–1900* (Chapel Hill: University of North Carolina Press, 1985); and Anne Firor Scott, *The Southern Lady: From Pedestal to Politics, 1830–1900* (Chicago: University of Chicago Press, 1970). In each of these classic texts, heterosexuality—or at least heterosexual marriage—is assumed and described as both the norm and the ideal, meeting Rich's definition of compulsory heterosexuality.

3. For northern women's friendships, see esp. Nancy F. Cott, *The Bonds of Womanhood: "Woman's Sphere" in New England, 1785–1835* (New Haven: Yale University Press, 1977); Carroll Smith-Rosenberg, "The Female World of Love and Ritual: Relations between Women in Nineteenth-Century America," in *Disorderly Conduct: Visions of Gender in Victorian America* (New York: Oxford University Press, 1985). On southern women's friendships, see Steven M. Stowe, "'The *Thing*, Not Its Vision': A Woman's Courtship and Her Sphere in the Southern Planter Class," *Feminist Studies* 9 (Spring 1983): 113–30; Melinda S. Buza, "'Pledges of Our Love': Friendship, Love, and Marriage among the Virginia Gentry, 1800–1825," in Edward L. Ayers and John C. Willis, eds., *The Edge of the South: Life in Nineteenth-Century Virginia* (Charlottesville: University Press of Virginia, 1991), 10–20, 28–29; Joan E. Cashin, "The Structure of Antebellum Planter Families: 'The Ties that Bound us Was Strong,'" *Journal of Southern History* 56 (February 1990): 64–65; Anya Jabour, "'It will never do for me to be married': The Life of Laura Wirt Randall, 1803–1833," *Journal of the Early Republic* 17 (summer 1997): 205–9.

4. See esp. Lillian Faderman, *Odd Girls and Twilight Lovers: A History of Lesbian Life in Twentieth-Century America* (New York: Columbia University Press, 1991), introduction and chap. 1 (quotation on 4). See also Nancy F. Cott, "Passionlessness: An Interpretation of Victorian Sexual Ideology, 1790–1850," in Nancy F. Cott and Elizabeth H. Pleck, eds., *A Heritage of Her Own: Toward a New Social History of American Women* (New York: Simon and Schuster, 1979), 162–81; Carroll Smith-Rosenberg, "The New Woman as Androgyne: Social Disorder and Gender Crisis, 1870–1936," in *Disorderly Conduct*, 245–96. Jane Addams is cited in Susan Ware, ed., *Modern American Women: A Documentary History* (Boston: McGraw-Hill, 1997), 36.

5. Blanche Wiesen Cook, "The Historical Denial of Lesbianism," *Radical History Review* 20 (spring/summer 1979): 60–65; Estelle Freedman, "Sexuality in Nineteenth-Century America: Behavior, Ideology, and Politics," *Reviews in American History* 10 (December 1982): 196–215.

6. Blanche Wiesen Cook, "'Women Alone Stir My Imagination': Lesbianism and the Cultural Tradition," *Signs* 4 (summer 1979): 738, 739; Leila J. Rupp, "'Imagine My Surprise': Women's Relationships in Mid-Twentieth-Century America," in Martin Duberman, Martha Vicinus, and George Chauncey Jr., eds., *Hidden from History: Reclaiming the Gay and Lesbian Past* (New York: Meridian Books, 1990), 398.

7. Wiesen Cook, "Historical Denial of Lesbianism," 64; Lillian Faderman, *To Believe in Women: What Lesbians Have Done for America—A History* (Boston: Houghton Mifflin, 1999), 2.

8. Notable exceptions are the essays included in John Howard, ed., *Carryin' On in the Lesbian and Gay South* (New York: New York University Press, 1997), esp. Elizabeth W. Knowlton, "'Only a Woman Like Yourself'—Rebecca Alice Baldy: Dutiful Daughter, Stalwart Sister, and Lesbian Lover of Nineteenth-Century Georgia," 34–53 (hereafter "Rebecca Alice Baldy"), and Katy Coyle and Nadiene Van Dyke, "Sex, Smashing, and Storyville in Turn-of-the-Century New Orleans: Reexamining the Continuum of Lesbian Sexuality," 54–72. For British scholarship, see Martha Vicinus, *Intimate Friends: Women Who Loved Women, 1778–1928* (Chicago: University of Chicago Press, 2004).

9. Christie Anne Farnham, *The Education of the Southern Belle: Higher Education and Student Socialization in the Antebellum South* (New York: New York University Press, 1994), chap. 7 (quotations on 156, 176).

10. Sharon Marcus, *Between Women: Friendship, Desire, and Marriage in Victorian England* (Princeton: Princeton University Press, 2007), 8, 25, 204.

11. See my recent study, *Scarlett's Sisters: Young Women in the Old South* (Chapel Hill: University of North Carolina Press, 2007), for young women's negative attitudes toward men, marriage, and motherhood and their positive experiences with female friendships. On "female marriage" and the phenomenon of British women using the language of family to describe their relationships, see Marcus, *Between Women*, esp. 196–204; Lisa Merrill, *When Romeo Was a Woman: Charlotte Cushman and Her Circle of Female Spectators* (Ann Arbor: University of Michigan Press, 2000); and Vicinus, *Intimate Friends*. In the late nineteenth-century United States, observers frequently characterized women's lifelong relationships as "Boston marriages."

12. Lizzie Grove to Laura Brumback, 19 November 1878, Grove Family Papers.

13. Anne Firor Scott, "Women's Perspective on the Patriarchy of the 1850s," in her book *Making the Invisible Woman Visible* (Urbana: University of Illinois Press, 1984), 178–79, quoted in Anya Jabour, "Marriage and Family in the Nineteenth-Century South," in Jabour, ed., *Major Problems in the History of American Families and Children* (Boston: Houghton Mifflin, 2005), 130.

14. Lizzie Grove Kennedy to Laura Brumback Grove, n.d., Grove Family Papers. For more on southern women's concerns about pregnancy, see Jabour, *Scarlett's Sisters*, 136–37, 218, 220.

15. Joan Cashin, "'Decidedly Opposed to the Union': Women's Culture, Marriage, and Politics in Antebellum South Carolina," *Georgia Historical Quarterly* 78 (winter 1994): 735–59.

16. Elise O. D. to Frances Bernard, n.d.; Adeline A. [Walker] to Frances Bernard, 23 December 1851,; and Elise O. D. to Frances Bernard, 15 April 1851, Bernard Family Papers, VHS. For more on southern women's doubts about marriage (particularly when juxtaposed with female friendship), see Jabour, *Scarlett's Sisters*, 89–94, 135–38, 165–67, 186–88.

17. Elise O. D. to Frances Bernard, n.d.

18. Erika L. Murr, ed., *A Rebel Wife in Texas: The Diary and Letters of Elizabeth Scott Neblett, 1852–1864* (Baton Rouge: Louisiana State University Press, 2001), 35, 40. For other examples of wives' displaced ambitions, see C. Vann Woodward and Elisabeth Muhlenfeld, *The Private Mary Chesnut: The Unpublished Civil War Diaries* (New York: Oxford University Press, 1984).

19. Faderman, *To Believe in Women*.

20. Marcus, *Between Women*, 204–12.

21. For quotations, see Martha Faison to Winifred Faison, 9 September 1889; Mollie Faison to Winifred Faison, 20 October 1889; and Aunt "Em" to Winifred Faison, 16 September 1889, Henry W. Faison Papers, Southern Historical Collection (SHC), University of North Carolina, Chapel Hill. For a more detailed discussion of the academy experience in the antebellum South, see Jabour, *Scarlett's Sisters*, chap. 2, and Jabour, "'College Girls': The Female Academy and Female Identity in the Old South," in Bruce L. Clayton and John A. Salmond, eds., *"Lives Full of Struggle and Triumph": Southern Women, Their Institutions, and Their Communities* (Gainesville: University Press of Florida, 2003), 74–92. For more on female friendship in southern schools, see Farnham, *Education of the Southern Belle*, chap. 7, and Steven M. Stowe, "The Not-So-Cloistered Academy: Elite Women's Education and Family Feeling in the Old South," in Walter J. Fraser Jr., R. Frank Saunders Jr., and Jon L. Wakelyn, eds., *The Web of Southern Social Relations: Women, Family, and Education* (Athens: University of Georgia Press, 1985), 90–106. On peer culture and romantic friendships in northern schools, see Jane H. Hunter, *How Young Ladies Became Girls: The Victorian Origins of American Girlhood* (New Haven: Yale University Press, 2002), 176–88; and Palmieri, *In Adamless Eden*, chap. 11. For the British context, see Martha Vicinus, "Distance and Desire: English Boarding School Friendships, 1870–1920," in Duberman, Vicinus, and Chauncey, eds., *Hidden from History*, 212–29.

22. Gerda Lerner, *The Creation of Feminist Consciousness: From the Middle Ages to 1870* (New York: Oxford University Press, 1993), 224, 226–27, 233. Lerner explains: "Since the locus of women's gender indoctrination has so often been the family, the social space necessary for liberating women has had to be a space outside the family" (233). See also Martha Vicinus, *Independent Women: Work and Community for Single Women, 1850–1920* (Chicago: University of Chicago Press, 1985), 7. In her study of American Victorian girlhood, Jane Hunter argues that "emotional bonds between student and teacher" offered a "profound challenge . . . to familial identification": see *How Young Ladies Became Girls*, 188.

23. Mary Frances Gray to Lolla, 3 November 1870, Gray Family Papers, SHC.

24. Vicinus, *Independent Women*, 199–200. On faculty-student relations and teachers' role as mentors at Wellesley College, see Patricia Palmieri, *In Adamless Eden: The Community of Women Faculty at Wellesley* (New Haven: Yale University Press, 1995), chap. 11, esp. 186–88, 191–95.

25. Josephine Simrall to Belle Simrall, spring 1892, Charles B. Simrall Papers, SHC.

26. Maria Duty to Bettie Joyner, ca. 1873, Joyner Family Papers, SHC. See also Palmieri, *In Adamless Eden*, chap. 8.

27. Lizzie Grove to Laura Brumback, 3 December 1871, 18 May 1872, and 3 October 1873, Grove Family Papers.

28. N. O. Wilkinson to Mattie Southgate, 27 January 1880; James Southgate To Whom It May Concern, 1 July 1881; Kate C. Sanborn to Lessie Southgate, 17 November 1881, James Southgate Papers, Duke University, Durham, N.C. For more on teaching, see Jabour, *Scarlett's Sisters*, 104–6, 279–80.

29. Palmieri, *In Adamless Eden*, chap. 8.

30. Farnham, *Education of the Southern Belle*, 163.

31. Josephine Simrall to Belle Simrall, 8 February 1892, Charles B. Simrall Papers.

32. William Benemann, *Male-Male Intimacy in Early America: Beyond Romantic Friendships* (New York: Harrington Park Press, 2006), xiv.

33. Kate C. Sanborn to Lessie Southgate, 17 November 1881; Lessie Southgate to Family, 25 December 1881, James Southgate Papers. See also Stowe, "The Not-So-Cloistered Academy," 90–106.

34. Aunt Em to Winifred Faison, 16 September 1889, Henry William Faison Papers; Lizzie Grove to Laura Brumback, 15 October 1878, Grove Family Papers; and "Bed Bug" to Mattie Southgate, 8 September 1882, with Southgate's comments, James Southgate Papers. See also Jabour, *Scarlett's Sisters*, 75.

35. Josephine Simrall to Belle Simrall, 26 October 1891, Charles B. Simrall Papers, SHC; Lizzie Grove Kennedy to Laura Brumback Grove, 27 September 1880, Grove Family Papers. See also Smith-Rosenberg, "Female World of Love and Ritual," 70–73.

36. Jabour, "Marriage and Family," 126.

37. Maria Duty to Bettie Joyner, ca. 1873 and 8 May 1873, Joyner Family Papers.

38. See Vicinus, *Intimate Friends*, xxvii. On "female marriage" in Victorian England, see Marcus, *Between Women*, chaps. 5 and 6.

39. Elise O. D. to Frances Bernard, n.d. On the language of romantic love, see Karen Lystra, *Searching the Heart: Women, Men, and Romantic Love in Nineteenth-Century America* (New York: Oxford University Press, 1989).

40. C. A. B. C. to Harriet Bowen, 31 December 1894, Southall and Bowen Papers, SHC; Faderman, *Odd Girls*, 19.

41. Eloise Whitaker to Liz, 1 March 1896, Eloise Whitaker Papers.

42. Willie to Mattie Southgate, 15 March 1882, James Southgate Papers. The fact that Willie was a woman is revealed in a letter from N. O. Wilkinson to Mattie Southgate, January 27, 1880, and also in Lessie Southgate to Family, 25 December 1881, James Southgate Papers.

43. For "darlings," see Maria Duty to Bettie Joyner, [ca. 1873], Joyner Family Papers. For other quotations, see Marcus, *Between Women*, 43, 51.

44. Kate Christian to Mattie Southgate, 12 October and 4 December 1882, James Southgate Papers; Faderman, *To Believe in Women*, 5.

45. Lizzie Grove to Laura Brumback, 19 November 1878, Grove Family Papers; Vicinus, *Intimate Friends*, xxix.

46. Mary Eddie to Mattie Southgate, 1 March 1883, and enclosed card; S. Eddie to Mattie Southgate, 30 January 1883, James Southgate Papers.

47. Marcus, *Between Women*, 20.

48. Maria Duty to Bettie Joyner, 27 January 1873, Joyner Family Papers; Marcus, *Between Women*, 51.

49. Many of the women used only first names or noms de plume and thus cannot be identified.

50. Knowlton, "Alice Rebecca Baldy," 42.

51. Ibid., 50.

52. Ibid., 44–45, 48.

53. Ibid., 50. On single women's familial roles in the South, see esp. Christine Jacobson Carter, "Indispensable Spinsters: Maiden Aunts in the Elite Families of Savannah and Charleston," in Janet Coryell, Thomas H. Appleton Jr., Anastatia Sims, and Sandra Gioia Treadway, eds., *Negotiating Boundaries of Southern Womanhood: Dealing with the Powers That Be* (Columbia: University of Missouri Press, 2000), 110–34; Joyce Linda Broussard, "Female Solitaires: Women

Alone in the Lifeworld of Mid-Century Natchez, Mississippi, 1850–1880" (PhD diss., University of Southern California, 1998). For Mary Telfair, see Betty Wood, ed., *Mary Telfair to Mary Few: Selected Letters, 1802–1844* (Athens: University of Georgia Press, 2007). I am suggesting not that the subjects of these works were lesbians but that options for women in the nineteenth-century South were severely limited.

54. Christine Jacobson Carter, *Southern Single Blessedness: Unmarried Women in the Urban South, 1800–1865* (Urbana: University of Illinois Press, 2006); Drew Gilpin Faust, *Mothers of Invention: Women of the Slaveholding South in the American Civil War* (Chapel Hill: University of North Carolina Press, 1996), 168–78; Clinton, *Plantation Mistress*, 85–86; Glenda Gates Riley, "The Subtle Subversion: Changes in the Traditionalist Image of the American Woman," *Historian* 32 (February 1970): 210–27. See also Letitia Anne Peplau, "Rethinking Women's Sexual Orientation: An Interdisciplinary, Relationship-Focused Approach," *Personal Relationships* 8 (March 2001): 1–19.

II

Measuring Families' Value

~

Quilting bees and other frolics provided venues in which the economic function of the household framed the affective relations of the family. At events like this 1854 quilting party, men and women, young and old, black and white, joined together in the frivolity and work of domestic productions, reinforcing the domestic order of southern life and the economic role of the southern family. Men governed their domestic dependents, and women contributed to the family economy through both productive and reproductive labor.

Fig. 5. "A Quilting Party in Western Virginia," *Gleason's Pictorial Drawing-Room Companion*, 21 October 1854. Courtesy of Library of Congress, Washington, D.C.

5

Out of Whole Cloth?

Sewing and Family in the Old South

LYNN KENNEDY

~

Mahala Roach, a resident of antebellum Vicksburg, Mississippi, sewed for her family. At first by hand, and then with the aid of a sewing machine, she created the sheets her family slept on and the clothes that they wore. On May 17, 1855, she made a typical entry in her diary, noting: "Sewing busily all day! I have accomplished a great deal of sewing lately—finished Nora's body, fixed 2 dresses, and made a jacket for Dick."[1] A seemingly endless pile of mending also occupied her time. So Mahala Roach sewed—but she did not always sew alone. As her daughters matured, they developed sewing skills. Further, the enslaved women who lived in the Roach household also took up their needles, or they took on other household tasks so that Roach could devote more time to sewing. The relationships created around the everyday tasks of sewing were complex. Sewing was a way for Roach to show that she cared for her family, both emotionally and physically. While her primary concern was for her white family members, sewing for and with enslaved women reshaped an understanding of "family" responsibility. The daily tasks of sewing intertwined the emotional and economic interests of the white southern family and often linked members of "our family, white and black."

Historians of the Old South recognize the household as a nexus of southern social relations. Within the plantation household, relationships between men and women, old and young, and free and enslaved found their most intimate articulation. The household formed the foundational unit of the southern power structure; within this patriarchal framework, all dependents—women, children, and slaves—fell under the authority of the white, male head-of-household. But the household also provided the site where sentimental family bonds formed. Peter Bardaglio suggests that linking the household and the family together held particular appeal for defenders of the southern social order because it suggested an "organic hierarchy" to their society. Eugene Genovese writes that although the slaveholders' discussions of familial relationships, particularly the relations between blacks and whites, may have largely been "self-serving cant," southerners still "assimilated that special sense of family to their self-esteem, their sense of who they were as individuals and as a people, their sense of moral worth, their sense of honor." Other historians, however, have argued that a clearer distinction must be made between household and family, between rhetorical and real relationships. Elizabeth Fox-Genovese, for example, stresses that southern household relationships rested on economic rather than emotional bonds, "with no necessary relation to family, although members of household may be related and many households may be coterminous with family membership."[2]

Plantation households undoubtedly acted as economic units, but they also engendered relationships far more complicated than those found in a factory or business. This study of the work of sewing shows that there was rarely a clear division between the household as a productive unit and as a site of affective relationships—the two were stitched together in a crazy-quilt pattern of interactions. Potential family ties between whites and blacks were tenuous and difficult to be sure, but the complexity of feelings and relationships between people who lived and worked together on a daily basis often resembled nothing so much as a family. Close and continual proximity created interactions and interdependencies that led to the formation of strong emotional ties (although the sentiment might as easily have been loathing as love). The blood and bonds of family coexisted, and sometimes overlapped, with the economic institution of slavery and the focus on domestic production. So while some southerners struggled to maintain distinctions between different familial groups within a single household, the divisions between household and family membership represented a site of complex and shifting boundaries.

Increasingly, historians have come to question the stark divisions between public and private interests suggested by "separate spheres," which has been a dominant model for understanding nineteenth-century gender relations. Separating market interests from domestic interests has the tendency to obscure the economic contributions made by the unpaid domestic labor of American women. Jeanne Boydston offered an important corrective to this model, creating a calculus of the economic value of women's household labor and suggesting that, although often beyond the realm of wage earning or the marketplace, "women's work" had an important economic value, contributing to the well-being of the household. Southern historians such as Elizabeth Fox-Genovese and Suzanne Lebsock have also noted women's economic contributions to their households within a distinctly southern social structure. The South's adaptation of capitalism to a slave-labor system made the plantation household the key productive unit. But an examination of white southern women's diaries, letters, and memoirs clearly suggests that their authors viewed their labor as essential to the comfort of their families. Thus the productive function of the household contributed to the emotional bonds created therein.[3]

The southern plantation household offered a distinct challenge to the physical understanding of "separate spheres." Unlike many of their counterparts in the increasingly industrialized North, men who owned southern plantations continued to work where they lived, and they could therefore maintain patriarchal control of domestic space. White men and women on the plantation generally performed different tasks, but they did so in close physical proximity and with the shared purpose of maintaining the economic viability of their plantation household.

Of course, the southern experience was also distinct because of the presence of enslaved individuals within the plantation household. Black residents labored, but they were often something more, tied to their owners by a complex set of social and cultural expectations. The position of enslaved women particularly illustrates the limits of the separate spheres model in the antebellum southern context. Sometimes black women were identified by their gender, when for example they were assigned work as seamstresses or caregivers to children. Yet often racial identity overrode this gendered identity, setting the expectation that black women should work in the fields "like men." Such inconsistency suggests the complex negotiations that members of the southern household undertook daily in relating to each other.[4] While both southern households and southern families, black and white, shared similarities with all antebellum American households and families, they also experienced distinct patterns and challenges, combining several blood-related families of different races and statuses under one roof. Within these households, antebellum southerners negotiated both economic and affective relationships.

Some southerners claimed clear and impermeable boundaries between racial groups; others lauded the loyalty and mutual regard that tied free and enslaved together. The reality probably lay between these extremes, reflected in the interactions and negotiations that occurred in everyday tasks like sewing. Such work was practical and productive, but it was also emotional—a way for some women to show that they cared for the physical comfort of those for whom they sewed. Northern women also sewed for their families, but the sewing done within the antebellum southern household negotiated a distinct set of boundaries and relationships. White women managed the production of clothing for the enslaved members of the household, and enslaved women sewed for white household members, suggesting the reciprocal relations of a family. Further, by training younger black and white women to sew, white southern women fulfilled another role of the family, replicating patterns of labor and sentiment for the next generation. But while the gendered task of sewing brought some women together across racial boundaries, white women's power to direct the labor and control the material allotted to black women also reinforced traditional race relationships. An examination of sewing in slaveholding southern households brings into sharper focus the often strained and complex interdependencies that shaped the southern family, black and white.

White southern women's sewing clothed their families, allowing for conservation of resources, specifically money spent on the labor of a seamstress or on purchasing garments. In addition, the clothing produced by women indicated the white family's stability and status beyond the household. In making white women both managers and producers, sewing blurred divisions between public and private and between work and family. This "women's work" and the interactions conducted around it fundamentally shaped the gendered, racial, and economic structures of the southern family. In her postbellum memoirs, Belle Kearney challenged the "popular delusion" that southern ladies did not work and pointed to the demands of sewing as evidence.[5] Historians too must seriously consider the immense labor undertaken by black and white women in keeping southern families clothed. This was their direct contribution to the family economy.

The tasks involved in the production of clothing altered over the course of the nineteenth century. In the early decades, many households still contained spinning wheels, looms, and other tools necessary to the production of cloth. Martha Ogle Forman lived on a plantation in Maryland with her husband and approximately fifty slaves. In the early years of her diary, kept from 1814 to 1845, she recorded the carding and spinning of wool and linen, although she often sent the resulting yarn out to be woven. In later years, she more often recorded the purchase of material that she, with the assistance of several enslaved women, cut out and sewed. She also occasionally purchased ready-made clothes for men on the plantation. Forman's experiences represent the typical trend. The production of homespun became increasingly less common in the antebellum period, as a growing number of textile mills produced machine-made material that was more available and more affordable. Ready-made clothing for men became increasingly available during this period, although the items were generally considered an option only for the lower classes, since the quality was often suspect. Women's clothing, with the exception of cloaks and corsets, was still made at home or by hired seamstresses until after the Civil War.[6]

Had Martha Forman kept her diary until the 1850s, she might also have discussed how the introduction of a sewing machine further altered her household labor, although sewing machines remained relatively rare in the antebellum period. Mahala Roach obtained her first sewing machine in May 1857 and spent weeks marveling at the speed it brought to her work. On June 8, she recorded that she had both started and finished a dress on the same day, something she had never accomplished when sewing by hand. Even more enthusiastic was Mary Sharpe Mallard of Georgia, who wrote what was virtually an advertisement in the summer of 1860: "I do not know how I would accomplish the work of the family if I did not have a Grover & Baker machine. Sewing machines are great inventions."[7] These women still used needle and thread to baste and mend clothing, and most southern women continued to have no other option than to sew by hand. For those who could afford it, however, the sewing machine seemed like a sound investment, increasing their productivity and thus their contributions to their families' needs. Whether moving toward mechanization or still working by hand, white women recognized sewing as an essential element in their families' material and social well-being, to accomplishing "the work of the family." Sewing in nineteenth-century America was a gendered task. Women, almost regardless of class status, were expected to have some skill with a needle.[8]

When women acted as consumers of cloth, rather than as producers, they were most often elite white women. Diaries and letters of elite women focused on the latest fashions and who wore what. As a teenager, Adele Allston Vanderhorst was enthralled by Charleston's social life and the opportunities it offered to dress up. In June 1859, she described a party at which she wore "my white double skirt muslin with Lilac ribbons." In the same entry, she described "a very pretty dress, my winter dress trimmed with green flowers," which she wore to another party. Vanderhorst's fascination with flounces and pretty things suggests a focus on consumption. But the outfits donned for the social whirl required a great deal of preparation work. As she wrote to her mother, "Oh but dear mamma I wish you would come to town and see about all the things for no one can get them as nicely as you can." Thus she suggests the work behind the public appearances that were essential for belles representing their families in elite southern society.[9]

Rather than viewing elite white women in the relatively passive role of consumer, however, we might more accurately see these women as managers of households and particularly of the wardrobes of those who lived therein. This was part of their economic contribution to the family. Just as southern planters were more likely to oversee plantation functions than to take up a hoe, so elite white women oversaw wardrobes, purchased materials, and supervised seamstresses to ensure family members were properly garbed within the family's means. In the case of Adele Allston Vanderhorst, managing a fashionable wardrobe occupied not only her mother but also her aunt, Harriette Lesesne, who visited Adele and her sister Bessie at school and then wrote to their mother: "I think they will require spring dresses before long, & it will give me great pleasure to get them & have them made up, if you say so."[10] Such service became a mark of family ties as well as an allocation of resources.

Often elite southern women relied on extended kin networks to obtain both materials for and information about the latest fashions. This was seen as a valuable service to those who felt "stuck" in the country and again marked the bonds of family. In 1830, Sarah Carter wrote her cousins Marion and Angelica Singleton, South Carolinians who were at school near Philadelphia. In her letter, Carter included an extensive list of desired clothes, including three dresses, bonnets, gloves, and bags. She also enclosed a draft for $150, but confessed, "I know so little of *fashionable* shopping that I think it probable that I have not supplied you liberally enough." Six years later, another cousin, Jane Coles, returned the favor to Marion Singleton, now Mrs. Deveaux and living on a South Carolina plantation, inquiring whether there was "anything I can do for you in the *Shopping* or *Millinery* line?"[11] Shopping commissions represented not just market transactions but also the maintenance of kinship networks that linked elite families together. Helping each other to create and manage their wardrobes became a means of strengthening valued family connections for the elite members of southern society.

Families who were not among the very wealthiest members of southern society also assisted each other, often through actually sewing pieces for a wardrobe. Generally, clothing sold as "ready to wear" fit poorly and required tailoring to make it passable. Only the poorest and most ill-cared-for men wore clothing "off the rack." And when a woman bought a "dress," she generally purchased a length of material or a pre-cut pattern, which required that either she hire a seamstress or, just as likely, that she or a family member complete the work. Mahala Roach

sewed almost every day for her children. In 1862 she expressed some of the sentiment behind her efforts. Noting that she was remaking one of her own dresses
to fit her daughter Nora, she concluded that "it gives me more pleasure to see
her lovely form dressed nicely, than to wear fine things myself." Roach's sacrifice
of "my beautiful blue brocade" was clearly motivated by the affection she felt for
her daughter.[12] The majority of white southern women regularly took up their
needles or in some cases their sewing machines to meet the clothing needs of
their families.

Some white women kept a reckoning of their work in their diaries, both to
note what kept them occupied and to record the value that they brought to their
family. Anna McCall Watson of Louisiana used the journal she kept in 1849 as a
progress report on her sewing projects. On January 20, for example, she began
to alter a dress that she completed two days later. By January 23, she had begun
attaching sleeves to another dress. While the projects varied, the continuing demand for more sewing did not. Mary Folger, who often attended a sewing circle
in New Orleans, recorded on April 1, 1859, that she had "finished making half a
dozen shirts." Mahala Roach sewed so regularly that *not* sewing was noteworthy
and duly recorded in her diary.[13] Over the years, each woman must have sewn
hundreds of pieces of clothing to meet the needs of her family. Her labor was of
value to the household economy, but it also often demonstrated affective ties.

Men, like women and children, were consumers of homemade clothes, but
they were rarely producers. While a few male tailors catered to an elite male clientele who demanded carefully fitted suits of clothing, sewing within the household fell entirely on the shoulders of its female members. Most southern men
relied on female family members when it came to completing wardrobes, albeit
with varying degrees of gratitude. In May 1832, A. T. Conrad of New Orleans
wrote to his sister, Mary Weeks. Although he urged her not to take any trouble,
Conrad was quite specific about his needs. Noting that he had sent her a shirt
"and am ashamed to say a dirty one too, as a pattern," he instructed that "those
that you have put the ruffles on you can make the collar like the one shirt." He
then critiqued some of her past efforts, commenting that "the button holes on
the bosoms of the last set you made me were a little too large. Please avoid this
fault—the holes in the shirt should be of a good size."[14] Although he could not
do for himself in this matter, a habit of command left him free to comment on
the efforts made in his extended family. Conrad needed the shirts made by his
sister, but he seems to have failed to fully recognize the labor that went into their
production.

Other men appeared more aware of the value of women's sewing work. Long after Charles Jones Jr. left his parents' Georgia plantation for Savannah, he continued to rely on the women in his family to meet some of his clothing needs. In May 1858, for example, he wrote home: "May I ask the favor of you, Mother, to have my summer clothes 'over-hauled,' as the sailors would say? They need repairs, I have no doubt. And when a suitable opportunity occurs, please send them to the city." His mother, Mary Jones, reported back just over a month later, "I have 8 shirts nearly done for you." But she asked whether he could get "*fine* good linen bosoms for the shirts" in Savannah. Problems with her eyes prevented her from completing the fine tuck work, and so Jones had to turn to the market to meet his needs.[15]

Jones's brother-in-law, Rev. Robert Mallard, similarly relied on female family members to provide clothing not only for him but also for his slaves. Fortunately for Mallard, his wife took care of such matters, and he appreciated it. In May 1859, he wondered "where this letter will find you" and then answered his own question by imagining: "it will be at the sewing machine, where the cloth with a 'click-click-click' slides rapidly over the burnished plate as Mrs. Mallard with a smile on her face exclaims: 'Grover & Baker's is the best!'"[16] The vision of his wife working productively in the interest of their shared household was an indicator that all was as it should be in his family.

Whether done out of love, duty, or economic necessity, the production of clothing in the southern household required a tremendous amount of work. Sewing was the primary, and seemingly interminable, task of many white women. Sarah Gayle of Alabama wrote in September 1832 that she had "an accumulation of work in my basket, sufficient to appall the stoutest heart." Mahala Roach sewed nearly every day but still felt unequal to the sheer amount of work. On April 17, 1856, for example, she wrote: "Tired—sad, and discouraged—have sewed as hard as I could all day—arose before 5—and have worked *all* the time—but cannot see any progress I make in my great quantity of work." The southern household was the workplace for these women. They used terms such as "the business of the family" to describe their sewing, and they described themselves as working industriously.[17] Use of such phrasing suggests a recognition of themselves not merely as consumers in the private sphere but also as producers and providers. Further, this was a "family" business; their sewing was their contribution to the material well-being of their families.

White plantation women did not, however, merely provide for the needs of their immediate family. Many also took an active role in providing clothing for enslaved members of the household, creating an expanded sense of family and familial duty. At times, providing clothing took the form of a purely economic exchange. When slaves were hired out, the provision of their clothes became part of a formalized contractual obligation. Hired-out slaves were only tangentially part of the household, and so their clothing became part of a market transaction. In 1825, for example, Sarah Thackeston not only agreed to pay $55 "for the hire of negroe man Oliver" but also promised to provide "one summer suit one winter suit of negroe cotton one pair double soled shoes & stockings and hat or blanket."[18] While the specific clothing allotments varied from contract to contract, the ability to provide the required apparel was an essential element of the household economy.

Slaves' clothing within the household, however, often went beyond mere economic obligation. Properly dressed slaves became, for many white southerners, a mark of their own beneficence as they provided for their black "family members." This effort was uniquely southern; wives of factory owners in the North would not have been expected to make such provisions for their husbands' employees. The production of clothing in the plantation household saved dollars by increasing self-sufficiency, but perhaps more important, clothing slaves suggested familial obligation or duty. Throughout her diary, Martha Forman recorded the demands of seeing to "the people's clothes." In general, she completed and distributed winter clothes in December or January and summer clothing in May or June—in either season, this provisioning required year-round work.[19] In wealthier families, white mistresses did not necessarily do all of the sewing themselves, but they managed the production of clothing for the enslaved labor force. Many also sought to personalize the distribution of this clothing, suggesting the sentiment embedded in this transaction. Adele Petigru Allston of South Carolina wrote of her sister Anne's trip to Pipe Down plantation, where she "gave out negro clothes and attended to plantation affairs." On another occasion, Allston commented on her own involvement in such matters, noting that "I gave out our little negroes clothes today, and hope to give out the grown peoples tomorrow night—I have everything of this kind to do as your Papa is not at home."[20] While Allston's words about her own actions indicate that she was not always responsible for this distribution of clothing, she clearly deemed it important that a member of the white family be present during this activity, suggesting a meaning beyond the mere provision of material goods.

Ensuring well-dressed slaves remained important to some white southerners because they believed slaves were part of the public face of the family, indicators of the status of the entire household. Elite Charlestonians, for example, often dressed enslaved men who served in a public role in fine livery. The Pringle family clothed coachmen and footmen in a dark green livery trimmed with yellow, while the Allston family clothed house slaves in "dark green broadcloth coats and vests trimmed in silver braid and red facings with trousers of green plush."[21] Finery had little to do with the needs or desires of the enslaved and more with the way that clothing created and maintained social appearances. Much of this livery may have been produced by a tailor, but the mistress often managed its purchase, and women within the household generally sewed the shirts and linens necessary to complete the outfit. Women's work to dress slaves helped to demarcate the public position of the household and the status of the family within southern society.

Similarly, the dress and appearance of white family members reflected the position and status of the household within the southern social hierarchy. Mary Bull Pringle counseled her sons away at college: "Neatness and attention to dress gives as little trouble and consumes as little time as would be required to arrange an awkward or a shabby suit of clothes." Similarly, in March 1856, Adele Petigru Allston wrote to her daughter, "You must be careful always to dress neatly and becomingly," reasoning that "at your age much depends on dressing appropriately."[22] Women who wanted the best for their families socially felt compelled to ensure they were properly garbed. This was not merely about providing for the physical comfort of one's family; it was about ensuring proper values and behaviors.

As much as southern family was about blood and emotional bonds, it was about inculcating and replicating social values, teaching the next generation how to be in the world. Through their sewing lessons, girls learned not only about their gendered responsibilities but also about the power relations of race. Ensuring white girls had the necessary skills with a needle replicated values of gender and duty within the family and ensured that daughters and nieces could offer valuable labor to their families. Differences in gendered expectations were illustrated in a letter from Ben Allston to his mother. He, like his sisters, relied on his mother to manage his wardrobe. From school he wrote: "My Dear Mother: I send these clothes to you to let you see what to do with them. My black coat wants some of the buttons sewed on more strongly as they are very nearly off."[23] While his sisters might also have made requests for clothing, they almost certainly would have been trained to sew on the buttons themselves. Allston's education in these family matters, in contrast, rendered him only a consumer of clothing.

Southerners envisioned sewing as a predominately female task and viewed the possession of sewing skills as intrinsic to female identity. Thus part of a plantation mistress's duties was to ensure that her daughters and other female members of the family acquired sewing skills. Letters between mothers and their daughters away at school suggested a growing skill set, as well as the bonds of affection expressed through sewing to meet family needs. The progress that girls made with their sewing became an object of praise or criticism. Mary McDuffie wrote to her grandmother, Rebecca Singleton, of her accomplishments in developing her skills with a needle: "I am now embroidering a pair of slippers for Papa Mac but I sew so slowly I fear I shall not finish them. I occupy my time here in practicing reading, and my needlework." Back at school in Philadelphia, she recorded more success, sending the completed slippers for her grandmother "to examine, as being the first pair I have ever made; but I hope you will not criticize them *too* closely. I must beg of you to send them by first opportunity to my dear papa at Cherry Hill." The slippers represented not only her growing skill but also McDuffie's increasing ability to contribute to the comfort of her family. Letitia Burwell remembered how the school she attended in Virginia emphasized domestic skills such as sewing, training intended to make southern women "an ornament to the drawing room," equipping them "for taking charge of an establishment and superintending every detail of domestic employment on a plantation—the weaving, knitting, sewing, etc.—for the comfort of the negro servants to be some day under her care."[24] While Burwell's assessment of the motivations may be suspect, clearly the schooling of southern girls ensured their ability to contribute to their families.

The training that occurred at school generally built on many years of instruction in the home. At an early age, southern girls were expected to model the behavior of older women in the family. Tryphena Fox noted with some amusement her daughter's inclination, writing to her own mother, "You don't know what a funny little body interrupts me with Ma-ma 'Fanny wants to sew' she has seen Adelaide sewing & nothing will do until *she* has thread & needle." In this case, Fanny seems to have been modeling her actions on an enslaved seamstress. Eliza Fisher, living in Philadelphia with her young family, reported back to her mother in South Carolina that her four-year-old daughter Lily was "busily employed *sewing* at my side, and will be very good, only occasionally interrupting me to have her needle threaded, or hem turned down—You will judge from this how much progress in the art of *stitching* she is making." Mary Norcott Bryan recalled how "I learned to sew by making the [enslaved] babies I had named clothes, and I am not ashamed even now of my sewing." Such skills made these girls not only proper young ladies but useful members of the household, able to contribute to the comfort of their families.[25]

While away at school, most young ladies would not have been expected to produce their own wardrobes, but young white women's discussions still expressed a deep interest in proper dress. This was part of their training in becoming ladies. The management of family members' wardrobes would be an important duty for these girls in their adult lives. Letters exchanged between mothers and their daughters suggested that young ladies gradually trained to manage their own wardrobes, so that they might ultimately take on larger household responsibilities. At the same time, mothers continued to provide for their daughters as part of their maternal duties. While these letters sometimes included discussions of purchased goods, more frequently they involved clothing produced within the household. In a bundle she sent to her daughter Marion, Rebecca Singleton of South Carolina wrote that she had included "a Cambrick under Frock, some Cambrick Kerchiefs, and 6 Towels." She had "been disappointed in procuring the silk to make your Aprons, but as soon as I can get it, I will have them made, and send them by Mrs. Converse, also some Muslin Capes."[26]

Similarly, Mary Townsend saw to the needs of her older daughters away at school in Barhamville, South Carolina. In January 1856, she wrote to her daughter Phoebe that she had included "various good things," adding, "I would have preferred waiting another month, when your clothes will be finished, but such things as the trunk contains will not keep so long." She continued: "My long cloth disappears so fast in the shape of coats, pantalets and nightgowns that I have none in the house." The same letter addressed her daughter Dame about the fit of some dresses that had been sent: "Is there no chance of you having the gingham altered? Maumer took so much pains to get them done in time, I was really in hopes that they would fit. If there is an opportunity send me the gingham and write me what ails it."[27] Townsend clearly saw the task not just as a duty but as a demonstration of her care for her daughters. However, the mention of Maumer, presumably an enslaved woman, indicates that she was not alone in the production of clothing. At the same time, reference to "my long cloth" suggests that she saw this as *her* work. Whether or not white mothers sewed every stitch themselves, they viewed their management as key to the comfort of their daughters. And they also hoped to train their daughters to replicate this role. The sewing done by and for these young women was all about the connections and duties of family life.

White girls who belonged to slave-owning families had to be trained not only to sew but to manage the labor of others. While gender expectations demanded that they possess skill with a needle, the racial hierarchy required that they direct enslaved women's sewing as well. Some girls showed a predisposition to supervise. Annie Deveaux, for example, wrote home to her mother in 1845 on the production of an enslaved woman: "Levinia finished Pick's and Richard's pantaloons last week and sent them down by Brutus, Richard's fit him very well, but Miss Pauline thinks that Pick's are too small in the seat."[28] Deveaux was not only learning to supervise the work of others but doing so with a critical eye.

Mary Townsend perhaps thought her daughters could use a similar lesson in supervision. She wrote to Phoebe in 1859, asking "if you have much needle work; when I have so many seamstresses and can send one down. Jane can easily go down, if the work comes to more than the passage money." Townsend undoubtedly recognized the importance of these supervisory skills because she herself had trained her daughters as well as several enslaved women to sew. She noted in a letter, "I have commenced this morning to teach Peggy how to embroider, she does so and so in the easiest part of the work; when she gets to the more difficult parts, I do not know what will be the fate of your coat."[29] Teaching and acquiring the skills involved in clothing production bound the women of this household together.

The training of enslaved seamstresses within the plantation household often suggested the complex interaction of economics and the potential for more familial sentiments. White mistresses trained black seamstresses like, and sometimes alongside, their daughters, much as colonial apprentices were taken into the home of craftsmen. Such actions implicitly recognized shared skills and the duty to train the next generation. White women also saw the training of black seamstresses as a valuable undertaking, since it promised relief from some of the burdens that rested on their own needles. Training began quite early, as it did for white girls. Sue Petigru King wrote that she had sent a young enslaved girl out to a "school to learn to sew. Miss Nell the distinguished instructress of little nigs has been in charge and I hope will make her a passable seamstress." Martha Forman noted how five-year-old Harriet, a member of her own household, trained to knit garters for her master and stockings for herself.[30] The intention of both mistresses was to ensure that these enslaved girls could contribute to the household economy, but in the process they replicated some of the gender expectations and training of white girls. Teaching these girls to sew suggested an expanded notion of "familial" responsibility.

The training of enslaved seamstresses illustrates that while sewing rarely crossed gender lines, it was a task that could and did cross racial boundaries, although neither the black nor white community intrinsically linked sewing to an enslaved woman's gender identity as it was for white women. While many enslaved women possessed some sewing skills, most served primarily as agricultural workers. This division in gendered labor expectations marked one of the ways that white southerners drew distinctions between black and white women, de-feminizing the former while constructing the latter as caretakers within southern society. The distinction extended to the provision of clothing for the enslaved family. While enslaved women may have wished to take responsibility for the clothing needs of their own families, both to ensure their comfort and as a mark of their emotional commitment, they generally lacked access to the necessary resources. Thus white mistresses could claim for themselves the responsibility for clothing enslaved men and children. But at times supplies distributed by slave owners reflected gender expectations about women and sewing. Mary Bull Pringle, for example, carefully recorded the clothing handed out to the male slaves who staffed her Charleston townhouse, but she did not keep similar records for female slaves. Instead, women received a length of material to make their own dresses. Former slave Mary Edwards of South Carolina confirmed the expectation that enslaved women made their own clothes, "which we done sometimes late in the evening," after the field labor had been completed. Common gender expectations coexisted with other labor expectations, complicating the boundaries that existed within the southern household.[31]

Where labor forces were sufficiently large, some enslaved women worked full-time at the tasks of sewing or clothing production for the household. Sharing the task with white women created close interactions and some potential for the formation of emotional bonds. Interviewed in the 1930s, Easter Jackson recalled that her mother, Frances Wilkerson, was "an unusually intelligent slave, able to weave, spin, and do all kinds of sewing, [who] cost Mr. Dix $1500.00. She received excellent care, never once being allowed to do any field work, and was kept at the 'Big House' to do the sewing for the household."[32] Jackson's memories assert that a degree of esteem accompanied Wilkerson's economic value.
Elizabeth Keckley suggested that a sense of connection could flow both ways. As a slave, she had used her skill with a needle to keep "bread in the mouths of seventeen persons for two years and five months," both black and white of all ages. Her memoirs suggest the interdependencies that often existed in the southern household. Although she bought her freedom when the opportunity arose, Keckley's autobiography suggests a surprisingly warm regard for her former owners.[33]

Some white women acknowledged their reliance on the labor of black women. Mahala Roach generally seemed to take for granted that her enslaved women would take on other household chores so that she could devote herself to her sewing. On occasion, however, she recorded her direct cooperation with these women. On September 2, 1858, she wrote: "I have almost finished Hala's green dress which Ailsie has been braiding." Although they may not have been work-ing side by side, the white woman and the slave labored together to complete the dress for Roach's daughter. Similarly, Kate Carney recorded sewing on a dress with her sister, and then added, "Betsy, the servant, assisted us yesterday on my other [dress], by hemming my ruffles."[34] While this sharing of tasks may not have grown into a close emotional bond, the daily interactions around sewing created a sense of mutual purpose that could, at least temporarily, link women across racial lines. Co-operation was not only useful but necessary if the house-hold was to function well.

On occasion, very skilled black seamstresses gained power within the house-hold, their work strengthening bonds of trust and dependency between women. For example, Mary Bull Pringle, who so carefully controlled the distribution of material to her seamstresses, trusted her personal maid Cretia to oversee the proper completion of this work. Mary Jones's letter to her daughter on October 21, 1858, praised a number of enslaved sewers. She wrote appreciatively of a down pillow completed by Patience, while Kate "has made and frilled the case very nicely." Jones could perhaps be generous with her praise because it reflected well on her own instruction and management, but her comments also indicate skills and sentiments that linked the women together. Perhaps the most notable ex-ample of sewing skills leading to independence is that of Elizabeth Keckley. Born into slavery, the skills she developed as a seamstress allowed her to acquire suf-ficient funds to purchase her freedom. Her dressmaking skills ultimately gained her celebrity and an invitation into the White House as dressmaker to Mary Todd Lincoln, a relationship portrayed in Keckley's own memoir as a familial bond.[35] While the needle symbolized servitude for many enslaved women, for a few it provided a route to freedom.

Undoubtedly, within the southern household, a clear hierarchy privileged the needs and desires of the white family and remained in place to challenge any notion of familial ties. Sewing replicated the power structures of the broader society in terms of controlling tasks and accessing materials. Frequently, the comforts of the white family were met at the expense of black women and their families. Even the Jones family of Georgia, who prided themselves on their Christian compassion and generosity as slave owners, carefully controlled the quality and amount of material available to enslaved members of the household. Mary Bull Pringle meted out tasks and material to her sewing women. She and her daughters cut out patterns and then placed them in a work box in the sewing room for distribution to the seamstresses. Martha Forman's main recorded task in the manufacturing of clothes for the slaves at Rose Hill plantation was "cutting out" the patterns that her enslaved assistants then sewed up.[36] Frequently, white women controlled the "cutting out," both because it was considered the most skilled task in clothing production and because it represented control of resources.

Although few rejected the aid of enslaved seamstresses, many white women cast aspersions on their skills. White women claimed sole domain over "fancy work," or embroidery, insisting that black women were only capable of "plain sewing": basting, seaming, hemming, and mending. On December 27, 1857, Tryphena Fox wrote that she was going to have the enslaved woman Mary "do coarse sewing for there are suits of clothes to be made for both Reuben & Susan & her children. I shall take the time to do up what fine sewing I can for the summer." These distinctions established difference in the face of a shared skill set. Mary Hering Middleton of South Carolina complained of the "filthy fingers" of her sewing women. In December 1843, she informed her daughter, "You may suppose how busy I have been since I came, giving work to 6 women who do not half as much as 2 whites would do in the same time." Slow work was a common complaint of white women. Rebecca Singleton griped to her daughters in 1830 that "altho there are 5 employed they make very slow progress" in making the requested clothing. Similarly, E. P. Lewis wrote from Louisiana in 1832 that the production of baby clothes proceeded slowly because an unnamed servant was "so good for nothing that she does scarcely anything."[37] These comments asserted the power that white women had over the labor of the enslaved women and the limits of common experiences and emotional ties.

Occasionally, disdain expressed for black seamstresses became more overt expressions of abuse. Their close proximity to the mistress probably left these enslaved seamstresses more exposed than other slaves to her temper or fits of pique. The story told by Hannah Jones about her grandmother may be unique in its extremity. Jones, born into slavery in 1850, recalled that her grandmother was "a fine seamstress" who sewed for the white people on the plantation. However, just three days after giving birth, her grandmother was forced to get up and make a dozen shirts for her mistress's son, who was going off to college. Weakened from childbirth, she stitched some of the shirts poorly, leading to a severe beating by the overseer. The end result, according to Jones, was that her grandmother was rendered "stone blind."[38] Such an outcome may have been unusual, but the complaints and assertions of control by white women were not. Such violent power dynamics, however, should not totally undermine the claims of affective familial sentiments in some households. Power and hierarchy were essential elements of antebellum southerners' conception of family. Although relationships were often troubled and tenuous, daily interactions within the household between black and white inhabitants resulted in a complexity of sentiments that historians have only just begun to untangle.

The southern plantation household was a distinct entity in antebellum America. Not only did it resist the market forces that gave middle-class northern women dominion in the domestic realm, but the presence of an enslaved labor force within the bounds of the household complicated interactions and relationships. Daily tasks involved in sewing and clothing production were shaped by these distinctions. Maria Inskeep, who had grown up in the North but lived her adult life on a Louisiana plantation, identified the particular southernness of sewing demands: "for in this climate and so long a continuance of warm weather, we are obliged to have a great many changes—and it is no trifle my dear sister to sit down and make from 15 to 20 dresses for myself and the girls, briches frocks for Marys children—and all the under cloaths which are obliged to be changed every day—and I hurry through it before the *hot* weather comes on—for then it is impossible to get through much sewing." Climatic demands allowed Inskeep to rationalize holding slaves. She wrote on another occasion: "here we are never without help, and if you treat them well they become very much attached to you, and the Family—and are serviceable."[39] For this transplanted northerner, the daily demands of the southern household and the maintenance of the slave system were fully intertwined, and sewing created a familylike attachment.

Enslaved women undoubtedly had a perspective distinct from white women on the attachments engendered by sewing. While some developed close, cooperative relationships with the white women alongside whom they worked, other enslaved women used their skills with a needle to surreptitiously assert a form of independence, artistically if not legally. The clothes that enslaved women made for their own black families when resources became available denoted their familial ties. Limited written evidence exists of the sentiments that enslaved women brought to the sewing they did for their own families. However, Rev. Isaac Williams in his antislavery memoir recalled his enslaved mother "sewing industriously to make or mend some needful garment, when so fatigued with the day's labor that she nodded between the stitches, and at last sat down in heavy slumber over her work." Williams clearly intended the effort his mother made to clothe her family, despite her great fatigue, to suggest the care and affection she had for them. Slave owners commented derisively on the makeshift, patchwork appearance of such creations, but to the wearers they represented both resourcefulness and affection. From clothing to quilts, an enslaved woman's sewing allowed for the expression of both individuality and black community values. This separation was a point often misunderstood by white masters and mistresses. Miriam Hilliard noted on January 13, 1850: "In the afternoon, we all made the rounds of the quarter—in honor of our coming many curiously patterned quilts displayed." In these efforts, Hilliard saw oddity rather than individual taste and style.[40] At such times, it was clear that there were two distinct familial interests and experiences living within the same plantation household.

The coming of the Civil War upset the structures of the southern household and destroyed any illusion of a single southern family, black and white. For many white southern women, the first reaction to the outbreak of war was a surge of sewing. As quickly as southern men enlisted in the army, white women formed societies to produce uniforms and other comforts of camp life. A member of the Lenoir family of North Carolina commented: "The ladies have been exceedingly busy sewing for the companies here & I expect they are better provided than any in the state." The women of Georgia also did their part. In August 1861, Mary Robarts informed her cousin Mary Jones that "the ladies are kept quite busy sewing for the soldiers. Whenever you call to see a lady now, you will find her with either a hickory or flannel shirt in her hands, making it or a pair of drawers." Meta Grimball of South Carolina worried about men who had already seen battle when she wrote in July 1861 that "the ladies are all as busy as possible forming themselves into relief societies for the wounded soldiers, and also to prepare clothing for them in the winter, which will soon now approach." Working with their needles became white women's contribution to the war effort and a way to show their support for the Confederacy.[41]

Plantation mistresses also sought to maintain the structures and relationships of their households during the war. The Jones family of Georgia viewed the provisioning of their slaves as a moral obligation despite the fact that the war made cloth difficult to obtain. Mary Jones began to fret that she would be unable to do her duty, even though she and her daughter had located an old loom and had begun to make homespun cloth. Other women had difficulties just providing for their white family members. Writing in 1864, Julia Johnson Fisher noted the shabbiness of her husband's attire, despite her best efforts: "I have used bedticking—sheets—curtains and the linings of my dresses to clothe him and now we know not where to get anything more." Besides the limited wardrobes, Fisher observed that lack of materials led to depression because it left her without employment and, therefore, without immediate purpose. Efforts to support the troops through sewing were also soon disrupted by a lack of material. Eliza Ripley lauded southern women's efforts to sew for the Confederate soldiers, but she conceded their ultimate failure in her region; the fall of New Orleans cut off a supply route, and thus "the 'Campaign Sewing Society' sadly disbanded."[42] Although white southern women found other opportunities to contribute both to their families and to the war effort, the disruption of their prewar activities amplified the chaos that the war created in their lives.

Ongoing shortages caused by the war, however, also allowed some white southerners to recognize the valuable contribution that sewing women made to the comfort and economic stability of their families in the antebellum period. When Mary Sharpe Mallard and her husband contemplated fleeing Atlanta in May 1864, she noted that they "sent away all of our winter clothing, comforts, carpets, my sewing machine, and most of Mr. Mallard's books to Augusta to Brother Joe, so that if the army does not make a stand at this place, we will not lose everything."[43] Stripped of most of the traditional southern measures of wealth, such domestic goods remained the last bastion of a white family's material well-being.

In contrast, the insecurity of war caused others to question their economic viability. Mahala Roach, who had been widowed before the war, worried about her ability to support her family. In 1854, she had recognized the value of sewing to the family economy when she offered extra work to a hired seamstress named Mrs. Kid, explaining that "when I saw the poor old woman with no other means of living—and I always busy—I gave her more work and paid her well for what she did." This gesture recognized the value of the work performed by Mrs. Kid and, by extension, Roach's own work. But in 1862, Roach expressed doubts about her own financial situation and any ability to support herself with her needle. Fretting over "how badly I sew," she concluded, "what a miserable life I would lead if I had to work for my children and my own living."[44] Such pondering suggests the significant turn in social situation that the war brought to many white families. Yet, despite her frequent bouts of self-doubt, her sewing remained essential to her family's comfort, public appearance, and status as postwar society unfolded. Both family values and the value to the family embedded in sewing remained important in the postbellum world, although the daily practice of this task, particularly labor relations, had changed.

In fact, in the postwar years many formerly elite southerners found themselves in significantly reduced circumstances. Once one of Charleston's premier families, the Pringles relied on relatives living outside of the South to provide luxuries that they had once taken for granted. White women in more desperate circumstances used their skills with a needle to earn what money they could to support themselves and their families.[45] But while many white women saw sewing for money as a reduction of the status that they had once enjoyed, newly freed black women seized the opportunities offered by their sewing abilities. Mary Jones noted that a former slave, Grace, had fled to Savannah and was now "sewing for her living." Frank Frost reported to his wife, Rebecca, that he had found a freedwoman who would work as a seamstress for three dollars a month.[46] While less than what she might have made as a field hand, the black seamstress made a choice to use the skills she possessed, perhaps asserting a claim to a newly available gender identity. Many white women complained bitterly about this new freedom, suggesting that they too were aware of shifts in gender ideas and not just in labor relations. In 1867, Tryphena Fox wrote that "the blacks are all growing more & more unreliable every day, & we are becoming very tired of them." She continued, "Had a girl to help me sew last week but she is very slow with her needle & I don't think she helps much only *she* is better than nothing."[47] No matter how much they complained, white women continued to rely on black women's aid, just as freedwomen needed the employment that sewing offered. Still, a significant change had occurred: negotiations had moved from a household interaction to a market transaction, and new ideas about gender, race, and power beyond the plantation household were being tested. Any sense of family bonds seemed to have disintegrated in the wake of war and emancipation.

With the rapid disintegration of household ties in the postbellum South, it may seem "our family, white and black" was a tale "made out of whole cloth" and never really true. Certainly, racial divisions ultimately became more central to southern society than the gender commonalities embodied in the tasks of sewing. But this is a perspective constructed in retrospect. The antebellum plantation household involved a complex interweaving of power relations and emotional bonds, somewhere between a purely economic interaction and the emotional ties of blood. Work done by all women within these households was certainly as essential to the economic viability and material comfort of their families as work done in the market economy. But the relationships forged in these tasks went beyond economic exchange of labor to involve close interactions, conflict, concessions, interdependence, and emotion. In other words, they resembled the negotiations that occur within the framework of family. Family is also about inculcating and replicating social values. The tasks involved in sewing and clothing production in the antebellum South became a means of teaching proper gender roles and power relationships. Sewing not only provided for the material comfort of the family; it also stitched together relationships, creating not just value for the family but an expression of family values. While these were not ready-made to fit clear definitions of family, they were tailored to meet the needs of those living within the antebellum southern household.

Notes

1. Mahala Roach Diaries, 17 May 1855, Roach-Eggleston Family Papers, Southern Historical Collection, Wilson Library, University of North Carolina at Chapel Hill.

2. Peter Bardaglio, *Reconstructing the Household: Families, Sex, and the Law in the Nineteenth-Century South* (Chapel Hill: University of North Carolina Press, 1995), 25; Eugene Genovese, "'Our Family, White and Black': Family and Household in the Southern Slaveholders' World View," in Carol Bleser, ed., *In Joy and in Sorrow: Women, Family, and Marriage in the Victorian South* (New York: Oxford University Press, 1991), 69; Elizabeth Fox-Genovese, *Within the Plantation Household: Black and White Women of the Old South* (Chapel Hill: University of North Carolina Press, 1988), 31.

3. The limitation of the separate spheres model is perhaps most clearly outlined in Linda K. Kerber, "Separate Spheres, Female Worlds, Woman's Place: The Rhetoric of Women's History" *Journal of American History* 75 (June 1988): 9–39; Jeanne Boydston, *Home and Work: Housework, Wages, and the Ideology of Labor in the Early Republic* (New York: Oxford University Press, 1990); Fox-Genovese, *Within the Plantation Household*, esp. chap 1; Suzanne Lebsock, *The Free Women of Petersburg: Status and Culture in a Southern Town, 1784–1860* (New York: W. W. Norton, 1984), 148; Elizabeth White Nelson, *Market Sentiments: Middle-Class Market Culture in Nineteenth-Century American* (Washington, D.C.: Smithsonian Books, 2004).

4. Deborah Gray White, *Ar'n't I a Woman? Female Slaves in the Plantation South* (New York: W. W. Norton, 1999), 5–7.

5. Belle Kearney, *A Slaveholder's Daughter* (New York: Abbey Press, 1900), 3.

6. See, for example, entries from August 1814 and April 1834 in W. Emerson Wilson, ed., *Plantation Life at Rose Hill: The Diaries of Martha Ogle Forman, 1814–1845* (Wilmington: Historical Society of Delaware, 1976); Ruth Cowan Schwartz, *More Work for Mother: The Ironies of Household Technology from the Open Hearth to the Microwave* (New York: Basic Books, 1983), 74; Susan Strasser, *Never Done: A History of American Housework* (1982; reprint, New York: Henry Holt, 2000), 126–29.

7. Varina Davis actually did endorse the Grover & Baker sewing machine in the September 1860 edition of *Harper's Weekly*. Joan Cashin, *First Lady of the Confederacy: Varina Davis's Civil War* (Cambridge, Mass.: Belknap Press, 2006), 88; Roach Diaries, May/June 1857; Robert Manson Myers, ed., *The Children of Pride: A True Story of Georgia and the Civil War* (New Haven: Yale University Press, 1972), 604. On the history of the sewing machine, see Ava Baron and Susan E. Klepp, "If I Didn't Have My Sewing Machine . . .": Women and Sewing Machine Technology," in *A Needle, a Bobbin, a Strike: Women Needleworkers in America*, ed. Joan M. Jensen and Sue Davidson (Philadelphia: Temple University, 1984), 20–53; and Strasser, *Never Done*, 138–41.

8. Rozsika Parker, *The Subversive Stitch: Embroidery and the Making of the Feminine* (London: Women's Press, 1984), 1, 138.

9. Diary of Adele Allston Vanderhorst, 15 June 1859; Adele Allston to Adele Petigru Allston, 16 March 1856, both in Adele Allston Vanderhorst Papers, 1859–1930, South Carolina Historical Society, Charleston; Anya Jabour, *Scarlett's Sisters: Young Women in the Old South* (Chapel Hill: University of North Carolina, 2007), 113–14.

10. Harriette Lesesne to Adele Petigru Allston, 6 March 1856, Adele Petigru Allston Papers.

11. Sarah Champs Carter to The Misses Singleton, 26 October 1830; Jane Coles to Marion Singleton Deveaux, 22 April 1836, both in Singleton Family Papers, Manuscript Division, Library of Congress, Washington, D.C.

12. Mary C. Townsend to Phoebe Townsend, 15 September 1871, Townsend Family Papers, 1850–1899, South Carolina Historical Society; Roach Diaries, 7 February 1862, 23–26 October 1855.

13. Journal of Anna McCall Watson, 1849, Cross Keys Plantation; Mary Folger Diary, 1 April 1859, both in Tulane University, New Orleans; Roach Diaries, 2 February 1853, 25 June 1859.

14. A. T. Conrad to Mary Weeks, 20 May 1832, Weeks Family Papers, Tulane University.

15. Myers, ed., *The Children of Pride*, 398, 423.

16. Ibid., 458, 481–82.

17. Journal of Sarah Ann Gayle, 26 September 1832, Denegre Family Papers, Tulane University; Roach Diaries, 17 April 1856; Miriam B. Hilliard Diary, 1 January 1850, Tulane University.

18. Agreement, 1 February 1825, box 1, Bruce Family Papers, Manuscript Division, Library of Congress; Keith C. Barton, "'Good Cooks and Washers': Slave Hiring, Domestic Labor, and the Market in Bourbon County, Kentucky," *Journal of American History* 84 (September 1997): 442–43.

19. Wilson, ed., *Plantation Life at Rose Hill*.

20. Adele Petigru Allston to Ben Allston, 20 November 1849, 14 November 1850, and 29 October 1849, Adele Petigru Allston Papers.

21. Richard N. Coté, *Mary's World: Love, War, and Family Ties in Nineteenth-Century Charleston* (Mount Pleasant, S.C.: Corinthian Books, 2002), 186; Maurie D. McInnis, *The Politics of Taste in Antebellum Charleston* (Chapel Hill: University of North Carolina Press, 2005), 13.

22. Coté, *Mary's World*, 104–5; Adele Petigru Allston to Adele Allston, 26 March 1856, Adele Petigru Allston Papers.

23. Ben Allston to Adele Allston, n.d. [prior to 1857], Adele Petigru Allston Papers.

24. Mary McDuffie to Mrs. R. Singleton, 29 July [1842–49] and n.d., Singleton Family Papers; Letitia M. Burwell, *A Girl's Life in Virginia before the War* (New York: Frederick A. Stokes, 1985), 194.

25. King, *A Northern Woman in the Plantation South*, 90; Eliza Cope Harrison, ed., *Best Companions: Letters of Eliza Middleton Fisher and Her Mother, Mary Hering Middleton, from Charleston, Philadelphia, and Newport, 1839–1846* (Columbia: University of South Carolina Press, 2001), 380; Mary Norcott Bryan, *A Grandmother's Recollections of Dixie* (New Bern, N.C.: Owen C. Dunn, Printer, [1912?]), 11.

26. Jabour, *Scarlett's Sisters*, 33–34; Mrs. R. Singleton to Marion Singleton, 5 May [1828?], Singleton Family Papers.

27. Mary C. Townsend to Phoebe and Lena "Dame" Townsend, 29 January 1856, Townsend Family Papers.

28. Annie Deveaux to Marion Singleton Deveaux, 2 December 1845, box 4, Singleton Family Papers.

29. M. C. Townsend to Phoebe Townsend, 2 April 1859, and letter fragment probably from February 1858, Townsend Family Papers.

30. Sue King to Adele Allston, 28 January 1846, Adele Petigru Allston Papers; Wilson, ed., *Plantation Life at Rose Hill*, 9.

31. Coté, *Mary's World*, 187; McInnis, *The Politics of Taste in Antebellum Charleston*, 262; George Rawick, ed., *The American Slave: A Composite Autobiography*, 24 vols. (Westport, Conn.: Greenwood, 1972), vol. 2, part 2 (South Carolina Narratives), 2.

32. Rawick, *The American Slave*, vol. 12, part 2 (Georgia Narratives), 299.

33. Elizabeth Keckley, *Behind the Scenes; or, Thirty Years a Slave, and Four Years in the White House* (1868; reprint, New York: Penguin Books, 2005), 20, 106–18.

34. Roach Diaries, 2 September 1858, 17 August 1859; Kate Carney Diary, 18 April 1861, http://docsouth.unc.edu/imls/carney/carney.html.

35. McInnis, *The Politics of Taste in Antebellum Charleston*, 262; Myers, ed., *The Children of Pride*, 454; Keckley, *Behind the Scenes*, 20–22, chaps. 5–9.

36. Myers, ed., *The Children of Pride*, 201, 264; Coté, *Mary's World*, 187; Wilson, ed., *Plantation Life at Rose Hill*, 79. On the skills needed for cutting out, see Marla R. Miller, "Gender, Artisanry, and Craft Tradition in Early New England: The View through the Eye of a Needle," *William and Mary Quarterly* 60 (October 2003): 751.

37. King, ed., *A Northern Woman in the Plantation South*, 68; Parker, *The Subversive Stitch*, 174; Harrison, ed., *Best Companions*, 336, 337n11; Mrs. R. S. Singleton to Marion and Angelica Singleton, 7 December 1830, Singleton Family Papers; E. P. Lewis to E.G.W. Butler, 13 May 1832, Custis-Lee Family Papers, Manuscript Division, Library of Congress.

38. Rawick, *The American Slave*, vol. 11, part 8 (Missouri Narratives), 218.

39. Maria Inskeep to Fanny Hampton, 22 April [1837?], 29 October 1832, Fanny Leverich Eshleman Craig Collection, Tulane University.

40. Isaac Williams, *Aunt Sally; or, The Cross the Way of Freedom: A Narrative of the Slave-Life and Purchase of the Mother of Rev. Isaac Williams of Detroit, Michigan* (Cincinnati: American Reform Tract and Book Society, c. 1858), 10; Hilliard Diary, 13 January 1850; McInnis, *The Politics of Taste in Antebellum Charleston*, 14.

41. Louis to Mame, 2 May 1861, Lenoir Family Papers, http://docsouth.unc.edu/imls/lenoir/lenoir.html; Myers, ed., *The Children of Pride*, 739; Journal of Meta Morris Grimball, 26 July 1861, http://docsouth.unc.edu/fpn/grimball/grimball.html; George C. Rable, *Civil Wars: Women and the Crisis of Southern Nationalism* (Urbana: University of Illinois Press, 1989), 93, 138–39; Drew Gilpin Faust, *Mothers of Invention: Women of the Slaveholding South in the American Civil War* (Chapel Hill: University of North Carolina Press, 1996), 24–25; and Jabour, *Scarlett's Sisters*, 253–55.

42. Myers, ed., *The Children of Pride*, 1054; Julia Johnson Fisher Diary, 3 January 1864, 1 February 1864, http://docsouth.unc.edu/imls/fisherjulia/fisher.html; Eliza Moore Chinn McHatton Ripley, *From Flag to Flag: A Woman's Adventures and Experiences in the South during the War, in Mexico, and in Cuba* (New York: D. Appleton, 1889), 14.

43. Myers, ed., *The Children of Pride*, 1174.

44. Roach Diaries, 4 April 1854, 15 May 1862.

45. Coté, *Mary's World*, 268; Rable, *Civil Wars*, 284.

46. Myers, ed., *The Children of Pride*, 1300; Coté, *Mary's World*, 305.

47. King, ed., *A Northern Woman in the Plantation South*, 210.

6

A Family Firm

The Marital and Business Partnership of Ann and Richard Archer

NIKKI BERG BURIN

~

As Ann Barnes Archer gazed upon the dull, frozen grounds of her Mississippi plantation in January 1856, she resigned herself to another day of dismal weather. "A cloudy day suits my feelings best," she wrote to her absent husband. One month had passed since Ann bade good-bye to Richard Thompson Archer and their four eldest children. Richard had left for an extended business trip and, along the way, conveyed two daughters, a son, and a nephew to their respective schools in Philadelphia and Richmond. Their collective absence compounded Ann's stress and dejection. In charge of five young children, two overseers, more than two hundred slaves, a large cotton ginning operation, and over two thousand acres of frozen land due to be plowed, Ann was overwhelmed with emotion and fatigue. She reached out to Richard, writing, "I feel so badly since my children left, I am unfitted to attend to matters at home as I would wish. In the last few weeks everything seems changed to me and everything makes me feel sad." Sitting in his hotel room in Washington, D.C., Richard regretted that business prevented him from returning home to comfort his wife. "I wish that money was not so necessary in this life," he lamented, "Much of our happiness is sacrificed to obtain it." Nonetheless, in a hastily scribbled postscript he reminded Ann of his responsibilities and her own: "I can give no thought to business at home[;] you must direct all as you wish."[1]

This episode captures the tenor of the Archers' thirty-three years of marriage. When Richard left to tend his distant plantations and nonagricultural investments, as well as his legal and political interests, he relied on Ann to manage business affairs at home. In addition to her regular round of maternal and domestic duties, she oversaw the operation of two plantations during such times, supervising the overseers' conduct and directing their labor as well as that of the slaves under their watch. The Archers' business arrangement had a profound impact not only on the operation of their family enterprise but also on their marriage.

A planter's decision to have his wife rather than a fellow planter or professional steward act as his agent was more than a matter of convenience; it was an implicit recognition of her competence and authority in business affairs. Women's supposed lack of these attributes formed, in part, the basis of the marital contract and much of society's general understanding of the differences between the sexes. As historian Brenda E. Stevenson points out, "Since the privileged position of free males clearly rested on the assumption that women could not function in the 'world,' a woman who did so challenged a basic premise of patriarchal power." Yet, like the colonial deputy-husbands described by historian Laurel Thatcher Ulrich, antebellum female managers did not declare their economic or social independence when serving as their husbands' agents, but rather fulfilled a spousal duty. To be a manager was to be a good wife. The rise of the companionate marital ideal in the eighteenth and nineteenth centuries facilitated planters' reliance on their wives as plantation managers and thereby fostered the development of more egalitarian marriages. While Ann occasionally undercut Richard's authority by overriding his decisions and censuring what she saw as his dubious ethics, her management did less to threaten his dominion than to augment their reliance on one another as life and business partners.[2]

However, the business partnership of spouses did not generate or sustain marital companionship. On the contrary, planter capitalism, which created the need for female management, drove a wedge between many husbands and wives. Absenteeism, a consequence of entrepreneurship and large-scale commercial planting, especially strained the emotional bonds of married couples and often created a climate of distrust, loneliness, and general unhappiness within their marriages. Richard and Ann both lamented the necessity of money in life and bemoaned their respective roles in the family business. Nonetheless, they thoroughly enjoyed their affluence and pursued greater riches despite the detrimental impact this priority had on their marriage. Aside from the Archers' mutual devotion to their children, the family firm was the pivot upon which their marriage turned. Ironically, the very thing that cemented their bond to each other put the greatest strain on their union, as well as their perception of each other's commitment to their gendered identities as responsible husband and dutiful wife, respectively. As their fluctuating relationship demonstrates, the forces of planter capitalism simultaneously brought Richard and Ann together and drove them apart.

Historians debate how common arrangements like that of the Archers were. Some scholars contend that plantation management by planters' wives was an infrequent occurrence. Yet recent research on the managerial abilities of slaveholding widows suggests that many white women had administrative experience prior to their husbands' deaths. Similarly, some scholars contend that female managers served as little more than figureheads, for their husbands and overseers alike assumed that women lacked the ability to manage plantations successfully. Others argue that the interim management of absentee planters' wives was essential to the productivity and efficiency of the plantation system. Finally, while some historians find that planters relied on their wives as managers only out of necessity, others maintain that they had confidence in their spouses' administrative capacity and deliberately chose them to serve as their agents rather than hire professional male stewards.[3]

While historians disagree about the extent to which female slaveholders served as managers and their ability to perform the duties associated with the job, it is clear that it was not uncommon for husbands to rely on their wives in this capacity. In fact, there was a long tradition of female plantation management in the South. From the colonial period through the Revolutionary era and well beyond the Civil War, the daughters, wives, and widows of absentee planters often assumed responsibility for the administration of their families' estates. While most women did not manage their families' plantations as often as Ann Barnes Archer and therefore did not have reason or the opportunity to wield as much authority over business matters as she did, most slaveholding women likely took over governance of their plantations at some point, whether it was for a day, a week, a month, or a year or more. To be a planter's wife was to be, potentially, a plantation manager.[4] Ann realized this within just a few months of her wedding.

In an affectionate manner characteristic of newlyweds, sixteen-year-old Ann penned two letters to her thirty-seven-year-old absent husband in December 1834. Assuring Richard that it was "not so pleasant" being without him, she declared that she had made up her mind never to let him leave again without her. After sharing the local news and expressing her desire that he would soon be home, Ann concluded her second letter by writing, "Every[thing] is going on pretty well at Pine Woods[.] I believe three or four of the negroes are sick[;] cotton is selling for 18¢ a pound of good quality." Richard, who was "very impatient" to return home to Ann, responded with an equally affectionate letter in which he regretted that she would "never know how *very very* much" he loved her, for she could not "witness the secret workings of the mind." Imploring her to take care of her health and promising not to stay away an hour longer than necessary, he closed his letter with instructions for Ann concerning his crop: "Tell [the overseer] to hurry the cotton to market as fast it is ready."[5] This seemingly insignificant exchange of letters signaled the beginning of a thirty-two-year business partnership in one of the largest slave-based agricultural enterprises in antebellum Mississippi.

By the end of the Archers' first year of marriage, Richard was the owner and co-owner of five Mississippi plantations—Chicopah, Archerlita, and Inno Albino on Honey Island in west central Holmes County, and Anchuca and Pine Woods in southwestern Claiborne County. Following the deaths of three male relatives in the mid- and late 1830s, he assumed managerial responsibilities for two additional plantations in Mississippi and ownership of one in Virginia. Richard and Ann held as many as five hundred African Americans in bondage on these eight estates until the end of the Civil War, many of whom they forcibly relocated from the Old Dominion to Mississippi. While cotton was the mainstay of the family's fortune, their bondspeople also grew corn and wheat, raised livestock, and processed lumber at Richard's mill.[6]

The Archer plantations were complex enterprises that required not only the labor of hundreds of slaves but also the constant attention of skilled administrators. A frequent traveler who was involved in a variety of business ventures, lawsuits, and political events, Richard could not manage all of his plantations all of the time. Like many planters, he was generally suspicious of the men he hired as overseers and preferred to have a manager look after his affairs in his absence. A plantation manager or agent occupied the administrative space between the overseer and the planter. In the proprietor's absence, the agent served as the resident master and was expected to act for and in the interest of the planter in all business concerns. Richard saw the ideal agent as a "trusty friend" who would protect his property—human and otherwise—from corrupt or incompetent overseers. As he explained to one of his managers, "The welfare of our negroes, and the safety and productiveness of our property will devolve on you."[7] Professional agents were usually white men with extensive managerial experience and a "respectable" social status, while amateur managers were typically kin, trusted neighbors, and fellow planters. Never satisfied with their performance, Richard went through a wide range of managers on his Holmes County plantations over the course of his life, including professionals, friends, cousins, and his son Abram. He had only one manager, however, on his home plantations in Claiborne County. That was Ann.

Entrepreneurial collaboration between husband and wife was a necessary component of many large-scale planting enterprises. Richard needed Ann to engage in their business at home so that he could sustain and expand it elsewhere. Although Ann had no experience in plantation management at the time of her marriage, she was the most convenient and trustworthy person for the job. Not only was she almost always at home—-child rearing, ill health, and domestic responsibilities necessitated this—but as a member of the Archer family she also had a personal investment in Richard's business interests. Her role as manager entailed the same duties as those required of her husband's agents in Holmes County. Richard wanted her to let him know "how the crop gets on" and to "let none of the negroes be maltreated." Ann sent regular reports to Richard informing him of the progress of the crop, the nature of the work in which the slaves were employed, and the performance of the overseers. "I write once a week," stated Ann, "to let you hear how the work on the two plantations gets along."[8]

The Archers' business arrangement was not only a product of their commercial needs but also a reflection of the emotional and legal framework of antebellum marriage. In the first half of the nineteenth century, popular sentiment held that men and women should marry on the basis of love and friendship rather than economic or social advancement, which had long served as the primary reason for marriage. Richard reflected this ideological transition when he professed to his wife in 1847, "I have loved you from the time I first courted you with my whole heart."[9] Ideally, antebellum husbands and wives would move away from the patriarchal structure of marriage and make familial, and in some cases, business decisions together. Companionate marriage was based on consensus, affection, and harmony. From the eighteenth century through the antebellum era and beyond, novelists, journalists, and moralists alike described how to achieve this new marital ideal. Moved by the romantic exploits of literary heroes and heroines, men and women searched for one with whom they could share and relish life. Richard and Ann found this in each other. Their family firm and Ann's role in it furthered their attempt to build a companionate marriage characterized by an egalitarian partnership. When Richard told Ann, "You are my only counselor," it was not a commentary on his lack of trustworthy male advisors but rather a statement of his faith in and reliance on her as a business and life partner.[10]

When couples stood before the altar, their ministers often emphasized the love between husbands and wives, but they also reminded couples about marital responsibilities. Embedded within nineteenth-century marital law was a labor agreement between husbands and wives, which involved an exchange of services and remunerations between superiors (husbands) and subordinates (wives). Wives were legally obligated to perform domestic services for their spouses, including cooking, washing, cleaning, and sewing—or managing the servants and slaves who completed these tasks. In cases where a husband owned a business, his wife also labored within it upon his request. The legality of this arrangement manifested in terms of husbands' rights rather than wives' duties. In his 1816 treatise on the laws of marriage or of "Baron and Femme," prominent lawyer and judge Tapping Reeve of Connecticut stated that if a wife was unable to fulfill her domestic duties as a result of injury from a third party, her husband could "bring an action in his own name, to recover damages which he sustained, by reason of the battery." The injury he suffered was "the loss of her service." The courts determined that for this grievance, compensation was due to the husband, not to the impaired wife.[11]

The labor contract between husband and wife may have privileged the former, but it also provided some protections to the latter. In exchange for their domestic labor, as well as the rights to their property, wives were entitled to financial support from their spouses. Husbands provided their wives with life's "necessaries"—food, clothing, and shelter, or at least the funds with which to procure them. If a couple separated, the courts defined the proper amount of support as that which would allow a wife to maintain the same quality of life that she experienced in marriage. The courts did not specify, however, how much support a husband was to provide his wife if they lived together. The judiciary assumed that if a wife continued to reside with her husband, she was adequately maintained or, in other words, he was fulfilling his spousal duties. This, of course, was not always the case. Even so, this economic arrangement defined the legal institution of marriage.[12]

Female plantation management, as in the case of the Archers, was one manifestation of the doctrine of marital service. However, husbands called on their wives to act as their agents not only because it was their legal right but also because it made sense to do so. What was probably a matter of convenience during short-term absences was a reasoned and informed solution to the potential problems that long-term absences posed. Business and politics frequently took wealthy men from home, but class prejudices and modern managerial philosophies dissuaded many from entrusting their overseers with their most valuable assets. New marital ideals stressing companionship and equality between husbands and wives encouraged men to trust their spouses above all others. All these factors pointed to wives as the wisest choice for managerial positions. That it was common for men to make this choice suggests not only that their wives were trustworthy but that they were also skilled managers.

While prevailing notions of femininity presented female plantation managers with certain challenges, it was ultimately because and not in spite of their womanhood that many women thrived in their administrative positions. Many female administrators saw plantation management as an extension of their domestic work as mothers, wives, mistresses, and the moral guardians of society. Approaching their administrative role in this way did not so much hamper their efforts to do "men's work," as plantation management redefined that work as the domain of women. Popular gender prescriptions posed unique challenges to female managers but also gave them firm ground to stand upon when put in a position of authority over affairs usually seen as outside the purview of the "feminine sphere." It also allowed them to use their real and presumed strengths as women—such as their reputed morality—to administer their plantations. As such, female managers realized their administrative goals without upsetting the social order and without compromising their sense of self. Moreover, it enabled them to act less as deputy-husbands than as autonomous managers of large-scale commercial plantations. For this reason, in addition to the fact that they were fulfilling one of their spousal duties, female plantation managers offset the patriarchal overtone of the marital contract without posing a threat to the sexual hierarchy and the larger social order. This was of particular importance in the South, where the hierarchical nature of marriage was routinely acknowledged if not celebrated by much of white society.

White southerners embraced the companionate ideal. But, as historian Peter Bardaglio observes, they also "clung to traditional notions of patriarchal authority that stressed the importance of harmony, dependency, and hierarchy." This was because the white family, in Drew Gilpin Faust's words, was "the essential foundation of Southern public life and values." The seemingly organic relationships of the white household were to serve as models for all social relations, especially that of masters and slaves. As such, the marital service of wives was understood by southern society to be a manifestation of the larger social order in which white patriarchs presided over all others.[13]

Yet in its ideal form, patriarchy was not to be an abusive or tyrannical social system, especially when applied to marriage. The meaning of patriarchy underwent revision in the antebellum South due in large part to rising antislavery sentiment. In the 1830s, there was a rhetorical shift in proslavery theory from a discussion of bondage as a "necessary evil" to a natural good. This change emphasized the paternalistic, benevolent nature of masters and challenged men to guide with a compassionate hand. The sentimentalization of male authority influenced not only the institution of slavery but also marriage. Southern society and churches in particular encouraged white men to let the forces of love and emotion guide their lives rather than the power of patriarchal privilege. The prescribed compassion of masters was to be exercised not only in the quarters and fields but also in the home. Although proslavery theorists and women's rights activists (and even some southern white women) made connections between husbands and masters, wives and slaves, and marriage and bondage, such comparisons were absent from nineteenth-century literature on the companionate ideal. As historian Anya Jabour found, "Literature in the new nation recommended that men and women should cherish equality, not hierarchy, in their relationships." Working as business partners in a family firm, absentee planters and their manager-wives mitigated the patriarchal structure of marriage and made palpable strides toward a partnership of equals.[14]

Despite its advantages, business arrangements like that of the Archers did not revolutionize the larger sexual hierarchy of the antebellum South. Female plantation management was, among other things, a manifestation of patriarchal privilege. It signaled to the world the male head of household's ability to leave his home at his leisure and his wife's obligation not only to labor for him but also to do so in his stead. Pointing to some female managers' lack of control over the family finances and lack of involvement in weighty business matters, some historians argue that women made few gains as "deputy-husbands." Laura Edwards argued that women "could step into the role of household head," but they "could never *be* household heads in the same way as free white men." Yet even though the limits on female managers' autonomy and power were manifest, they were not a pressing concern for such women. It was not in terms of women's rights, but rather spousal duty that Ann understood her role in the family business. She was far more interested in the implications of her management on her relationship with her husband than on the sexual hierarchy. With respect to the former, her administrative work was often advantageous.[15]

The Archers' respective roles in the family firm became part and parcel of their marriage. Their business partnership fostered the development of a more egalitarian union by increasing Richard's reliance on Ann in a common commercial endeavor. However, despite its positive influence on the Archers' relationship, this abstract advantage was countermanded by a variety of concrete disadvantages. The very circumstance that generated the Archers' partnership—Richard's absence from home—also pushed it to its limits.

Seven months into her sixteenth pregnancy in October 1856, thirty-eight-year-old Ann anxiously awaited the arrival of a letter from her husband. Richard had recently left home to attend a directors' meeting for the Texas Western Railroad in New York City and to escort the Archers' two eldest daughters to Patapsco Institute in Maryland. Despite her delicate physical condition, Ann was left to care for five children, manage the household, and guide her inexperienced twenty-year-old son in the business of plantation administration. When Ann heard from a relative that Richard was too busy to write to her, she became infuriated. She penned an angry missive to her husband. "Busy as I am and unwell all the time and only seven weeks to be up to prepare the clothing for the children I have & for one expected, I still take time to write to you though I much doubt if you care to get letters from me except to hear from the children and crops." Recalling her brush with death in her most recent labor and delivery two years earlier, Ann thrust her dagger of words even deeper into Richard's heart by reminding him, "My time may be short on earth." In his response, Richard accused Ann of questioning his love for her. "You have never credited the affection I bear you," he charged. Defending himself and his absences from home, he declared, "I have provided as well as I have been able for you and my children."[16]

This tense exchange between Ann and Richard took place during a prolonged stretch of marital difficulties in the mid-1850s. The family firm was doing well, but the cost of achieving financial success was physical and, subsequently, emotional separation between the Archers. Richard's recurring absence from home was the primary cause of the growing fissure in their relationship. While he lamented the "necessity" of leaving his wife throughout his life, his professed devotion to Ann only strengthened his commitment to that which took him away from her. Like many husbands, Richard felt the pressure to fulfill his end of the marital contract—to support his wife financially. It was common for husbands to be pulled between the desire to be with their families and the need to make money, which often required an absence from home. Many focused on the latter, while their wives attended to their domestic and local business affairs even as they endured the physical and emotional stress of frequent pregnancies. For the Archers, this arrangement became increasingly troublesome as their marriage faltered. While their partnership as absentee planter and plantation manager brought them closer together by making Ann a more prominent player in the family enterprise, it undermined their marital bond by producing feelings of loneliness, fatigue, and distrust.[17]

Throughout their marriage, the Archers expressed discontent with their separation in different ways. Although Ann claimed that she "never expressed [her] feelings as much as most persons," her letters to Richard were not void of sentimentality. In the fall of 1847, when Ann was pregnant with the couple's ninth child, she apologized for not writing to her cousin Fanny, with whom Richard stayed. Ann explained that she had felt so badly about Richard's absence that she had not been able to compose herself enough to write. She wrote to her husband, "Tho I am in the midst of eight children & others I feel a void that no one can fill till your return." The next month she commented that as Richard's trip neared completion, time moved even more slowly than when he first left. "I have received four letters from you," she wrote, and "every one I have read over again & again hoping to find something new that may have escaped me in the previous readings[.] So you see 'tho I have so much to occupy me that needs attention I will be a little self indulgent[.] A very grateful thing to your vanity I suppose." Indeed it was, for Richard—like other husbands in antebellum America—often complained that his wife did not readily profess her love for him.[18]

While Richard's letters to Ann were relatively brief and hurried (those to his business and political associates were usually lengthy, if not interminable, and he was meticulous in writing them), they were not without affection. This was especially true of those written when Richard, away for months at a time, became increasingly mindful of both his advancing age and the discomforts of traveling. Missing his wife and children while on Honey Island in the fall of 1849, Richard contemplated selling the property so that he could spend more time with his family and told Ann, "I wish I had a balloon in which I could fly home nightly like a bird." A few months later, he was distressed at the poor state of affairs on his Honey Island estates (a consequence of bad management, in his opinion) and ached for Ann's comfort. "But for a sense of duty," he wrote, "no amount would reconcile me to be absent from you when I do so need your sympathy. All at Fanny's show the most sincere affection and kindness but there are none who can supply your place. . . . God grant us a speedy reunion."[19]

Despite his evident affection for his wife, Richard did not experience the couple's separations in the same way that Ann did. Even though Richard grieved when apart from his wife, he had many opportunities to find emotional, social, and even sexual fulfillment away from her. Because rural white women spent most of their lives within the boundaries of their households, their happiness was usually tied to their relationships with family members. Surrounded by her many children and slaves, as well as some friends and acquaintances, Ann wrote often about feeling isolated when her husband ventured away from home.[20]

Such feelings were a consequence of the kind of family enterprise that Richard built and that Ann's management helped sustain. Her loneliness was compounded, however, when her eldest children went away to school. Abram, her first-born child, and Edward, her nephew and ward, left in 1854 for the University of Virginia, where they studied for nearly two years. In December 1855, Mary and Ann Maria, the Archers' two eldest daughters, departed for Mrs. Gardel's boarding school in Philadelphia, which Ann had attended twenty-four years earlier. Mary stayed for only a few months, while Ann Maria remained for eight months. In 1857, both girls attended Patapsco Institute in Maryland for less than a year. All four children left home for school with Ann's support. When Mary contemplated leaving school because of debilitating headaches, her mother encouraged her to stay, writing, "I have felt the want of a finished and thorough education to[o] painfully and frequently . . . not to wish you to do what you are able to bear to get one." The absence of her children, however, was painful to Ann. Only a few weeks before she advised Mary to stay in school, she confided in Richard, "A separation from my children this fall has been the next most severe trial I have ever had, and I have had many." Over the course of their absence, Ann referred in her correspondence to instances when she was too sad to leave the house or to visit relatives and friends. When her children went back to school after their winter break in 1856, she told her husband, "I have now lost the power to be cheerful or look on the bright side. The sight of my own changed face is painful to me." A month later she sadly acknowledged, "My children are beyond my reach."[21] Being apart from her children made Ann's loneliness more acute, her separation from her husband more difficult to bear, and her support of their business arrangement less secure.

After years of recurring separations from Richard, Ann gave way to fatigue and frustration. When she was still a newlywed, she expressed concern that she had only received one letter from her absent husband, but told Richard that she would not write again, for she was certain he would "come without any more *persuading*."[22] It seems, however, that Ann misplaced her confidence, as she spent much of her married life trying to persuade Richard to come home. There was a shift in the tone of her appeals when his absences grew in length and frequency, particularly after 1850 as business, lawsuits, and the secession debate demanded more of his attention. Rather than expressing loving sentiments, Ann most often conveyed feelings of despondency, anger, and resentment. For his part, Richard grew increasingly defensive and forlorn. Over time it became easier for both to lament their individual burdens than to secure the loosened bonds of their marriage. The family firm was taking its toll on their relationship.

Ann's managerial responsibilities on the plantation lengthened her day and increased her workload. Her management duties became particularly onerous when she was pregnant, which was at least seventeen times during a period when American women bore an average of 5.4 children. Her first child was born in 1836 and her last known pregnancy was in 1857. While Ann's frequency of pregnancy differed from that of the average American woman, it was not unusual in the antebellum South. Historian Sally McMillen found that many southern women "exceeded [the national] rate and often devoted thirty or more years of their lives to bearing, nursing, and raising children."[23] This took a great toll on women's emotional and physical health.

Like most antebellum women, Ann experienced incredible anxiety in the months leading up to the birth of her children. She described one of her pregnancies to her mother-in-law by saying, "My hand was very tremulous from constant fever & my spirits were bad as they always are at such a time." Southern mothers were particularly fearful, for the frequency of their pregnancies, the region's unhealthy environment, and the limited availability of proper medical care made them more susceptible to complications in labor than northern women. As Catherine Clinton observed, when the time for childbirth drew near, a woman "literally prepared to die."[24]

Not surprisingly, Ann was most distraught when Richard left home during the latter stages of her pregnancies and put her in charge of the plantations at those precarious times. After composing a particularly melancholy letter to Richard during her ninth pregnancy in 1847, Ann added an apologetic postscript: "I must beg you will not grow uneasy of my pregnant writing. I feel as if I wanted to hold communion with you by letter every time I feel so heavy hearted which is most of the time." Rather than try to explain the source of her despondency, she simply said, "Thoughts come pressing on me you will hardly be able to understand." Perhaps Richard could not comprehend Ann's feelings, but her oldest daughter Mary seemed to grasp her mental state. During the last trimester of Ann's sixteenth pregnancy, Mary sent her a letter. "It makes my *heart ache*," she wrote, "to know that my *dear Ma* is at home *sick*, and *suffering*, without some one to help her, in her business, or to take care of the children, and servants as well as her. Ma, I will study very hard, so that I can come home, in two *years* to take your place, in attenting [*sic*] to all of Pa's, the children, & plantation affairs that you have to attend to now."[25] No doubt Ann would have welcomed such assistance, for her recurring depression and physical weakness during and after her numerous pregnancies had a significant impact on her ability and willingness to perform her administrative role on the family's home plantations.

Fatigue and depression caused Ann to reevaluate the nature of her business partnership with her husband. At her most vulnerable moments, she resisted the autonomy and authority that came with her administrative post. "I feel as if I was almost if not quite without a Protector," she told Richard in 1847, "as if all devolved on me & I was incapable of acting from a sense of it." Partnership or not, Ann made it clear that while it was her customary duty to sacrifice her happiness for the family, it was his duty to protect and support her. This was a well known and accepted bargain outlined in conventional gender ideology and, depending on one's interpretation, marital law. After numerous pregnancies, Ann expressed concern that Richard was not holding up his end of the bargain, suggesting that he reneged on his spousal duties by leaving her in charge of the plantations when she was physically and emotionally exhausted. Ann tried to make Richard aware of this by emphasizing her frailty. "You know how weak my mind is now," she wrote while pregnant in 1849, "[and] my body so inert that I cannot keep up my regular round of duties without finding each day something left undone or defered [sic] too long. I do so much wish I had the energy & pleasure in business I had a few years since, but all I do seems a drag & as if I were in a dream & waiting for something."[26]

Like many southern women in their childbearing years, Ann seemed obsessed with the possibility of dying.[27] Richard took note of Ann's "gloomy apprehensions" and expressed concern about his wife's emotional and physical health. He entreated her to resist giving in to depressing thoughts and instead to think of him and their children. "When would you find a family whose peace and well being would be so wrecked as ours would be if you were to die?" asked Richard. "I am wholly unfit to supply your loss . . . you must not think of leaving those to whom you are so necessary." He agreed that Ann was overextended, but rather than hire another agent to relieve her of her managerial duties, Richard encouraged Ann to discontinue one of her more traditional and pressing tasks: sewing. Female managers' domestic responsibilities did not cease when they assumed an administrative role on the plantation. In Ann's case, sewing proved more physically exhausting than managing, and the fatigue it created affected all of her work. On more than one occasion Richard pleaded with Ann to put down her needle and thread, beseeching her to "stop sewing if you love me." He promised her that he would try to find a northern seamstress to bring to Anchuca, but most of the women whom he contacted did not want to move to Mississippi. In 1854, an overseer's wife came to Anchuca to "cut and sew" for Ann and to assist her in all "domestic matters." However, two years later, Ann was again unwell and overwhelmed with work. This time Richard took to scolding her. "I wish very much you would stop sewing and lead a more active life," he wrote. "I am very uneasy about you, but fear my wish that you will change your hibits [sic] will not be pleasant to you. I could better be spared by our children than you, yet I put myself under many restraints on their account."[28]

Ann knew far better than Richard how much her children relied on her. The exhaustion she experienced upon carrying and delivering numerous babies increased with the responsibility of raising and caring for a household of toddlers and adolescents. Although she had the assistance of slaves, Ann frequently complained about the amount of physical and emotional energy it took to look after the children, particularly when they were ill. "I am very much fatigued having to nurse night & day," she told Richard, "added to which I am anxious about my children." Such anxiety was not unfounded. When Ann wrote this letter she had already lost three children and would go on to lose at least five more. Earlier that summer, she informed Richard that "the baby looks very badly & seems to suffer very much with his gums & Bowels & I fear he will suffer as much as our poor & beloved one we lost last Summer." Although this child survived, the Archers lost their next born the following year. As historian Laura Edwards observes, "The high rates of still births, infant mortality, and death during childbirth made motherhood an extremely difficult, potentially tragic experience" for southern women.[29]

Given her pressing maternal responsibilities, in addition to her domestic and administrative ones, Ann often had little patience with Richard's absences and little vigor for her work. Fearing that she might have a premature birth in September 1856 (her sixteenth pregnancy), Ann told Richard, "My spirits are so depressed all the time, it is with very great difficulty I can force energy enough to attend to what is necessary." Abram was assisting with the management of Anchuca and Pine Woods plantations at this time, but Ann was responsible for guiding his efforts. The business details that she included in her letters suggest that she was as busy as ever as manager. Richard responded to Ann's melancholy epistle with an equally glum note. He had recently received notice of the death of two of his cousins, he had experienced an emotional parting with his daughters upon dropping them off at boarding school, and he suffered from a bad cough. All of this depressed Richard and caused him to develop a romanticized view of life back in Mississippi. Upon declaring that "Home is infinitely dear," Richard told Ann, "I never more felt your absence."[30] To be sure, fatigue and depression were not unique to Ann in this marital and business partnership, for Richard too suffered from the stress of absenteeism.

While traveling on business in 1855, an aging and weary Richard told Ann, "I feel so overworn with business and care and the sorrows of life that it appears that death is often a luxury." He went on to say that if "Abram was more impressed with the importance of improving himself . . . I might surrender into his hands the care of you all." Richard endured what historian Carol Hammond termed the "burdens of proprietorship"; he became responsible for the care and support of both his immediate and his extended family. When his older brother died in 1837, Richard became the family patriarch. He not only managed his own plantations and those of his deceased brother but also assisted managing those belonging to kin in Mississippi and Virginia. He also took responsibility for his brother's debts, as well as those of his mother, uncles, aunts, and cousins, in addition to some of Ann's extended relations. He assumed guardianship for his orphaned nephew and spent much time and money protecting Edward's inheritance in a drawn-out legal battle. He also financially supported his wife and nine surviving children. In other words, as Hammond has argued, Richard "worked tirelessly not only to further his own fortunes but also to secure the well-being and happiness of the many people who depended on him." The "burdens of proprietorship" were a source of privilege and status for southern planter-class men, but they could be exhausting as well.[31]

By the mid-1850s, Richard's fatigue was apparent. When he sent his nephew Edward and eldest son, Abram, to the University of Virginia in 1854, he expected them to study hard so as to be able to assist him in his planting business. "When you [Edward] and Abram consider how much I have on my mind with no one except your Aunt Ann to counsel with or aid me," wrote Richard, "and how burdensome business is to an old man who cannot undergo the fatigue of mind or body as of old, I trust you will feel the importance of hard study and good preparation to undertake the duties of life."[32] Only five months later, Richard contemplated taking the boys out of school to help him manage his Holmes County plantations. "The sooner young men devote themselves to business the more useful citizens they generally become," Richard explained to Ann. "Your father I believe never had a college education, and if they make such men as he I shall be satisfied."[33] In June 1855, he announced to Abram and Edward, "I shall probably live but a few years, or if longer am now so failing in memory & business capacity that the management of the property & care of and education of the family must devolve on both of you."[34] Both boys returned home within a year.

While Ann desperately wanted Abram and Edward to get a good education (she believed both medical and legal studies were essential for a successful planter), she recognized the pressing need for them at home. As Ann informed Edward, Richard "is getting old & losing his capacity for business & cannot bear up against trouble as he once could & cannot go through much fatigue of mind or body & he has no one to assist him, & is so anxious for you & Abram to be here to assist him." A few months later she told her son, "Your Pa is overburdened with business and thinks he may not live much longer, and needs you and Edward at home very much indeed to assist him." Ann also realized, more so than any others, that age was not all that caused Richard's troubles. He was stressed about fluctuations in the market and was disappointed when his crops did not do as well as expected. Richard also faced a variety of lawsuits over the course of his life, many of which dealt with disputes over land and slaves. In one of the greatest disappointments of his adult life, Richard invested several thousand dollars and traded one of his plantations for over seven thousand shares in the Texas Western Railroad. Although he believed this venture would provide financial security for his entire family (he thought it would earn them millions of dollars), he ultimately lost his entire investment when the company faltered in the late 1850s. Finally, Richard was a difficult man to please and continually felt that his overseers, managers, and many other business associates were untrustworthy and often inept. As Richard got older and more fatigued, the stress of all of these troubles made him question his own abilities as a planter/businessman. Years of work-related frustrations and disappointments plagued him with self-doubt. When contemplating taking the boys out of college, he told Ann, "I wished much to have given them a thorough education, but I feel my own incompetency to manage, and it may be better for them to give up a college education than that they and all the children should be ruined. I am the worst judge of mankind I know. I am always deceived and plundered."[35]

Disappointments in business usually encouraged Richard to press forward, albeit with depressed spirits. His desire to relieve his family of debt and provide for their current and future needs kept him away from home. Such a lifestyle wore not only on his mind and body but also on his relationship with his wife. According to Richard, the suffering that the couple's separation brought him was so great at times that he could not bear to think about Ann or their home. When visiting Honey Island in December 1852, he wrote, "I wish I could be with you, but wont [sic] allow myself to think much about it, if I can help it." Away from home around Christmas again in 1855, Richard explained, "I cannot allow myself to think of home it being out of my power now to say when I can return."[36]

As loneliness and fatigue overtook both Richard and Ann, their faith in each other faltered. Ann grew distrustful, and Richard became defensive. At the root of the Archers' faltering relationship was misunderstanding. Neither Richard nor Ann appreciated fully the demands of the other's life—a common problem for absentee husbands and their wives. In her analysis of Betty and Robert

Conrad of Virginia—a plantation mistress and absentee husband, respectively—Brenda E. Stevenson asserts that Robert, like many men in his situation, was unwilling to understand his distressed wife's needs and the pressures that she faced at home. "It was necessary for him to dismiss his wife's depression as unreasonable," contends Stevenson, "because of his need to feel that he was providing a happy and satisfactory lifestyle for her and their children." Similarly, Anya Jabour contends that Virginian and absentee husband William Wirt found it difficult to understand his wife's depression because of his romanticized visions of home. He identified home with leisure; it was a place for him to rest and recuperate from the trials of life. Elizabeth Wirt had an entirely different view. "Because her own labor was located in the household," Jabour explains, "the ease and retirement that her husband identified with being at home were in short supply for her." The stark differences in their perceptions of home made it difficult for William to understand the source of his wife's unhappiness, increasing Elizabeth's frustration with her absent husband, who did not help ease her burdens. The Archers faced similar problems.[37]

In the fall of 1856, Mary Archer wrote a revealing note to her mother in which she bemoaned her father's lack of appreciation for the sacrifices Ann made and the difficulties that she endured for him. While it is not clear if Mary was responding to a particular incident or the general state of her parents' marriage, she clearly understood the disadvantages of their partnership, at least from her mother's perspective. Noting that Ann had sacrificed much of her happiness to meet Richard's "every wish," Mary expressed dismay that "any one could treat you unkindly[,] particularly one who owes so much to you." She explained that she loved her father, but she could see his faults. Mary believed that Richard's seeming ingratitude for Ann was due to the fact that he "has never had any one to make him give up every wish or comfort for their sake whether it suited him or not as you & we children have had to do." Her daily and nightly prayer was that "God will so direct things that all may come wright [*sic*] some day & that you will be appreciated as you should & is due you."[38]

Replacing Richard as her mother's confidante and supporter, Mary provided the sympathy that Ann sought from her husband. Although not a planter's wife, Mary was close to her mother and perceived the difficulties that Ann endured. Both women were likely exasperated by the differences between the separate lives Ann and Richard led. Richard filled his letters home with accounts of socializing with friends, family, and new acquaintances, while Ann's typically held accounts of her isolation and work. Reading her husband's descriptions of travels and parties must have made it difficult for Ann to believe Richard's complaints about leaving home and, even more so, his contention that he did it all for her and their children.[39]

Richard frequently took a defensive posture in his correspondence to Ann, trying to make it clear that his travels were not enjoyable but laborious. They were not something he chose to do, but something he had to do out of duty. He frequently expressed his desire to be home with Ann and their children and to be free of the burdens of business. While the enormity of his land and slave-holdings, as well as the diversity of his investments, suggest that Richard was a genuine entrepreneur who enjoyed business, he told Ann that he did not desire money. While away on a three-month trip, he explained to his wife in a series of letters, "I care not for money except for my children," "I do not love money but as the power to minister to my childrens and your wants," and "our children are raised in the expectation of fortune." He could not let them down.[40]

Ann also wanted her children to have a secure future, and she certainly enjoyed the luxuries that wealth afforded her. However, Richard's persistent absence, combined with her own continual fatigue and despair, caused her to question his reasons for leaving as well as his affection for her. In January 1857, Ann confronted Richard just as he was preparing to leave for Honey Island. It must have been an unpleasant scene as she accused him of preferring to spend time at the Honey Island plantations to being at home with her. Richard's defensive response, written upon his arrival in Holmes County, reveals not only his elitism, but also his sense of duty and of the sacrifices he made for his family. "You made me uneasy on leaving home," Richard wrote to Ann. Pointing out what he saw as the absurdity of her accusation, he explained:

My situation on the Island is at best extremely uncomfortable. There is but a single servant there that is even tolerably cleanly. They are disagreeable in odor from want of cleanliness, smell of dirty children, and dirty clothes, and are attendants on those of their family who have bothersome diseases. . . . Even the most cleanly of all of them is less so than our house servants, as field hands will of necessity be. But you overlook these considerations and ascribe to partiality, my endeavor to be as little annoyed as I can by the contrast between home comforts and the discomforts of a dirty overseers house. I feel these discomforts so much that my business is almost ruinously neglected in consequence of my being so little on the plantations. But it must suffer for I cannot go or stay there more than is absolutely necessary, to pay taxes and accounts and see what the condition of the negroes.[41]

One of the most striking elements of Richard's letter is the difference between his perception of how much time he spent on the island and Ann's perception of the time he spent there. Richard claimed his Holmes County plantations suffered from his absence. Ann believed he spent enough time there to develop a penchant for them. However, Ann's sense of Richard's partiality for the Honey Island plantations may not have been due solely to the amount of time that he actually resided there. Two years prior to their confrontation in 1857, the Archers had another tense exchange that sheds light on Ann's growing distrust of her husband and dislike of his travels. While her correspondence from this exchange was not preserved, Richard's response was. "Ah my wife," he wrote, "because I have many faults you never give me credit for the deep and abiding love I bear you. The torture of feeling that you do not love me often goads [me] to conduct which still more alienates your affections."[42] The conduct to which he referred was likely infidelity. Absentee planters, who spent a considerable amount of time away from their wives, had numerous opportunities to engage in extramarital activity. While some planters had white mistresses, it was more common for them to have sexual relations with their female slaves.[43]

There is evidence to suggest that Ann discovered Richard's probable affair with a slave woman named Patty who lived on Walton's Bend plantation. After the Civil War, Richard relied on Patty's services as a nurse, as she was reportedly the only person who was willing to care for him. He explained to Ann that he tried to avoid the plantation as best he could, but being seventy years old and very sick, he had to go where he could find someone to nurse him. Proclaiming that he was "in such health as to be *impotent*," Richard explained why he had come into contact with his former slave. "And now Ann," wrote Richard, "I know you will dislike my having Patty to attend to me. It was the leading reason for my staying at the lower place. But I can control no servants on either place unless they voluntarily serve me." In a postscript written the next day, Richard explained: "I sent for Patty to know if she would nurse me through the night. She said she would do so, but she feared you would be angry if she did. . . . I told her I had written you about it, and the necessity I was under."[44] While it is unknown what exactly occurred between Richard and Patty that would make Ann so angry, it is plausible that the incident was sexual in nature. What Richard may have perceived as a consensual encounter, Patty may have seen as coercive and Ann may have seen as a betrayal on Richard's part and insolence on Patty's. Given Ann's aversion to Richard spending time at Walton's Bend at the nadir of their relationship, it is likely that the episode took place in the mid-1850s.

While Richard's probable infidelity was not a consequence of his absenteeism, his persistent work-related travels and Ann's loneliness at home exacerbated her pain. When Ann confronted him about the matter, their marriage was already faltering due to frequent separations and mutual fatigue. A blatant act of duplicity on Richard's part likely made his frequent absences suspect in Ann's eyes, thereby making their working arrangement even more disagreeable to her. For Richard, the pain of Ann's growing coldness toward him was difficult to bear, especially in his old age when he most desired the comfort of loved ones. His business trips became increasingly unwelcome to him as he lamented the difficulties that his business created for his marriage. Wishing that his daughters would never experience such grief, he complained to them in 1857, "I feel your mothers absence as one feels a heavy calamity, and I feel no true enjoyment even of the society of most dear friends when she is far away."[45]

In 1856, Ann offered marital advice to her daughter Mary. Marriage, she wrote, was "such an important step in life." She encouraged Mary "not to enter very young on the duties and assume the cares of life too soon." "I speak from experience," advised Ann; "let it be a guide to my dear children." That same year, she told her son that in marriage, "much, very much depends on congeniality of tastes, disposition, and all on true and abiding tender love in each one." When Ann married Richard in 1834, she had just turned sixteen. For the next thirty-three years the Archers struggled to maintain the emotional connection that sparked their love for one another as they took on the responsibilities of marriage, parenthood, and a large-scale cotton venture.

The Archers' relationship turned on the vicissitudes of their enterprise. Like most nineteenth-century Americans, they sought a companionate marriage in which they would share life as friends, lovers, and partners. Their business arrangement facilitated such a marriage by enabling them to work together, thereby increasing their reliance on and respect for one another. Richard's business-related travels were manifestations of his gendered and marital identity and obligation as a devoted and responsible husband, while Ann's plantation management (in addition to her traditional domestic duties) was an expression of her gendered and marital self as a loving and dutiful wife. Working together, the Archers not only created an empire in slaves and cotton, but also a strong foundation for a companionate marriage. Yet, while the Archers made palpable strides toward companionship on account of their business partnership, the nature of their enterprise also prevented them from living the marital ideal.

Frequent separations and demanding responsibilities increased Richard and Ann's frustration with one another and their dissatisfaction with their working arrangement. Both came to regret the amount of time and energy that they devoted to the family firm. Ann's persistent poor health and Richard's repeated disappointments in business enhanced the fissure in their marriage by magnifying their respective unhappiness when apart. A probable act of infidelity on Richard's part further strained their marriage and symbolized, for Ann at least, all that their attention to matters outside of their emotional relationship had cost them. Richard eventually came to a similar realization. In his last known letter to Ann, written eight months before his death in 1867, he told his wife, "I have loved & wished to make you happy. I wish I had been a better husband."[46] For the Archers and many of their contemporaries, business was a core element of marriage that carried the promise of companionship, but in practice it often struck at the foundations of the marital bond.

Notes

1. Ann Barnes Archer to Richard Thompson Archer (hereafter Ann and Richard), 1 January and 4 January 1856, box 2E649; Richard to Ann, 19 January 1856, box 2E646, all in Richard Thompson Archer Family Papers, Natchez Trace Collection, Center for American History, University of Texas at Austin. Ann's despondency is similar to that expressed by slaveholding women during the Civil War as they grew frustrated with the disorder and deprivation caused by the conflict. Drew Gilpin Faust, *Mothers of Invention: Women of the Slaveholding South in the American Civil War* (New York: Vintage Books, 1996).

2. Brenda E. Stevenson, *Life in Black and White: Family and Community in the Slave South* (New York: Oxford University Press, 1996), 78; Laurel Thatcher Ulrich, *Good Wives: Image and Reality in the Lives of Women in Northern New England, 1650–1750* (New York: Alfred A. Knopf, 1980).

3. On female plantation management in the antebellum period, see Nikki Berg Burin, "A Regency of Women: Female Plantation Management in the Old South" (PhD diss., University of Minnesota, 2007); Kirsten E. Wood, *Masterful Women: Slaveholding Widows from the American Revolution through the Civil War* (Chapel Hill: University of North Carolina Press, 2004), 25–33; William Kauffman Scarborough, *Masters of the Big House: Elite Slaveholders of the Mid-Nineteenth-Century South* (Baton Rouge: Louisiana State University Press, 2003), 109–11; Marli F. Weiner, *Mistresses and Slaves: Plantation Women in South Carolina, 1830–1880* (Urbana: University of Illinois Press, 1998), 35–37; Elizabeth Fox-Genovese, *Within the Plantation Household: Black and White Women of the Old South* (Chapel Hill: University of North Carolina Press, 1988), 203–207; Leah Rawls Atkins, "High Cotton: The Antebellum Alabama Plantation Mistress and the Cotton Culture," *Agricultural History* 68 (spring 1994): 92–104; Catherine Clinton, *The Plantation Mistress: Women's World in the Old South* (New York: Pantheon Books, 1982), 30–33. On female managers during the Civil War, see Faust, *Mothers of Invention*; Joan Cashin, "'Since the War Broke Out': The Marriage of Kate and William McLure," in *Divided Houses: Gender and the Civil War*, ed. Catherine Clinton and Nina Silber (New York: Oxford University Press, 1992). On female managers in the colonial period, see Cynthia A. Kierner, *Beyond the Household: Women's Place in the Early South, 1700–1835* (Ithaca, N.Y.: Cornell University Press, 1998), 12–13.

4. Some planters, of course, had an aversion to leaving their property in their wives' hands, preferring instead to see them as passive and dependent on male protection. A notable example is William McLure of South Carolina, who refused to acknowledge that his wife, Kate, administered their plantation during his service in the Confederate army. See Cashin, "'Since the War Broke Out.'"

5. Ann to Richard, 15 December 1834, box 2E649; Richard to Ann, 16 December 1834, box 2E646, both in Archer Family Papers.

6. The Archers were among the elite of southern planters (those individuals who owned 20 or more slaves). Scarborough identified only 338 planters in the entire South, including the Archers, who owned over 250 slaves. Yet while the Archers' wealth was unusual, their values were not. Allegiance to slavery, capitalism, family, and "proper" gender roles was a defining characteristic of the planter class, which accentuated the predominate beliefs and practices of antebellum slaveholding society. Scarborough, *Masters of the Big House*, 6.

7. Richard to Ann, 8 January 1850; Richard to Abram Barnes Archer, 28 May 1856, both in box 2E646, Archer Family Papers.

8. Richard to Ann, 16 May 1849, 26 December 1855, box 2E646; Ann to Richard, 5 October 1856, box 2E649, all in Archer Family Papers.

9. Richard to Ann, 7 November 1847, box 2E646, Archer Family Papers.

10. Richard to Ann, 4 May 1855, box 2E646, Archer Family Papers. On companionate marriage, see Stephanie Coontz, *Marriage, a History: How Love Conquered Marriage* (New York: Penguin Books, 2005); Nancy F. Cott, *Public Vows: A History of Marriage and the Nation* (Cambridge, Mass.: Harvard University Press, 2000); Anya Jabour, *Marriage in the Early Republic: Elizabeth and William Wirt and the Companionate Ideal* (Baltimore: Johns Hopkins University Press, 1998); Steven M. Stowe, *Intimacy and Power in the Old South: Ritual in the Lives of the Planters* (Baltimore: Johns Hopkins University Press, 1987); Ellen K. Rothman, *Hands and Hearts: A History of Courtship in America* (New York: Basic Books, 1984).

11. Tapping Reeve, *The Law of Baron and Femme; of Parent and Child; of Guardian and Ward; of Master and Servant; and of the Powers of Courts of Chancery with an Essay on the Terms Heir, Heirs, and Heirs of the Body* (New Haven, Conn.: Oliver Steele, 1816), 63.

12. Hendrik Hartog, *Man and Wife in America: A History* (Cambridge: Harvard University Press, 2000), 157; Cott, *Public Vows*, 12.

13. Peter W. Bardaglio, *Reconstructing the Household: Families, Sex, and the Law in the Nineteenth-Century South* (Chapel Hill: University of North Carolina Press, 1995), xiii; Drew Gilpin Faust, "Epilogue," in *In Joy and in Sorrow: Women, Family, and Marriage in the Victorian South*, ed. Carol Bleser (New York: Oxford University Press, 1991), 253.

14. Jabour, *Marriage in the Early Republic*, 9.

15. Laura F. Edwards, *Scarlett Doesn't Live Here Anymore: Southern Women in the Civil War Era* (Urbana: University of Illinois Press, 2004), 3.

16. Ann to Richard, 5 October 1856, box 2E649; Richard to Ann, 15 October 1856, box 2E646, both in Archer Family Papers.

17. For an extended treatment of this dynamic, see Jabour, *Marriage in the Early Republic*; see also Stevenson, *Life in Black and White*, 83.

18. Ann to Mary Cocke Archer, 3 December 1842, box 2E649; Ann to Richard, 8 October, 11 November 1847, box 2E649, all in Archer Family Papers. On correspondence between court-

ing, engaged, and married couples in the North, see Karen Lystra, *Searching the Heart: Women, Men, and Romantic Love in Nineteenth-Century America* (New York: Oxford University Press, 1989); Rothman, *Hands and Hearts*; for the southern context, see Jabour, *Marriage in the Early Republic*.

19. Richard to Ann, 14 November 1849, 8 January 1850, box 2E646, Archer Family Papers.

20. Clinton, *The Plantation Mistress*, 38. This was true as well for women in the urban South, as indicated in Jabour, *Marriage in the Early Republic*.

21. Ann to Mary Catherine Archer, 23 January 1856; Ann to Richard, 1 January, 4 January 1856; Ann to Edward Stephen Archer, 11 October 1854, all in box 2E649, Archer Family Papers.

22. Ann to Richard, 15 December 1834, box 2E649, Archer Family Papers.

23. Sally McMillen, *Southern Women: Black and White in the Old South*, 2nd ed. (Wheeling, Ill.: Harlan Davidson, 2002), 60; McMillen, *Motherhood in the Old South: Pregnancy, Childbirth, and Infant Rearing* (Baton Rouge: Louisiana State University Press, 1990), 32.

24. Ann to Mary Cocke Archer, 7 September 1843, box 2E649, Archer Family Papers; McMillen, *Southern Women*, 65; Clinton, *The Plantation Mistress*, 151.

25. Ann to Richard, 8 October, 15 October 1847, box 2E649; Mary Catherine Archer to Ann, October 1856, box 2E650, both in Archer Family Papers (emphasis is original).

26. Ann to Richard, 8 October 1847, 22 May 1849, box 2E649, Archer Family Papers.

27. See, for instance, Drew Gilpin Faust's discussion of Texan Lizzie Neblett's fears about childbirth. Faust, *Mothers of Invention*, 124–26.

28. Richard to Ann, 7 November 1847, 7 February 1854, and 25 January 1856, box 2E646, Archer Family Papers. For more on women's sewing, see Lynn Kennedy's essay in this volume.

29. Ann to Richard, 22 May and 3 June 1849, box 2E649, Archer Family Papers; Edwards, *Scarlett Doesn't Live Here Anymore*, 25.

30. Ann to Richard, 28 September 1856, box 2E649; Richard to Ann, 15 October 1856, box 2E646, Archer Family Papers.

31. Richard to Ann, 18 December 1855, box 2E646, Archer Family Papers; Carol Hammond, "Richard Thompson Archer and the Burdens of Proprietorship: The Life of a Natchez District Planter" (PhD diss., University of North Texas, 2001), 289.

32. Richard to Edward Stephen Archer, 14 December 1854, box 2E646, Archer Family Papers.

33. Richard to Ann, 4 May 1855, box 2E646, Archer Family Papers.

34. Richard to Edward Stephen Archer, 14 December 1854, 4 May 1855; Richard to Edward Stephen Archer and Abram Barnes Archer, 1 June 1855, all in box 2E646, Archer Family Papers.

35. Ann to Edward Stephen Archer, 4 April 1855; Ann to Abram Barnes Archer, 13 June 1855, both in box 2E649, Archer Family Papers; Richard to Ann, 4 May 1855, box 2E646, Archer Family Papers.

36. Richard to Ann, 29 December 1852, 22 December 1855, box 2E646, Archer Family Papers.

37. Stevenson, *Life in Black and White*, 76; Jabour, *Marriage in the Early Republic*, 44.

38. Mary Catherine Archer to Ann, 18 September 1856, box 2E650, Archer Family Papers.

39. On southern women's perception of the lives their absentee husbands led away from home, see Stevenson, *Life in Black and White*, 84.

40. Richard to Ann, 21 December 1855, 19 January and 27 January 1856, box 2E646, Archer Family Papers.

41. Richard to Ann, 30 January 1857, box 2E646, Archer Family Papers.

42. Richard to Ann, 15 December 1855, box 2E646, Archer Family Papers.

43. Catherine Clinton argued that sexual relationships "were not rare aberrations, but a built-in subculture within the slave owner's world." Catherine Clinton, "'Southern Dishonor': Flesh, Blood, Race, and Bondage," in Bleser, ed., *In Joy and in Sorrow*, 66.

44. Richard to Ann, 10 November, 11 November 1866, box 2E646, Archer Family Papers (emphasis is original).

45. Richard to Mary and Ann Maria Archer, 3 May 1857, box 2.325/V36, Archer Family Papers.

46. Ann to Mary Catherine Archer, undated [likely 1856]; Ann to Abram Barnes Archer, 12 April 1856, box 2E649; Richard to Ann, December 28, 1866, box 2E646, all in Archer Family Papers.

7

Making a Home in Public

Domesticity, Authority, and Family in the Old South's Public Houses

KIRSTEN E. WOOD

~

For many, if not most, whites in the Old South, "family" included a tangle of parents, children, siblings, cousins, in-laws, and other more remote relatives. No matter where they lived, no matter how small the chance of meeting in person, white southerners cherished the memories of, and correspondence with, distant family members. But the core of their family usually consisted of the people with whom they shared a household, such as a spouse and children, siblings, or parents. While spatially confined, the co-residential white family was dense with day-to-day interactions and expectations, pleasant and unpleasant alike.[1]

Profoundly shaping those interactions was the expectation that family members who shared a household had mutual obligations, particularly a duty to contribute to the household economy. For some, wealth stripped this obligation of manual labor: the sons and daughters of the South's great planters performed far more cultural than manual work, pursuing educations, careers, marriages, and leisure activities that would advance their family's reputation and financial prospects.[2] For most, however, contributing to the domestic economy meant hard physical work.[3] This was especially true for the region's thousands of yeoman and tenant farmers, overseers, and artisans. It also applied to those families who kept public houses, establishments that depended heavily upon the indoor labor of women and children.

The dynamics of slavery in the region added another layer of complexity to the links between household economy and family. While only some slave owners professed to believe that the family included black and white members of their households equally, they all expected slaves, like their own children, to work for the good of the household as defined from the top down. This obligation, almost without exception, forced slaves to work double shifts in order to have any time to devote to their own families.[4] Despite slave owners' routine manipulation of family ties where slaves were concerned—traducing them one minute and exploiting them the next—ideas about familial responsibilities profoundly inflected household interactions. In particular, patriarchal authority shaped both personal and labor relations in most southern households. Even beyond the slaveholding minority, southern whites generally agreed that women, children, and slaves owed both obedience and work to husbands, fathers, and masters, respectively. These overlapping dynamics of obligation and authority, often encapsulated in the term *mastery*, took particularly hierarchical form in the South as compared with the North. That is, in the South, the extent, the exercise, and the discourse of men's power within their own families and households were generally broader, often harsher, and more frequently absolutist.[5]

Even so, a host of antebellum notions usually associated with the North, like domesticity and privacy, also took root in southern families and households. Because both the plantation and the farmhouse remained workplaces, they departed markedly from the idealized home as a private haven of leisure and domesticity. Nevertheless, these values became increasingly familiar and even popular in the Old South, especially among elite southerners who read magazines, newspapers, and novels. Many white southerners sought to combine mastery, domesticity, and privacy, an awkward combination that complicated the task of raising families and running households in the early nineteenth century.[6]

Nowhere in the South was this more evident than in the region's many public houses. Like most white southern households, taverns, inns, boardinghouses, and even some hotels combined the functions of residence and workplace. Families who kept public houses developed gendered divisions of labor and experienced internal conflicts quite similar to those in other white southern families.[7] However, the distinctive demands and requirements of tavern keeping shaped family life in key ways. Among the most important was the impact of public accommodations on the financial and cultural value that accrued to different forms of household labor, especially to conventionally feminine housewifery. Women—typically the tavern keeper's wife and daughters, sometimes servants and slaves as well—occupied a central place in the antebellum tavern. Popular opinion attributed taverns' quality and comfort largely to women's efforts, and publicans accordingly made much of their money from women's work: house-keeping, domestic production, and intangibles like genteel manners and maternal coziness.

Of equal importance, and closely related to the value of female labor, was the impact of keeping a public house on the structure of authority within tavern households. The public house departed in distinctive ways from the idealized southern household, where a man's word was law and where both neighbors and the legal system resisted intervening in domestic affairs. Public accommodations—taverns, inns, and hotels in particular—were subject not only to their patrons' critical gaze but also to legal scrutiny, especially through licensing requirements.[8] Some faced an additional and quite particular set of constraints by virtue of being near colleges and universities. The public house was open to public view and public comment, which aggravated daily familial and household conflicts and threatened the authority of the household head in ways that most white southern patriarchs never encountered.[9]

This essay relies extensively on travelers' comments on taverns, and so its conclusions may not apply as well to taverns that rarely entertained travelers. For the historian, however, it is precisely those travelers' accounts that provide the richest glimpses into the domestic workings of tavern families; most surviving tavern records are account books that give little or no indication of who lived and labored in a particular tavern. Since tavern keepers pursued the trade only intermittently, it is difficult to catch them in the decennial snapshots provided by the federal census. Moreover, licensing procedures made no inquiries into male applicants' familial situation.[10] Travelers are particularly valuable interlocutors for historians because their presence often created situations that revealed the cracks and strains in domestic authority and labor relations. Their opinions, meanwhile, mattered not simply because their custom could be lucrative but also because their pleasure—or, more often, displeasure—could make or break an establishment's reputation. In the first decades of the nineteenth century, men traveling on politics or business from Charleston to Philadelphia, for example, traded recommendations about where to stay (or to avoid), supplementing the bare lists of taverns in contemporary almanacs.[11] In later decades, published travel writings proliferated, many of them quite splenetic about the accommodations they encountered. A traveler's opprobrium might have no bearing on local custom, of course, but the innkeeper's exposure to public and published comment distinguished these households from those of most other southerners. Thus, while travelers' reports speak to intermittent rather than constant conditions in tavern households, they reveal the pressure that keeping a public house placed on southern understandings of family and household mastery.

In the course of an 1822 tour through Indiana, Ohio, Kentucky, and Virginia, visiting Scotsman James Flint remarked that, "like its owner," the backwoods tavern "commonly makes a conspicuous figure in its neighbourhood." This was not due to distinctive architecture, since the building could be "a log, a frame, or a brick house." More characteristic was the "tall post" and "sign-board" that stood out front, depicting "a Washington, a Montgomery, a Wayne, a Pike, or a Jackson." Equally notable, Flint suggested, was the roof's "small bell, which is twice rung before meals."[12] While the sign and the bell did communicate "tavern" to antebellum southerners and travelers alike, most rural public houses in the Old South differed little from the other homesteads around them, in part because many, if not most, encompassed other functions like farming, retailing, or crafting. In southern towns, the principal inns and taverns tended to be larger structures, two or more stories, with significant frontage on a commercial street, but even so, these buildings generally blended with those around them. Boardinghouses were even more characteristically nondescript, lacking exterior signs and bells.

In contrast, public accommodations that truly deserved the name of hotel were quite different. Purpose-built and expensive, the hotel was primarily business—not a familial residence that from time to time became a public house as the family's needs and interests permitted.[13] As a distinct form of public accommodation, hotels developed slowly in the southern states, but they did crop up across the region's cities and resort areas. Hotels promised more privacy, specialized space, attentive service, and physical comfort than was available in other public accommodations. Hotels worthy of the name also boasted a bevy of specialized public rooms, such as parlors, bars, coffee rooms, and reading rooms, as well as vast ballrooms and dining rooms.[14] The best had elaborate interior decorations, including fancy carpets, wallpaper, and plaster work, while some even featured gas lighting. These establishments had staffing to match their size, with numerous waiters, chambermaids, porters, dishwashers, and laundresses, creating problems of management that far exceeded those of private life. By this definition, hotels were distinctly in the minority among southern public accommodations. However, many proprietors adopted the name, probably seeking the cachet the term connoted to both American and European ears even before the hotel had emerged as a distinct type of public accommodation. That the term was often more aspirational than descriptive may be gauged from travelers' re-characterization of many so-called hotels: a particular place might be named a hotel, but if travelers called it a tavern or inn in their letters and journals, then it likely had little in common with the great hotels. Dubbing one's establishment a tavern, conversely, did not always suggest modest ambitions or meager accommodations. Sometimes the chief "public hotel" in an antebellum southern city was still styled a tavern, such as the Eagle Tavern in Augusta, Georgia.[15]

In the Old South, another important type of public house was the boardinghouse, which properly speaking was not even legally public. Boardinghouses typically had no signposts, because they did not need to be identified from the street. Instead of throwing open their doors to drinkers and travelers, boardinghouse keepers could pick and choose their lodgers. This helped make them attractive to women, both as residents and as landladies, since exclusivity implied respectability (not always accurately). In addition, since boardinghouses typically did not have liquor licenses, they could serve alcohol only to lodgers, not to casual passers-by.[16]

In contrast, taverns and inns—legally equivalent in the early national and antebellum United States—faced quite different regulations. Tavern licensing laws passed long before the American Revolution had established an implicit quid pro quo: licensees could sell liquor by the drink for immediate consumption in exchange for the public service of sheltering and feeding travelers and their livestock. Colonial statutes had typically barred licensees from selling alcohol to Indians, slaves, servants, apprentices, and sailors. Some of these restrictions persisted in the new nation, especially concerning slaves, but by the late antebellum period, the constraint upon the innkeeper arguably came from the opposite direction. As an 1855 *Traveler's Legal Guide* put it, the publican "is bound to receive all guests who come" unless they were drunk, disorderly, or diseased. Similarly, he or she must provide guests with "board and convenient lodging-room," "take proper care of their goods and baggage," and meet all "reasonable wants and requests, for a reasonable compensation." Most significantly, an innkeeper could not "lawfully refuse to receive guests to the extent of his reasonable accommodations."[17] These regulations did not prevent racial discrimination, for example, nor were they intended to, but they did require tavern keepers to accept as lodgers both types and numbers of people they might never have accepted as guests in their home.

Inns and taverns ran the gamut from marginal establishments that could sleep one or two lodgers to substantial concerns that resembled small hotels in their size and physical comforts. Despite their differences, the boardinghouse resembled a tavern at least insofar as the proprietor had opened his—or more typically her—home to outsiders, and is occasionally included here for that reason. However, because they were not fully public, boardinghouse families avoided much of the disruption that tavern families often encountered. Conversely, the hotel, while fully public in the legal sense, was not typically a family's residence; hotels had the potential to disrupt family life, but in different ways and for different reasons than taverns, hotels, and boardinghouses. However, the standards associated with newly built—not just renamed—hotels had substantial implications for tavern families and for the gendered division of authority in antebellum public houses, and so they, too, inform this analysis.[18]

As James Flint's description implies, setting up a tavern rarely required any significant redesign, which was one reason many families serially entered and left the trade. Nor did keeping a public house necessarily require a substantial revision of domestic responsibilities. Like farmsteads, taverns relied on the labor not just of the household head but also the household's dependents, namely, children, women, and servants or slaves. In all but the richest families, tavern keepers' children became integral parts of the household economy as soon as they could be trusted not to fall into the fireplace or break whatever they touched. Boys at least ten years of age helped with stabling horses, for example, while their older brothers tended bar or waited at table. Grown sons provided invaluable assistance by stepping up whenever their fathers had to be away or by taking charge after they died.[19] The youngest girls assisted their mothers with simple tasks, while older daughters helped with everything from cooking and serving food to laundering sheets, mending clothing, and spinning cotton. By their teenage years, some tavern daughters had taken over most of the feminized aspects of tavern keeping. In one unlicensed Virginia tavern, the landlord's "bright eyed daughter" waited at table, serving the guests a meal of "fine corn bread and yellow butter[,] mountain venison, a chicken that not an hour before reposed in quiet on his roost, fine gingerbread, and *hoecake*, and *last* not *least* a good dish of Tea." At another Virginia tavern, the widowed keeper relied on his two daughters to wait on tables and work in the kitchen, saving him the expense of hiring a housekeeper. More unusual was a tavern keeper's daughter near Wheeling, Virginia, who ferried her father's customers back and forth across the river.[20]

Keeping a public house complicated family dynamics in distinctive ways. Infants and toddlers were particularly disruptive for tavern keepers because they interrupted their mothers' remunerative work. In the spring of 1776, Mrs. Crockatt had to tell a group of wealthy South Carolinians bound for the Continental Congress that she could not give them breakfast right away because "she must take care of her Child" first. Years later, James Flint reported a similar experience near Lexington, Kentucky. "We could not procure breakfast," he recalled, "because the family had a sick child." One Mrs. Edwards, who kept a tavern near the foot of the Blue Ridge in the late 1830s, juggled "nine small children and one at the breast." Pregnancy also complicated tavern keeping. A "poor pale" and heavily pregnant landlady in Florida, for example, struggled to cope with "domestic management" while raising five little children. She had only as much help as a "single little negro wench" could provide, since her husband was often away. A tavern full of guests also aggravated the cramped quarters commonly found in rural households. At Turner's near Fredericksburg, Virginia, "half a dozen children" shared their bedroom with overnight customers. Some travelers complained about having to share rooms and beds, but few stopped to wonder where their hosts and children slept. Indeed, guests often had little sympathy for tavern-keeping parents. Anne Royall, author of several gossipy travel books, went so far as to assert, "No man who has children ought to keep a tavern," since parents "never hear the noise of their *own* children."[21]

Royall's suggestion was arrant nonsense, of course, since tavern keepers relied on their dependents' labor. But Royall did have a point, at least indirectly: tavern keepers really needed adult helpers, and most relied heavily on their wives and grown daughters.[22] This reliance creates an instructive contrast with the South's yeoman farmers, who could disguise their households' reliance on women's labor. White women's work in the house, garden, dairy, and sometimes fields produced goods that could be sold as well as consumed, but the primary function of female labor in this context was to avoid cash expenditures. Similarly, women's work in maintaining the household's labor force—keeping the residents fed and clothed, for example—was essential yet difficult to value in monetary terms.[23] In contrast, tavern women's work had a clear price.[24] The importance of women's work to their households' cash flow was all the more marked in families that combined innkeeping with farming. The combination made perfect sense because the farm supplied the tavern with foodstuffs and provender and kept the family busy whenever tavern business flagged. Thus Martin Browne kept a tavern near Winchester, Virginia, but he was also a grain farmer, and his wife wove cloth when she was not working in the house. Martin's sons assisted him on the farm, while daughter Juliana helped her mother.[25] Tavern keeping similarly coexisted easily with keeping a store or with ancillary trades like blacksmithing. In these households, the explicit financial significance of women's service labor in the tavern became obvious because the men spent so much time working in the fields, the store, or the smithy.

The centrality of women's labor to public houses meant that the tavern landlady bore substantial responsibility for traveling patrons' satisfaction. As their remarks make amply clear, items like clean linens, plentiful and well-prepared food, and reasonable beds came first on patrons' list of desirables, and all of them owed much to the female members of the establishment. While a male tavern keeper might cut "a conspicuous figure" in the neighborhood and typically mattered a great deal to local drinking customers, he often was not the most important person in the eyes of travelers. For example, when J. B. Dunlop's stage pulled into Darien, Georgia, he observed that the locals gathered eagerly to hear the news, and to them, the tavern keeper was a key figure—all the more so if he also served as postmaster.[26] For travelers like Dunlop, however, the news was nothing compared with the "neat supper awaiting us," almost certainly the product of female hands.

At a Kentucky tavern, New Yorker Andrew Lester delighted in finding that "every thing looked neat and we had a good breakfast and were not detained long in getting it." He concluded that the innkeeper must have "a smart wife." Charles Stuart likewise attributed a tavern's comfort to its women. While spending the night at an unlicensed Virginia tavern, he remarked in his diary on the "snug" house, "furnished plain and neat, and all arragned [*sic*] with that neat style of taste, and order of convenience, which distinguishes the accomplished housewife, and which will be sufficient to demonstrate the character of the female inmates of these premises." Anne Royall provided another testament to women's importance in describing an Alabama landlady as "the life and soul" of not only her tavern but also the surrounding neighborhood. Giving credit (and blame) to women for tavern conditions was particularly common among travelers who were not southern. While southerners generally recognized housekeeping as women's work, they were more likely to compliment a man on his wife's accomplishments than to give her credit for the household's success.[27] But this does not mean that outsiders' recognition of women's contributions warp our perspective on southern taverns. Instead, they permit us to identify one of the ways that ideas about domesticity filtered into the South and to recognize that taverns were a kind of vanguard in the region's adoption of new ideas about women's work and sphere.

As travelers' comments make clear, tavern women's domestic services earned not only a financial but also a cultural wage. Calling a woman the heart of the home would rapidly become a worn-out trope in antebellum America, but in taverns this association had distinctive meaning. Viewed through the lens of contemporary domestic ideology, housekeeping expressed women's identities as caretakers and loving mothers and wives. Yet, in crediting women for tavern comforts, travelers altered terms of the woman–and–home equation. Not only did most antebellum women earn no money for keeping their own houses, but also any reputation they gained for good housekeeping tended to reinforce the linked ideas that domestic work was not really work and that the home itself was a refuge from the cutthroat workaday world. In taverns, however, women's housework both earned cash and made reputations that directly affected the family's financial prospects.[28]

As travelers also made clear, the domestic comforts that southern tavern mistresses provided varied considerably.[29] In some cases, the hostess presided over an environment that bespoke what taste and money could secure in the way of furniture, tableware, carpets, and decorative objects. Mrs. Calder's 1806 advertisement for her Planter's Hotel in Charleston boasted not only of "cleanliness through every department of the house" but also of bedrooms amply "furnished with *entire new Furniture, Bedding, Carpeting*, &c. &c.," and a table stocked with "the best the markets afford." Both the name and the interior of the Calder establishment suggest that the proprietress sought genteel customers and a refined reputation. Most rural taverns, by contrast, displayed a more humble understanding of domestic comfort. At a rural Virginia tavern in the early 1830s, for example, some woman of the household, undoubtedly, had crafted the "home-made rag carpet" and "sprigged muslin [table] cover" that adorned Charles D. Stuart's room. Neither elegant nor refined, these adornments were nonetheless decorative rather than strictly functional, and they indicated a woman's investment of time and care in the room. Some tavern landladies earned praise—or blame—for their manners far more than for their housekeeping, and here, too, expectations were deeply gendered. A visitor to Planter's Hotel in 1810 praised the landlady—possibly still Mrs. Calder—not for her refined surroundings but for the motherly affectation of calling her "favorites" by "the maternal appellation of *My Son*."[30]

Keeping a public house had distinct consequences for women's reputation. A poorly kept house made visitors think ill not only of the landlady's taste and industry but often of her morals as well. The taint of sexual impropriety easily attached itself to any disorderly house, and public houses by their very nature seemed especially prone to disorderliness. In Charleston, for example, another female proprietor of the Planter House, a Mrs. Street, was imagined to prostitute her female slaves to her hotel's guests, while Cornel June, a male boardinghouse keeper, was known to prostitute both slaves and free women. Also in Charleston, another landlady's "suspicious" conduct meant that her coffeehouse was "not under the best character."[31]

Even in taverns with no detectable involvement in the sex trade, landladies and their daughters were vulnerable to unguarded flirtation and suggestive talk simply by virtue of their exposure to strangers. Male and female guests discussed tavern women's comeliness in print as well as in private. Men often flirted with them in ways that had everything to do with their status as transients who could not be held fully accountable for indiscreet behavior. When the married Col. John Boykin traveled from New Jersey to his South Carolina home in 1833, he enlivened the journey by flirting with nearly all the landladies he encountered on the way. His traveling companion, Francis Lee, recorded that he "succeeded pretty well" in "engaging" one landlady's affections, to the extent that she "tearfully bade him goodbye" and seemingly "wished for widowhood." Boykin's behavior suggests the kind of freedoms tavern guests sometimes took with their hosts. Even a simple description of a landlady's looks could focus attention on her person and distract the mind from her marital status and her husband's rights. We can only imagine what Colonel Pettis, who kept a tavern near Huntsville, Alabama, thought when he learned that Anne Royall had described his wife as "young, active, genteel, and sprightly, with a sparkling black eye."[32]

Unmarried women in a public house were even more likely targets for customers with flirtation—or more—on their minds. A Chapel Hill girl who lived in her mother's boardinghouse caught the eye of at least one of the boarders. As J. O. B. described to his cousin, this "pretty" girl made his lodgings "so much the more pleasant, for you know what a gallant I am." Calling himself a gallant may have been only so much bravado in a letter to a peer, but it is equally likely that this young man saw the young Miss Lewis as someone on whom to practice a kind of proto-courtship without consequences, at least not for him. For widowed tavern keepers, good looks were an equally mixed blessing. When Anne Royall warmly recommended a "fine" widowed landlady to her readers and praised her "regular round features, soft, full blue eye, and bright auburn hair," she probably intended a compliment, but that kind of public notice was likely the wrong sort of advertisement.[33]

Associating a public house with public women was alarmingly easy. Indeed, the linkage was ubiquitous in both the public print and the public record, with newspaper anecdotes and court proceedings testifying repeatedly to the dubious character of tavern landladies.[34] Yet it was not the only behavioral or moral attack against them. Travelers also sharpened their pens to sketch those landladies who acted more like elegant planters' ladies than motherly housewives. At a recently opened tavern near Lynchburg, the landlady felt unprepared to cope with guests—perhaps she had resisted her husband's decision to keep a tavern in the first place—and an irritated Anne Royall found that she had to cook her own breakfast as a result. When this woman finally did appear in the public rooms, Royall grumbled that she did no useful work but simply loitered in the dining room gaping at the guests. To Royall's way of thinking, even if there were servants aplenty, the landlady ought to cater to her guests personally: "Imagine my surprise," she wrote of another tavern, "to find the landlady seated in an elegant parlour, on an easy sofa, dressed like a princess, all in white." Rather than lounging and acting "scornful" and "consequential," this woman "had better be in the kitchen," Royall sniped.[35] In other words, the behaviors that marked planter ladies—chief among them an appearance of leisure—did not befit a tavern landlady, however wealthy her husband or genteel her household.

The importance of women to tavern patrons—for better or for worse—did not necessarily enhance women's domestic authority, however. As in many slaveholding households, the master and mistress of a tavern household faced resistance from slaves and servants that sometimes pitted them against each other. The public nature of tavern keeping made these tensions far more visible to outsiders than in most southern homes, which raised the stakes for all parties concerned and constituted a sort of supervision that most southern householders sedulously avoided. At one Fayetteville tavern, a long-standing quarrel between an enslaved woman, the landlady, and her son—the landlord—provided a sour sort of entertainment for visitors. The enslaved woman, whose name no one recorded, used the expectations of tavern hospitality as a pretext for criticizing her mistress, Mrs. Wells. She openly quarreled with Mrs. Wells in front of guests, rebuking her, for example, for not offering tea or coffee to go with dinner. Mrs. Wells retorted that the strangers could take what she had offered or go without. In refusing to alter her behavior, even to suit paying customers, Mrs. Wells signaled her disdain for the bondwoman's opinions—and also, evidently, for her son's preferences. When the enslaved woman warned her mistress that the master of the house would disapprove of her behavior, Mrs. Wells dismissed both of them: "Who cares for your Massa Tommy, or you either?" In the eyes of the tavern's visitors, this set-to—featuring an assertive slave, a surly mistress, and an ineffective master—totally distorted the ideal southern household. Of course, countless private households contained the same toxic mix of personalities, but only in taverns could a complete stranger so easily get a ringside seat.[36]

At a tavern in Melton's Bluff, Alabama, a chronic disagreement between the mistress of the house and another enslaved woman illustrates the particular tensions of keeping house in the public view. Here, the bondwoman was a high-ly trained—and expensive—cook from Baltimore; she represented a significant investment in the tavern's quality and reputation. Unfortunately for the tavern keeper, her skills and consequent sense of prideful authority led to quarrels with his wife. Whereas some landladies disdained to labor in the kitchen, Mrs. Melton repeatedly tried to displace the cook. In turn, the cook—and again we do not know her name—acted much like the Wells family's slave, claiming that she "was responsible to her master" and not, presumably, to her mistress. In this case, competing foodways aggravated the quarrel: Cherokee-born Mrs. Melton prepared the dishes of her childhood, while the Baltimore-trained cook tailored her meals to citified eastern tastes. Mr. Melton had to intervene repeatedly to ensure that his guests would get a meal at all. Similar conflicts disrupted meal-times in private households as well, but only in taverns did they erode both the householder's authority and earning potential. Ironically, scenes like these were such staples of travel literature that it seems the tavern keeper's loss was the au-thor's gain. Inadvertently encapsulating the problems that tavern management posed for domestic authority, Anne Royall observed that she actually preferred taverns kept by bachelors, because in those establishments, "I am always mis-tress of the servants."[37]

Royall's expectation that she should be able to command tavern servants threatened a basic element of household governance which tavern men and women alike were loathe to relinquish. When New Yorker Andrew Lester ar-rived at Clover Dale near Staunton, Virginia, one of his party ordered the ser-vants, "of which there appeared to be plenty," to take their horses to the stable and feed them at once. The "boys" declined, explaining that they "had no orders from their master & did not dare to go without them."[38] This household's en-slaved boys were caught between demanding visitors and an owner who clearly was determined to have the first and last word on the disposition of his domes-tic labor force.

An even more dramatic instance of how keeping house in public view com-plicated domestic authority comes not from a tavern but from a boardinghouse memorialized by the Duke of Saxe-Weimar in his 1828 *Travels*. Madame Herries of New Orleans employed a number of slaves to clean the rooms and attend the boarders in her large house, and one morning a chambermaid fell afoul of another male lodger. According to the duke, when the serving woman re-sponded slowly to an order, this man "struck her . . . in the face" hard enough that "the blood ran from her forehead." When Mme. Herries heard of the affray, she forced the chambermaid's "sweetheart"—a waiter in the boardinghouse—to beat her "with a cowhide." This sort of beating was by no means uncommon in slaveholding households, especially since the enslaved woman had apparently struggled with her attacker, nor was it unusual that a slave owner would have a slave punished to satisfy a guest. Yet the public nature of the Herries board-inghouse ensured that this incident had far greater consequences than in a private home. It appears that Mme. Herries felt constrained to punish her slave swiftly and harshly in order to keep her boarder's business. Yet because another boarder—the duke—was offended by the whipping, her actions backfired, for he made the incident into an unflattering anecdote in his popular travel narrative. Once she learned of his account, Herries felt obliged to rebut it in the newspapers. The sordid business came to light once again several years later when Anne Royall referenced the duke's criticism in one of her own books. All households with slaves experienced quarrels and usually violence of some kind, but running a public house was unusual in requiring masters and mistresses to factor outside opinion into their slave management.[39]

Another distinctive constraint on tavern keepers' domestic authority affected only those establishments near a college or university. At the University of North Carolina, for example, the faculty passed an ordinance in 1801 prohibiting students "from eating or drinking at Taverns or Public Houses" without a faculty member's permission. In practice, this translated into a ban on selling alcohol to students within two miles of the campus. Often violated, the ban nonetheless restrained the tavern keeper's trade and created an external, extragovernmental layer of supervision to which private householders were not subject. The faculty also monitored whether boardinghouses "permitted" students to live in an "irregular manner" or exposed them to "disorderly & pernicious examples." The university imposed price controls on public houses as well. In 1845, the board of trustees prohibited students from lodging with anyone who charged more than ten dollars a month, at a time when there was no legal price control on what boardinghouse keepers could charge. In addition, students who boarded out had to get faculty permission to change their residence. Unlike the other aspects of university paternalism, this one had some potential benefits for landlords. For example, the landlord who complained that a student boarder had left without notice and written him an "abrupt and abusive" letter may have gained some satisfaction from knowing that the faculty compelled the student to answer for his conduct. Similarly, another landlord might have been pleased to learn that students John Bragg and John Allison were suspended because of the "anonymous, menacing & scurrilous" letters they had written him.[40] Yet university paternalism of this sort, like the more overt restraint on innkeepers' access to student patrons, tended to undermine rather than enhance tavern keepers' ability to rule their own roosts.

Male and female, southern tavern keepers struggled with the many ways that their public work eroded their domestic authority. As a result, travelers found the truly "accommodating," "obliging," and "attentive" innkeeper rare enough to deserve lavish praise. Not incidentally, travelers used the latter words about tavern servants and slaves as well, a clear indication of why an innkeeper might cavil at courting his customers' favor too openly. To be sure, some tavern keepers deliberately positioned themselves as willing servitors in newspaper advertisements.[41] John G. Ballard of Camden promised to use "every exertion" to please his guests. Charleston's Mrs. Calder boasted about her "obliging, obedient, and orderly servants" and pledged to make "the utmost efforts to give satisfaction."[42] Taverns advertised in this way clustered in market centers or county seats and generally aspired to higher standards for both furnishings and service than the typical country tavern.

Sometimes, however, landlords who acted masterfully benefited tavern patrons, especially women traveling alone. At the U.S. Hotel in Columbia, South Carolina, the proprietor policed his household by ensuring that no one could enter Anne Royall's parlor without his "presence and permission." Similarly, an Augusta proprietor took offense when a local newspaper mentioned his house in a piece concerning Royall's arrival in that city. Instead of welcoming the free publicity, he paid an angry call on the publisher—cane at the ready—demanding, "How dare you name my house, you old s——l . . . or any person in it." Protecting a guest in this way was the arguably masculine version of the mothering that some travelers found so congenial in a landlady, but the landlord seems to have been more concerned with his patriarchal rights as a householder than with his reputation as a host.[43]

Yet as Mme. Herries learned, the attempt to act as "the master of the house" more often offended than pleased travelers. When disappointed travelers accused tavern keepers of barbarism, rudeness, laziness, sloth, filth, and ignorance, sometimes they groused with good reason. But reading between the lines, we can guess that some innkeepers whom travelers depicted as sullen or stupid had simply rejected the idea that tavern families should act like servants. These tensions were often most obvious in the writings of European travelers, whose notions of service evolved from far more rank-bound societies than the republican United States, but they also appeared in American writings. James Clitherall capped a fault-finding anecdote about a particular South Carolina innkeeper with what he sarcastically considered "convincing Proofs of his high breeding & good Manners": "his House was at the Bottom of a very pretty Hill, & being asked by Mrs. Middleton why he did not build it up there, he answered that if she was big bellied she would not like to carry Water from the Valley up to the House." While the man's wife might well have appreciated this consideration, the visiting ladies were shocked by the innkeeper's honest but indelicate answer. Compounding the supposed offence, the man then rubbed his long beard, and said "It['*]s almost time to take off my Beard for it feels very itchy," which the party apparently took as a reference to lice or other vermin.[44] This innkeeper may have been deliberately playing on his guests' preconceptions, but it is equally likely that he simply saw no reason to alter his manners in his own house.

Like this innkeeper, many of his ilk asserted their independence in ways that confused or even offended their clientele. An unknown proportion simply flouted the laws governing their establishments. Technically, refusing to feed travelers, as happened to James Flint in Lexington, Kentucky, violated licensing rules, but travelers' diaries contain countless examples of taverns that could not or would not provide meals. The lice-ridden landlord whom James Clitherall's group encountered in South Carolina let them know that "ourselves & Horses would get nothing to eat" unless they were "on our very best Behavior"—a strange experience indeed for elite women like Mary Izard Middleton and Henrietta Middleton Rutledge, but one which speaks to this man's certainty that he was master of his own house. Several decades later, another innkeeper flared up in anger when a customer criticized the "stinking meat" he had provided and, worse, mistook him for a waiter. "If you don't choose to eat such as there is on the table, you may go without!" retorted the landlord, who refused to be lectured under his own roof.[45]

On some occasions, tavern keepers were even more aggressive. A ferry keeper who encountered James Clitherall's party in 1776 was not only "surly, swearing [and] impertinent"—was he perhaps a Tory acting out at people connected to the Continental Congress?—but also ready to take advantage of their temporary dependence. Instead of taking them directly across the river, he toyed with them, rowing up and down the river instead. One of the escorts longed to "reward the Bear according to his Deserts," but the women in his care insisted on avoiding a confrontation in an isolated and unprotected spot. Decades later, innkeepers in Vicksburg and Louisville flatly refused to house Anne Royall, throwing both the traveler and her bags into the street. (By this time, she was a household name, having been convicted as a common scold in Washington, D.C., on the basis of intemperate remarks to members of a local evangelical church.) Facing such hostility, vexed customers usually felt freer to work out their frustrations on servants and slaves than on the proprietors. When Clitherall's party had another troublesome encounter at a Virginia ferry, for example, "the impertinence of a Negro Ferryman obliged Mr. M. to exercise his fist."[46] This time, the women made no objection.

Even such seemingly mundane matters as the organization of the dinner table pitted innkeepers against their guests. For tavern-keeping families, providing three meals a day, consisting of whatever the family was going to eat and served whenever the family chose to eat, posed the least disruption to their own routines. In addition, set meal times allowed innkeepers to try to synchronize schedules with railroad, steamboat, and stagecoach companies. But requiring guests to eat at a common table also affirmed innkeepers' standing as masters in their own households. As Fanny Wright told fellow Briton Frances Trollope, for example, the landlady they met in Memphis regarded any request for a separate, private meal "as a personal affront," which suggests the importance she accorded to presiding at her own table. Whatever the reason behind a particular establishment's choices, the *table d'hôte* system produced many conflicts with customers. Foreign visitors particularly disliked the large or promiscuous assemblage of people they found at the table. While in Memphis, for example, Frances Trollope had to dine with her servant, William.[47]

On the other side of the coin, tavern families lost privacy and access to their own domestic spaces when they lodged travelers, often without any offsetting convivial company. When innkeepers took advantage of their company to trot out favorite stories over the common table, travelers often felt offended. James Clitherall resented one "greasy" South Carolina landlord for chattering on about his children and his adventures with the Scopholites (a group of South Carolina Loyalists). He also disliked having to share a bed—which he clearly considered *his*— with the landlord. A few decades later in Georgia, a tavern daughter who sat down at the table with British visitors Captain Basil Hall and his family was later memorialized as a ill-mannered rustic who plopped down uninvited in a "vacant chair" and, "planting her elbows on the table," made "no effort to entertain us, but continued staring at us, as if we had been so many wild beasts feeding." Half a continent away in Texas, the sight of her innkeeper's son drawing his chair up to the fireplace and initiating a conversation with her husband prompted another Briton to remark, "How surprised we should be in England at such familiarity as this."[48] Even tavern-raised children paid a price, albeit a small one, if they acted as if their homes were their own.

Conversely, paying guests disrupted familial life and domestic space without a second thought. A tavern-keeping family had to expect its customers to wander all over their house rather than confining themselves to the dining room, kitchen, parlor, and barroom. For example, when John Melish stopped at a tavern outside Savannah, "hearing the noise of a wheel upstairs . . . I went to see what was going on." Looking into a room, he found "a daughter of the landlord" spinning and "a black girl carding cotton." Once he came back downstairs, he began asking questions, and his landlady told him that everyone in the neighborhood spun cotton at home "for family use." Many other travelers joined Melish in quizzing tavern families, even though they often took offense when their hosts reciprocated. European travelers in particular expected conversational and spatial privacy that they denied to their hosts. "An Englishman certainly feels," Matilda Houstoun wrote, "when he pays for his room at an inn, that even the landlord has no right to enter it." In her experience, no such expectation existed in the South, and white southerners' notions of household mastery and domestic authority were largely responsible.[49]

The presence of outsiders affected tavern families in ways well beyond the loss of domestic privacy and the scrutiny—so often hostile—to which patrons subjected them. Long-term guests became virtual members of the family, while even brief visitors often became enmeshed in familial dynamics. The impact that this had on tavern families may be guessed from the records of Martin Browne, a tavern keeper near Winchester, Virginia, at the turn of the nineteenth century. Like most early republican and antebellum innkeepers, he ran a family business: his wife, sons, and daughters assisted in the tavern and with ancillary activities like farming and textile production. His household also included long-term hired servants and boarders. When serving woman Minty Johnson quit after more than six months with the family, Browne recorded that she left "in a dirty manner," suggesting a sense of betrayal at her unexpected departure. That reaction was a typical reaction to a servant's quitting, but Browne responded similarly when two of his boarders left unexpectedly. In his notes, he called them "Blackguards & unworthy Villains," for not only had they absconded from his house without paying their bill, but they also departed without "taking any leave of the Family."[50] To Browne, their rudeness to the family with whom they had lived for so long was a separate and perhaps equal offence to their financial crime.

Browne's reaction differed somewhat from the way many tavern keepers would have responded thirty or forty years later, when inns and taverns had begun to develop a slightly different relationship to their customers. Similarly, Matilda Houstoun's experiences in 1840s Texas departed from what she might have encountered at the same time in the Southeast, where public houses had begun to accommodate travelers' demands in new ways. In the first decades after the Revolution, travelers knew that they could expect to share their bedroom (and like as not their bed) with their hosts or fellow guests. In 1801, Adam Alexander shared a bed near Fayetteville with his traveling companion, while his host and hostess had another bed in the same room, and their daughter slept on the floor. Alexander "thought this was equal to half bundling, as partitions & curtains were out of the Question," but he was unusually fastidious. Most seasoned travelers of this era who complained about such intimacies did so on account of noisy bedmates or roommates rather than objecting to the idea. Strangers slept in close proximity as a matter of course, and familial dynamics easily encompassed those who spent more than a few days in the household. Similarly, the rudeness that James Clitherall's party encountered en route to Philadelphia in 1776 was relatively typical for the time, but would have been somewhat surprising thirty years later. As early as 1810, Virginia's Martha Cocke took it for granted that if her husband became a tavern keeper, she would have to provide separate dinner tables "as genteel travellers would not like to eat with waggoners . . . nor either would it be reasonable to expect it." A few years later, Margaret Steele enjoyed a special ladies' parlor at a tavern on her way through the Carolinas. Her observation that it was "entirely separated from the rest of the house and boarders" strongly suggests that the tavern keeper's family considered the room off limits. By the antebellum decades, sharing beds and rooms had become far less common, at least in the eastern states, for those willing and able to pay for privacy. Truly private parlors or sitting rooms also became available in select taverns in the larger towns and cities.[51] Travelers rarely if ever stopped to consider that this increased privacy, which made them feel more at home, meant that tavern families were less at home in their own houses.

This displacement of tavern-keeping families reflected the competition taverns faced from an entirely new kind of public accommodation: the hotel. From around 1800, American innkeepers with aspirations (or pretensions) to refined accommodations increasingly adopted the word *hotel*, whose European associations suggested—but often did not deliver—a more elegant establishment than the typical American tavern. Tunis Campbell's 1848 book of advice for hoteliers indicates how different the hotel was, or at least could be, from the traditional tavern. For example, he recommended that hoteliers drill their staff daily in an elaborate system of synchronized table-waiting. Campbell suggested that his methods could be applied at home, but his system had little to say to most southern householders, because it effectively reduced the proprietor to the position of head servant. Indeed, hotels were perhaps most different from taverns and boardinghouses in not being first and foremost the homes of their keepers; they were businesses on another scale. Typically funded by a group of investors, hotels were often managed on a day-to-day basis by a hired hotelier—who was a man virtually without exception—sometimes with the help of assistant clerks, as well as many servants. Unlike the men and, rarely, women who worked as hired hotel keepers, the tavern master and mistress wielded economic, legal, coercive, social, moral, and above all familial power in their own homes. Hired housekeepers in large modern hotels possessed significant power over the servants and slaves they managed, and their position reflected gendered preconceptions drawn from family life. However, they were not acting as members of a family or even as masters of a household, and they drew no authority from the intersecting roles of master, husband, and father—or mistress, wife, and mother—that shaped both the familial lives and the domestic management of most southern whites. Complicating the hotelier's authority still further, some southern hotels hired white men and women—often immigrants—for highly visible positions like dining room attendants or chambermaids, although they still used enslaved or, sometimes, free African Americans as dishwashers, laundresses, and porters.[52]

Ironically, women's truncated managerial responsibilities in modern hotels may have been a factor in their popularity. Antebellum travelers continued to laud those wives and daughters who made taverns homelike and cozy, yet growing numbers hungered for public accommodations that offered more privacy, exclusivity, and comfort. Men and women alike valued hotels for their well-appointed bedrooms, private parlors, and lavish meals. Both sexes also enjoyed the attentive service that hotels offered, free from the demands of familial or household intimacy. In fact, at its best, a hotel may have felt like an idealized home: a well-appointed domestic sanctuary without any of the bother of managing servants and keeping accounts. But it usually was men who took advantage of the host of semiprivate and specialized rooms where they could gather with their peers, in a setting that offered exclusivity and privacy without the concomitant expectations of familial bonds, domesticity, and female authority that middling and wealthy Americans increasingly found in their own homes.[53]

For thousands of southern tavern keepers after the Revolution, their taverns were their homes as well as their livelihoods. In all of these taverns, the ideological distinctions that Americans—South and North—increasingly drew between the place of business and the familial realm had little practical effect. For historians, taverns serve as an extreme case of the physical porosity of all southern households, notwithstanding the legal and political potency of the ideal of the private and inviolable household in the region. Similarly, the multiple and constant challenges to a tavern keeper's mastery are a magnified instance of the many barriers to personal mastery that all white southerners faced, no matter their collective power in the region. The central position of the tavern mistress in the social and economic aspects of tavern keeping also demonstrated in concentrated form the key roles that white women played in southern families, despite the South's overwhelming patriarchalism.[54]

Antebellum ideas of public and private were always far more complicated than the simple equation of the family with private space and the feminized "domestic sphere," particularly in the nation's rural areas. There, many equated the family with the household, a socio-spatial construct in which the husband and father had mastery over his dependents, kin and non-kin alike. Outsiders—and their opinions—were often tolerated more than welcomed, an attitude which complicated running a public house. Some outsiders viewed rural families through a nostalgic or romantic lens, imagining a simpler time when families gathered around the domestic hearth for shared and sociable labor. Travelers who envisioned this sort of family tended to be charmed rather than appalled by rustic, rural taverns. For a vocal subset of urban Americans and foreign travelers, however, family increasingly meant the nuclear family and excluded servants or slaves, even if they shared the same house. For these people, privacy vied with comfort as the hallmark of domestic space. For some, not only was privacy possible in the public sphere but it was arguably more possible in a hundred-room hotel—where they had servants on call, space to entertain visitors, and the ability to exclude anyone they chose—than in a small country tavern, where travelers' needs sometimes ran a distant second to the demands of children and household production.

While historians delight in teasing out the constant border-crossings between the public world of commerce and politics and the supposedly sacrosanct private terrain of the family, white southerners did not view their surroundings in quite the same way. Few would have disagreed that keeping a tavern took a family down "a very public road," and that public entertainment differed significantly from the hospitality offered to family and friends. Some surely saw in taverns the antithesis of all they cherished in family life. On the one hand, a woman who made a business of providing homelike comfort and maternal care reaffirmed popular stereotypes about women as natural caretakers. On the other hand, by commercializing the skills and the space of housewifery and maternity, tavern keeping arguably contaminated or even prostituted the supposedly sacrosanct domestic sphere. But most tavern keepers rarely brooded over the gap between separate spheres ideology and the daily work of maintaining a family.[55] And at the end of a long day on the road, most antebellum travelers gave little thought to such boundary-crossings either, as long as someone could provide them with a clean bed and a hot supper.

As the subset of tavern families suggests, understanding southern families requires a broad perspective on the cultural and ideological meanings of both family and home. The familiar and convenient distinctions that historians often draw between southern households and northern homes obscure the circulation of ideas and people across the Mason-Dixon line. That very circulation made the tavern a place where historians may track the advance of northern-identified ideals like domesticity. It also made taverns a common terrain of contestation between competing versions of proper familial organization, domestic authority, and gender roles.[56]

Notes

1. For the impact of white understandings of family upon enslaved southerners, see Brenda E. Stevenson, *Life in Black and White: Family and Community in the Slave South* (New York: Oxford University Press, 1997), 214.

2. For elite southern youth, see Lorri Glover, *Southern Sons: Becoming Men in the New Nation* (Baltimore: Johns Hopkins University Press, 2007); Anya Jabour, *Scarlett's Sisters: Young Women in the Old South* (Chapel Hill: University of North Carolina Press, 2007); Cynthia M. Kennedy, *Braided Relations, Entwined Lives: The Women of Charleston's Urban Slave Society* (Bloomington: Indiana University Press, 2005), ch. 4.

3. See esp. Stephanie McCurry, *Masters of Small Worlds: Yeoman Households, Gender Relations, and the Political Culture of the Antebellum South Carolina Low Country* (New York: Oxford University Press, 1995); D. Harland Hagler, "The Ideal Woman in the Antebellum South: Lady or Farmwife?" *Journal of Southern History* 46 (August 1980): 405–18; Laura F. Edwards, *Scarlett Doesn't Live Here Anymore: Southern Women in the Civil War Era* (Urbana: University of Illinois Press, 2000), chap. 2; Michele Gillespie, *Free Labor in an Unfree World: White Artisans in Slaveholding Georgia, 1789–1860* (Athens: University of Georgia Press, 2004); Susanna Delfino and Michele Gillespie, eds., *Neither Lady nor Slave: Working Women of the Old South* (Chapel Hill: University of North Carolina Press, 2002).

4. See, for example, Deborah Gray White, *Ar'n't I a Woman? Female Slaves in the Plantation South*, rev. ed. (New York: W. W. Norton, 1999). I use the term *slave owner* in preference to *slaveholder* in order to underline the property claim—and the attendant violence and state power required to uphold it—on which chattel bondage depended. Slave owners did not simply "hold" slaves; they repeatedly and continually enslaved them in an ongoing process of legal, economic, social, and physical oppression. *Enslavers* captures this more clearly still than *slave owners*, but this term suffers from the distracting homophony with the verb *slaver*.

5. For an analysis that explores the psychological and physical cruelties of mastery, see Drew Gilpin Faust, *James Henry Hammond and the Old South: A Design for Mastery* (Baton Rouge: Louisiana State University Press, 1982). For the ideal of "corporate" paternalism, see Jeffrey Robert Young, *Domesticating Slavery: The Master Class in Georgia and South Carolina, 1670–1837* (Chapel Hill: University of North Carolina Press, 1999).

6. The best recent study of "middle-class" and supposedly northern values in the South is Jonathan D. Wells, *The Origins of the Southern Middle Class, 1800–1861* (Chapel Hill: University of North Carolina Press, 2004). On the construct of the household, see McCurry, *Masters of Small Worlds*; Elizabeth Fox-Genovese, *Within the Plantation Household: Black and White Women of the Old South* (Chapel Hill: University of North Carolina Press, 1988); Peter W. Bardaglio, *Reconstructing the Southern Household: Families, Sex, and the Law in the Nineteenth-Century South* (Chapel Hill: University of North Carolina Press, 1995); Marli F. Weiner, *Mistresses and Slaves: Plantation Women in South Carolina, 1830–80* (Urbana: University of Illinois Press, 1997); Jasper Adams, *Elements of Moral Philosophy* (Charleston: Folsom, Wells and Thurston, 1837). On gender in the context of family, see Jane Turner Censer, *North Carolina Planters and Their Children, 1800–1860* (Baton Rouge: Louisiana State University Press, 1984); Joan E. Cashin, *A Family Venture: Men and Women on the Southern Frontier* (New York: Oxford University Press, 1991); Steven M. Stowe, *Intimacy and Power in the Old South: Ritual in the Lives of the Planters* (Baltimore: Johns Hopkins University Press, 1987); Bertram Wyatt-Brown, *Southern Honor: Ethics and Behavior in the Old South* (New York: Oxford University Press, 1982). On southern consumption of northern and English ideas about authority and responsibility, see Young, *Domesticating Slavery*. The classic article on domesticity and true womanhood is Barbara Welter, "The Cult of True Womanhood, 1820–1860," *American Quarterly* 18 (summer 1966): 151–74. See also Nancy F. Cott, *The Bonds of Womanhood: "Woman's Sphere" in New England, 1780–1835* (New Haven: Yale University Press, 1997). For southern domesticity, see Weiner, *Mistresses and Slaves*; Kennedy, *Braided Relations*, 68, 82; Young, *Domesticating Slavery*; Stephanie Cole, "Servants and Slaves: Domestic Service in the Border Cities, 1800–1850" (PhD diss., University of Florida, 1994), 14–16, 35, 39, 205, 271n3; but see also Hagler, "Lady or Farmwife"; Fox-Genovese, *Within the Plantation Household*.

7. Although some tavern keepers were black or Indian, I have not considered them here for want of a sufficient number of cases. On labor conflicts within families, see Cole, "Servants and Slaves," esp. chap. 5. Southerners had several names for public houses: inns, taverns, ordinaries, and hotels. In this essay, I use *tavern* as a shorthand to indicate all public accommodations that were managed and staffed (at least in part) by the proprietor's family, as opposed to an exclusively hired staff of slaves, servants, and managers. This definition excludes the largest hotels, which often had salaried managers and relied on no family labor.

8. Paton Wesley Yoder, "Tavern Regulation in Virginia," *Virginia Magazine of History and Biography* 87 (July 1979): 273.

9. On southern families and the law, see Bardaglio, *Reconstructing the Southern Household*; Victoria E. Bynum, *Unruly Women: The Politics of Social and Sexual Control in the Old South* (Chapel Hill: University of North Carolina Press, 1992).

10. Sarah Hand Meacham, "Keeping the Trade: The Persistence of Tavernkeeping among Middling Women in Colonial Virginia," *Early American Studies* 3 (spring 2005): 140–63.

11. "Route to Charleston . . . Recd from Mr Poinsett Nov 22nd 1813," "Routes to & from

Charleston, 1815 & 1816," "Road from Philad. to Pittsburg recd from the Chief Justice Sep 27 1824," Roads and Travel Notes Collection, Historical Society of Pennsylvania, Philadelphia; Robert Andrews, *The Virginia Almanack, for the Year of Our Lord, 1794* (Richmond, Va.: T. Nicholson, 1793); Andrews, *The Virginia Almanack, for the Year of Our Lord, 1792* (Richmond, Va.: Augustine Davis, 1791).

12. James Flint, *Letters from America, Containing Observations on the Climate and Agriculture of the Western States* (Edinburgh, Scot.: W. and C. Tait, 1822), 135.

13. Andrew K. Sandoval-Strausz, "For the Accommodation of Strangers: Urbanism, Space, Travel, and the American Hotel, 1789–1908" (PhD diss., University of Chicago, 2002); Sandoval-Strausz, "A Public House for a New Republic: The Architecture of Accommodation and the American State, 1789–1809," in *Perspectives in Vernacular Architecture*, vol. 9: *Constructing Image, Identity, and Place*, ed. Alison K Hoagland, and Kenneth Breisch (Knoxville: University of Tennessee Press, 2003); Sandoval-Strausz, *Hotel: An American History* (New Haven, Conn.: Yale University Press, 2007).

14. Sandoval-Strausz, "For the Accommodation of Strangers," 96, 119–20; Doris Elizabeth King, "The First-Class Hotel and the Age of the Common Man," *Journal of Southern History* 23 (May 1957): 173–88; Charlene M. Boyer Lewis, *Ladies and Gentlemen on Display: Planter Society at the Virginia Springs, 1790–1860* (Charlottesville: University Press of Virginia, 2001); Thomas Chambers, *Drinking the Waters: Creating an American Leisure Class at Nineteenth-Century Mineral Springs* (Washington, D.C.: Smithsonian Institute Press, 2002); Hon. Gibson Lamb Cranmer, comp. and ed., *History of Wheeling City and Ohio County, West Virginia, and Representative Citizens* (1902; reprint, Apollo, Penn.: Closson Press, 1994), 203; Donna-Belle Garvin and James L. Garvin, *On the Road North of Boston: New Hampshire Taverns and Turnpikes, 1700–1900* (Hanover, N.H.: University Press of New England, 1988), 28, 35.

15. Garvin and Garvin, *North of Boston*, 28, 35; *The Falls of Niagara: Being a Complete Guide to All the Points of Interest Around and in the Immediate Neighbourhood of the Great Cataract* (New York: T. Nelson and Sons, 1858), 26, Wyck Association Collection, American Philosophical Society, Philadelphia; Lady Emmeline Charlotte Elizabeth (Manners) Stuart-Wortley, *Travels in the United States, Etc., during 1849 and 1850* (London: R. Bentley, 1851), 46, 148; Mildred McConnell and Carr Liggett, *Wheeling's First 250 Years: A Short History Done in Celebration of Service to Our Neighbors in Wheeling for Half That Period, 1817–1942* (Wheeling: National Bank of West Virginia at Wheeling, 1942), 36; Accounts, 1841–1849, Jacob A. Kline Account Books and Letters, Southern Historical Collection, University of North Carolina, Chapel Hill; Cole, "Servants and Slaves," 132–33; unknown, diary, 1817, Samuel Rowland Fisher Diaries and Account Books, 1767–1856, Historical Society of Pennsylvania.

16. Kym S. Rice, *Early American Taverns: For the Entertainment of Friends and Strangers* (Chicago: Regnery Gateway, 1983), 42; Alexander S. Davis, *The Traveler's Legal Guide and Business Men's Directory* (Rochester, N.Y.: D. M. Dewey, 1855), 82.

17. Sharon V. Salinger, *Taverns and Drinking in Early America* (Baltimore: Johns Hopkins University Press, 2002), chap. 1; Shirley V. Baltz, "Annapolis on the Threshold," *Maryland Historical Magazine* 81 (fall 1986): 224; Cranmer, *History of Wheeling*, 20–21; Davis, *Traveler's Legal Guide*, 80, 81.

18. Swaim Curran, "Diary, 1852," Lyndon Swaim Papers, 1844–72, sec. A, 34, Special Collec-

tions Library, Duke University, Durham, N.C.; 11 November 1810, J. B. Dunlop Diary, 1810–11, New-York Historical Society, New York City; Peter Adolph Grotjahn Memoir, 67, American Philosophical Society; 10 September 1835, Robert Patterson Diaries, 1835, vol. 2, Historical Society of Pennsylvania; unknown, diary, 1817; J. Conard to Roberts Vaux, 24 August 1832, 684, Vaux Family Papers, Historical Society of Pennsylvania. American's early nineteenth-century licensing laws drew no distinctions among taverns, inns, and hotels, to the confusion of inexperienced visitors from England, where those terms had legal meaning. For customer belief that hotels ought to offer better-than-average accommodations, see Anne Newport Royall, *Mrs. Royall's Southern Tour; or, Second Series of the Black Book*, 3 vols. (Washington, D.C., 1831), 1: 30, 110. For northern taverns and their evolution, see Garvin and Garvin, *North of Boston*. The rise of the hotel was not the only source of change in tavern family life in this period, but others lie beyond the scope of this essay.

19. Matilda Charlotte (Jesse) Fraser Houstoun, *Texas and the Gulf of Mexico; or, Yachting in the New World* (London: J. Murray, 1844), 226; Royall, *Mrs. Royall's Southern Tour*, 1: 76; John Green to Martin Browne, 27 February 1799, Martin Browne Papers, 1770–1830, Southern Historical Collection; Eliza Schley to Henry Jackson, 22 April 1837, Jackson and Prince Family Papers, Southern Historical Collection; Mary (Grey) Lundie Duncan, *America as I Found It!* (London: J. Nisbet, 1852), 162; 28 April 1776, James Clitherall Diary, 1776, Southern Historical Collection; William Burke, *The Mineral Springs of West Virginia; with Remarks on Their Use, and the Diseases to Which They Are Applicable. To Which Are Added a Notice of the Fauquier White Sulphur Spring, and a Chapter on Taverns, Also a Review of a Pamphlet Published by Dr. J. J. Mooreman*, 2d ed. (New York: Wiley and Putnam, 1846), 392.

20. Fortescue Cuming, *Sketches of a Tour to the Western Country: Through the States of Ohio and Kentucky; a Voyage Down the Ohio and Mississippi Rivers, and a Trip through the Mississippi Territory, and Part of West Florida. Commenced at Philadelphia in the Winter of 1807, and Concluded in 1809.* (Pittsburgh: Cramer, Spear & Eichbaum, 1810), 94; Charles D. Stuart Journal, 1832, 36, 38, Woodson Research Center, Fondren Library, Rice University, Houston; 27 August 1836, Andrew Lester Diary, 1836, New-York Historical Society.

21. 17 April 1776, Clitherall Diary; Flint, *Letters from America*, 93; John L. London Diary, 1838, Calder Family Papers, Southern Historical Collection; Duke of Saxe-Weimar Eisenach Bernard, *Travels through North America, during the Years 1825 and 1826*, 2 vols. (Philadelphia: Carey, Lea and Carey, 1828), 2: 50; Roberts Hunter, *Quebec to Carolina in 1785–1786, Being the Travel Diary and Observations of Robert Hunter Jr., a Young Merchant of London*, ed. Louis B. Wright and Marion Tinling (San Marino, Calif.: Huntington Library, 1943), 200; Royall, *Mrs. Royall's Southern Tour*, 1: 115. On Anne Royall, see Alice S. Maxwell and Marion B. Dunlevy, *Virago! The Story of Anne Newport Royall* (Jefferson, N.C.: McFarland, 1985); Elizabeth J. Clapp, "'A Virago-Errant in Enchanted Armor?' Anne Royall's 1829 Trial as a Common Scold," *Journal of the Early Republic* 23 (Summer 2003): 207–32. On early American guidebooks, see Richard Gassan, "The Birth of American Tourism: New York, the Hudson Valley, and American Culture" (PhD diss., University of Massachusetts, Amherst, 2002); Richard Gassan, "The First American Tourist Guidebooks: Authorship and the Print Culture of the 1820s," in *Book History*, ed. Ezra Greenspan and Jonathan Rose (University Park: Pennsylvania State University Press, 2005), 51–74.

22. Royall, *Mrs. Royall's Southern Tour*, 2: 114. Female licensees did not have an advantage over men in the business, however, because male labor was hardly dispensable. Female tavern keepers sometimes—but not always—hired barmen, for example, to handle the liquor trade, and men and women alike often needed a hostler or two to handle the horses.

23. On southern women in the paid labor force, see essays by Stephanie Cole, Barbara J. Howe, Timothy J. Lockley, Bess Beatty, Michele Gillespie, and Susanna Delfino, in Delfino and Gillespie, eds., *Neither Lady nor Slave*. For the eighteenth century, see Cynthia A. Kierner, *Beyond the Household: Women's Place in the Early South, 1700–1835* (Ithaca, N.Y.: Cornell University Press, 1998), 17–22; Julia Cherry Spruill, *Women's Life and Work in the Southern Colonies* (Chapel Hill: University of North Carolina Press, 1938), esp. 255–313.

24. On the question of women's work in yeomen households and the blurring of domestic and commercial production, see Stephanie McCurry, "Producing Dependence: Women, Work, and Yeoman Households in Low-Country South Carolina," in Delfino and Gillespie, eds., *Neither Lady nor Slave*, 55–71; McCurry, *Masters of Small Worlds*; Hagler, "Lady or Farmwife."

25. Volumes 1789–1808, Martin Browne Papers, 1770–1830. In contrast, boardinghouses, which tended to be urban, also housed fewer competing activities and little or no domestic production. Cole, "Servants and Slaves," 133.

26. For a useful reading of a tavern scene and the importance of the mail, see Richard R. John and Thomas C. Leonard, "The Illusion of the Ordinary: John Lewis Krimmel's *Village Tavern* and the Democratization of Public Life in America," *Pennsylvania History* 65 (winter 1998): 87–96.

27. See 13 February 1811, Dunlop Diary; 2 September 1836, Lester Diary; Stuart Journal, 37; Anne Newport Royall, *Letters from Alabama on Various Subjects: To Which Is Added, an Appendix, Containing Remarks on Sundry Members of the 20th & 21st Congress, and Other High Characters, &c. &c. at the Seat of Government. In One Volume* (Washington, D.C., 1830), 66; Bernard, *Travels through North America, during the Years 1825 and 1826*, 1: 185, 208; 2: 49; 5 May 1776, Clitherall Diary; Royall, *Mrs. Royall's Southern Tour*, 2: 37. Both a contrarian and self-contradictory, Anne Royall proclaimed elsewhere that in the South, men were the "life and soul" of a good tavern and filled the role occupied by women in northern taverns. Royall, *Mrs. Royall's Southern Tour*, 2: 107. For colonial tavern landladies, see Spruill, *Women's Life and Work*, 293–303.

28. On the rise of wage labor and its impact on women's domestic work, see Jeanne Boydston, *Home and Work: Housework, Wages, and the Ideology of Labor in the Early Republic* (New York: Oxford University Press, 1990); Cole, "Servants and Slaves," 16.

29. Patrons' expectations depended in part on location. Expectations for sexy, sinful New Orleans differed wildly from those for the sand hills of Georgia or the remotest parts of West Virginia. Cole, "Servants and Slaves," 205–6. See also Virginia Bartlett, *Keeping House: Women's Lives in Western Pennsylvania, 1790–1850* (Pittsburgh: Historical Society of Western Pennsylvania, 1994), 19–38, 53–66; Garvin and Garvin, *North of Boston*; Alecia Long, *The Great Southern Babylon: Sex, Race, and Respectability in New Orleans, 1865–1920* (Shreveport: Louisiana State University Press, 2004).

30. Richard L. Bushman, *The Refinement of America: Persons, Houses, Cities* (New York: Alfred A. Knopf, 1992); *City Gazette and Daily Advertiser* (Charleston, S.C.), 17 October 1806; *Anti-Monarchist and South-Carolina Advertiser* (Edge-field Court House), 2 November 1811;

Camden (S.C.) *Gazette*, 30 January 1817; *Falls of Niagara*, 26; Stuart-Wortley, *Travels*, 128; Hannah Haines Journal, 24 June 1812, Wyck Association Collection; Stuart Journal, 53–54; 12 November 1810, Dunlop Diary.

31. Kennedy, *Braided Relations*, 121; Royall, *Mrs. Royall's Southern Tour*, 2: 5, 14.

32. See 26 August 1833, John Boykin and Francis P. Lee Journal, 15 August–5 Sept. 1833, American Philosophical Society; Royall, *Letters from Alabama*, 66. Servants and slaves were, of course, far more vulnerable, as the references to Mrs. Street above make clear. My point is not to minimize their plight but to highlight the impact of innkeeping on women who in other contexts would have been comparatively protected in their own homes. Glover, *Southern Sons*, 129. My research does not yet permit me to comment on local men's attitudes toward and treatment of tavern landladies and daughters.

33. [Cousin J. O. B.] to Theodore B. Kingsbury, 13 March 1846, Theodore Bryant Kingsbury Papers, 1840–1915, Southern Historical Collection; Glover, *Southern Sons*, 104; Royall, *Mrs. Royall's Southern Tour*, 1: 122; 2: 19.

34. The association of public houses with disorder was a national or even international phenomenon, not a southern one. See Thomas Fairfax, *Journey from Virginia to Salem, Massachusetts, 1799* (London: private printing, 1936), 25–26; Harriet Martineau, *Society in America, in Two Volumes* (New York: Saunders and Otley, 1837), 1: 384; John William Willcock, *Laws Relating to Inns, Hotels, Alehouses, and Places of Public Amusement* (London: Saunders and Benning, 1829), 12, 99, 111; September Session, 1783, General Quarter Sessions of Peace Docket, Philadelphia County, December 1780–December 1785, Historical Society of Pennsylvania; Tavern Licenses, Alfred J. Liebmann Collection of Historical Documents, Manuscripts Division, New York Public Library, 53M150; Tavernkeepers' Bonds, Montgomery County, New York, Deeds, Commission 1786–1817, New-York Historical Society; Complaints—Taverns, April 1822, Stephen Allen Mss, New-York Historical Society; "Liquor Licenses," Beer—Taverns Research File, Library Company of Philadelphia; [Humane Society of New York], *A Report of a Committee of the Humane Society, Appointed to Inquire into the Number of Tavern Licenses . . .* (New York: Collins and Perkins, 1810), 8; Mrs. Lincoln Phelps [Almira Hart], *Caroline Westerley; or, The Young Traveller from Ohio: Containing the Letters of a Young Lady of Seventeen, Written to Her Sister* (New York: J. & J. Harper, 1833), 64–65; Bernard, *Travels through North America, during the Years 1825 and 1826*, 108; Joshua R. Rothman, *Notorious in the Neighborhood: Sex and Families across the Color Line in Virginia, 1787–1861* (Chapel Hill: University of North Carolina Press, 2003), 109; Yoder, "Tavern Regulation in Virginia," 260.

35. Royall, *Mrs. Royall's Southern Tour*, 1: 97; 2: 199–200.

36. Royall, *Letters from Alabama*, 36–37; Cole, "Servants and Slaves"; Weiner, *Mistresses and Slaves*, 37–43, 73–74, 84–87; Fox-Genovese, *Within the Plantation Household*, 135–40, 163–66; John Hammond Moore, ed., *A Plantation Mistress on the Eve of the Civil War: The Diary of Keziah Goodwyn Hopkins Brevard, 1860–1861* (Columbia: University of South Carolina Press, 1993), 71, 86–87, 89, 95, 105; 25 entries for July, 7 August, 17 August, 27 August, 15 September, 6 October, 8 October, 11 November, 6 December 1840, 23 January, and 4 February 1811, Natalie de DeLage Sumter Diary, South Caroliniana Library, University of South Carolina, Columbia. On legal regulation of southern families, see Bardaglio, *Reconstructing the Southern Household*; Bynum, *Unruly Women*, 59–110.

37. Cole, "Servants and Slaves," 211; Royall, *Letters from Alabama*, 60; Royall, *Mrs. Royall's*

Southern Tour, 3: 97. On the transition from enslaved to free domestic servants, see Cole, "Servants and Slaves," 66, 68, 70, 73. For Royall's politics, see Clapp, "Virago-Errant." I draw the term *foodways* from David Hackett Fischer, *Albion's Seed: Four British Folkways in America* (New York: Oxford University Press, 1989).

38. 19 August 1836, Lester Diary.

39. Bernard, *Travels through North America, during the Years 1825 and 1826*, 3: 82; Royall, *Mrs. Royall's Southern Tour*, 3: 88. I have not yet located Mme. Herries's rebuttal. For evidence of the role of outside opinion in slave management, see Weiner, *Mistresses and Slaves*; Fox-Genovese, *Within the Plantation Household*; Nell Irvin Painter, "Soul Murder and Slavery: Toward a Fully Loaded Cost Accounting," in *Southern History across the Color Line* (Chapel Hill: University of North Carolina Press, 2002), 15–39.

40. Board of Trustees Minutes, vol. 1: 1789–97, 221; vol. 3: 1801–10, 9; vol. 6: 1841–68, 62; vol. 15: Executive Committee 1835–73, 291; General Faculty and Faculty Council, Records of the General Faculty, vol. 1.2: 1814–21, 17; vol. 1.3: 1821–41, subgroup 1: 5, 19, all in University Archives, University of North Carolina; J. Johnston Pettigrew to E. Pettigrew, 19 April 1844, Pettigrew Family Papers, Southern Historical Collection.

41. Doris Elizabeth King, "Hotel Life in the Old South, 1830–1860" (MA thesis, Duke University, 1947), 176; 8 October, 14 October 1835, John Wight Bill Diary/Account Book, 1835–38, New-York Historical Society; Stuart-Wortley, *Travels*, 105; Curran Diary, 31; Houstoun, *Texas and the Gulf of Mexico*, 222; Basil Hall, *Travels in North America, in the Years 1827 and 1828*, 2 vols. (Philadelphia: Carey, Lea & Carey, 1829), 2: 183; Flint, *Letters from America*, 93; Royall, *Mrs. Royall's Southern Tour*, 1: 55, 121; 2: 57; 3: 5; John Melish, *Travels in the United States of America, in the Years 1806 and 1807, and 1809, 1810, and 1811*, 2 vols. (Philadelphia: privately printed, 1812), 1: 268; 17 April, 29 April, 1 May 1776, Clitherall Diary; Martineau, *Society in America*, 173; Burke, *Mineral Springs of West Virginia*, 387.

42. Stuart-Wortley, *Travels*, 80, 128; Royall, *Mrs. Royall's Southern Tour*, 1: 110; 13 August 1845 bill; *Camden Gazette*, 6 July 1820; *City Gazette and Daily Advertiser*, 17 October 1806.

43. Royall, *Mrs. Royall's Southern Tour*, 2: 57, 74.

44. Frances Trollope, *Domestic Manners of the Americans* (London: Whittacher, Treacher, 1832), 165; 16 April 1776, Clitherall Diary.

45. Yoder, "Tavern Regulation in Virginia"; Complaints—Taverns, April 1822; Salinger, *Taverns and Drinking in Early America*, 183, 203; Daniel B. Thorp, "Taverns and Tavern Culture on the Southern Colonial Frontier: Rowan County, North Carolina, 1753–1776," *Journal of Southern History* 62 (November 1996): 670, 680; 16 April 1776, Clitherall Diary. This landlord did not have the last word, for the customer happened to be Anne Royall, and she threatened to have him "prosecuted as a swindler" for failing to provide "edible meals." Royall, *Mrs. Royall's Southern Tour*, 1: 155–56.

46. See 12 April, 5 May 1776, Clitherall Diary; Royall, *Mrs. Royall's Southern Tour*, 3: 116, 206; Clapp, "Virago-Errant," 222–26.

47. Trollope, *Domestic Manners*, 41.

48. See 16 April 1776, Clitherall Diary; Hall, *Travels in North America*, 258; Houstoun, *Texas and the Gulf of Mexico*, 226.

49. Melish, *Travels in the United States*, 1: 32; Houstoun, *Texas and the Gulf of Mexico*, 226; King, "First-Class Hotel," 177.

50. Tavern Ledger, 1797–1804, and Memorandum Book, 1793–98, 1803, 1805, Martin Browne Papers.

51. See 9 November 1811, Adam Alexander Travel Diary, 1801, Alexander-Hillhouse Family Papers, Southern Historical Collection; James Gibbons Journal, 1804, 10, 99, Historical Society of Pennsylvania; Martha Lewis Cocke to Caroline Lewis Cocke, 19 November 1810, Cocke Family Papers, Virginia Historical Society, Richmond; Margaret Steele to Mary Steele, 9 October 1814, John Steele Papers, 1716–1846, Southern Historical Collection; Hall, *Travels in North America*, 2: 99, 180; Trollope, *Domestic Manners*, 154; Harriet Martineau, *Retrospect of Western Travel* (London: Saunders and Otley, 1838), 143.

52. Bushman, *Refinement of America*, 164; Garvin and Garvin, *North of Boston*, 34; Tunis G. Campbell, *Never Let People Be Kept Waiting: A Textbook on Hotel Management. A Reprint of Tunis G. Campbell's Hotel Keepers, Head Waiters, and Housekeepers' Guide*, ed. Doris Elizabeth King (1848; reprint, Raleigh: King Reprints in Hospitality History, 1973), xvi, 5, 8–26, 27–28, 29; King, "First-Class Hotel," 180; Sandoval-Strausz, "Accommodation of Strangers," 126; Cole, "Servants and Slaves," 15, 70. For immigrants in New Orleans, see Lady Victoria Welby, *A Young Traveller's Journal of a Tour in North and South America during the Year 1850, with Numerous Illustrations by the Authoress* (London: T. Bosworth, 1852), 131; Stuart-Wortley, *Travels*, 123, 128; Mississippi River Travel Diary, 1838, Special Collections Library, Duke University, 13. I do not necessarily endorse Andrew Sandoval-Strausz's view that the "modern" hotel was on the "leading edge" of "American modernity"; Sandoval-Strausz, "Accommodation of Strangers," 2; Sandoval-Strausz, *Hotel*.

53. Sandoval-Strausz, "Accommodation of Strangers," 3. For another perspective on white southern men's reactions to female authority, see Edward E. Baptist, "'Cuffy,' 'Fancy Maids,' and 'One-Eyed Men': Rape, Commodification, and the Domestic Slave Trade in the United States," *American Historical Review* 106 (December 2001): 1645–46. On families choosing to board, see Duncan, *America as I Found It!* 165.

54. Kirsten E. Wood, *Masterful Women: Slaveholding Widows from the American Revolution through the Civil War* (Chapel Hill: University of North Carolina Press, 2004), 90–93; McCurry, *Masters of Small Worlds*. For elite women occupying nominally masculine roles in the Old South, see Wood, *Masterful Women*; Nikki Berg Burin, "A Regency of Women: Female Plantation Management in the Old South" (PhD diss., University of Minnesota, 2007).

55. Cocke to Cocke, 19 November 1810; Anya Jabour, "'The Privations and Hardships of a New Country': Southern Women and Southern Hospitality on the Florida Frontier," *Florida Historical Quarterly* 75 (winter 1997): 259–75. For historians' use of the separate spheres metaphor, see esp. Linda K. Kerber, "Separate Spheres, Female Worlds, Woman's Place: The Rhetoric of Women's History," *Journal of American History* 75 (June 1988): 9–39; Kim Warren, "Separate Spheres: Analytical Persistence in United States Women's History," *History Compass* 5 (January 2007): 262–77.

56. For regional and cross-regional understandings of family in the mid-nineteenth century, see Glover, *Southern Sons*; Amy Murrell Taylor, *The Divided Family in Civil War America* (Chapel Hill: University of North Carolina Press, 2006).

III

Family Values and Social Order

~

The presence of both black and white family members at rituals, holidays, and celebrations, as depicted in this 1857 illustration of Christmas on the plantation, reinforced the notion of an organic racial hierarchy within "our family, black and white" and thus supported the slaveholding South's social order. The text accompanying this illustration concluded, "The 'stately mistress' and her 'aristocratic daughters' may be seen assisting, by every act of kindness, and displaying in the most charming way the family feeling and patriarchal character of our Southern institutions."

Fig. 6. "Winter Holidays in the Southern States: Plantation Frolic on Christmas Eve," *Frank Leslie's Illustrated Newspaper*, 26 December 1857. Courtesy of Library of Congress, Washington, D.C.

8

Family Ties

Indian Countrymen, George Stinson, and Creek Sovereignty

ANDREW K. FRANK

∽

In 1823, George Stinson established an unlicensed store in the heart of Creek country. Stinson understood that federal regulations required "white men" to apply for and obtain licenses from the United States before they could trade with the Creeks and that they had to post bond to ensure good behavior. Nevertheless, Stinson defied these laws, reportedly asserting to his neighbors and clients that "he would shed blood if an attempt was made to arrest him." The location of Stinson's store magnified his transgression. It stood precisely where it would most irritate U.S. Indian agent John Crowell, "in the vicinity of the *stand* occupied by [Crowell's brother and sometimes business partner] Thomas." As if agent Crowell needed further motivation to close the store down, rumors persisted that Stinson plied his clients with alcohol before offering them access to his merchandise and that he extended vast lines of credit in order to attract and control Creek hunters.[1]

Under normal circumstances, Crowell would have quickly and efficiently shut down this illegal store. Events over the next few months, however, demonstrated that the circumstances surrounding Stinson's store were hardly typical. Stinson's family connections within Creek society made every maneuver more complicated than the Indian agent could have imagined. Crowell struggled to apprehend Stinson and confiscate his merchandise, initially proved unable to confine him after his arrest, and then ultimately failed to secure a conviction in a U.S. federal district court in Savannah, Georgia. Exonerated by the court, Stinson returned to the Creek nation, retook possession of his confiscated property, and went back to business. At every step, family ties prevented Crowell's pursuit of justice.

The peculiarities surrounding the trial of George Stinson reveal the importance of family in southeastern Native American communities. As an intermarried white man, what nineteenth-century Americans commonly called an "Indian countryman," Stinson had kinship ties to many of the most powerful and often controversial Creeks and white southerners in the antebellum South. These cross-cultural familial relationships enabled him to open the trading store, fund its operation, find interpreters and partners to assist him, and ultimately attract Creek clients. Stinson's family ties also provided him with enough legal cover to escape conviction, as he defended himself by asserting his familial connections and his social standing as an adopted member of the Creek nation prohibited the need for a license. This essay explores these realities, demonstrating how the Creek Indians in antebellum Georgia, Florida, and Alabama used marriage and the resulting family obligations to control interactions with southern society and to otherwise assert political and legal sovereignty. These ties to the outside shaped Creek society and family life even as they helped natives control their future. In addition to demonstrating the interconnectedness of kinship and self-determination, it reveals how family ties remained the central aspect of determining identities in Native American societies in the pre-removal Southeast. Although racial identities and paternal ties increasingly influenced the behavior of southeastern Indians, matrilineal clans and familial ties remained the final arbiters in determining membership in these Indian societies. As a result, Crowell could fully believe in his right to prosecute an American-born citizen who traded among the Creek Indians while Stinson could believe that his kinship connections in native society made him Creek enough to avoid prosecution.

Scholars have long recognized the importance of kinship for Indians of the Southeast. Several generations of research have demonstrated how a matrilineal system of kinship structured Creek and neighboring Indian societies and organized their daily lives. Every member of Creek society belonged to one of about a dozen clans; village residents who did not have a clan identity may have been invited guests, but they were not members of the community. Clans—not residence or paternity—determined communal membership. Creeks believed that these clans, usually named for an animal or natural phenomenon, extended back through the female line to a single progenitor, making all of its members family. These families provided Creeks with a series of social relations and obligations, helping determine who hunted, farmed, danced, cohabited, advised, tutored, or traded together. Kinship also structured native legal systems, as Creeks practiced a system of clan vengeance, whereby they extracted "satisfaction" on a member of the clan responsible for the death of one of their relatives. At the same time, an incest taboo prevented clan members from marrying one another, even as the children of the same biological father could marry without sanction. In short, by structuring society with a range of daily and lifelong social obligations, a system of matrilineal clans separated insiders from outsiders and citizens from visitors. The children of Creek women were *este muskoke* (fellow Muskogee people); the children of non-Creek women were not.[2]

Despite a plethora of often nuanced and insightful studies on the nature and importance of kinship in the Southeast, the connections between sovereignty and kinship have seldom been explored for the eighteenth century. This may be surprising considering the nearly universal scholarly acceptance that kinship and native identities were tightly connected. In the case of Stinson, several scholars have avoided the familial details of his actual defense in lieu of other rationales for his acquittal. One historian focused on Stinson's role as a "clerk" rather than a trader, thus presuming that Stinson successfully avoided conviction by being a "lesser employee." Such an explanation avoids both the argument of the defense and prosecution and instead assumes that Stinson successfully passed for a "clerk." Another historian attributed the verdict to local political influences, particularly the "influence and popularity of the two star defense witnesses," federal agent and former Georgia governor David B. Mitchell and Creek chief William McIntosh. Stinson's status and the ability of Creeks to assert control over their territory could not explain the jury's actions because "it would probably be safe to say that no non-Indian in Georgia in 1824 believed the Creek Nation was sovereign." This may be an overstatement, as the verdict and other evidence explicitly seem to imply. Even if this characterization of Georgian society were true, however, it does not negate the reality that Creeks considered themselves to be a sovereign people and repeatedly used kinship ties to defend their society.[3]

Perhaps more important, Stinson had kinship as well as economic and political connections to Mitchell and McIntosh, the two men that many scholars and some contemporaries claimed had undue influence over the jury. Stinson had earlier married one of McIntosh's sisters; he thus became attached to his immediate family and the highly influential Wind Clan. He also opened the store in partnership with one of McIntosh's sons, Chilly. William McIntosh's kinship connections permeated Georgian society. McIntosh's biological father, a Tory who fled to the Creek Nation during the American Revolution, provided his son with several prominent white relatives. Through his connection to Chief McIntosh, Stinson was half-brother both to William R. McIntosh, the two-term member of the House of Representatives, and to John McIntosh, the collection agent for the Treasury Department at the port of Savannah. Stinson also benefited from McIntosh's continued efforts to use his own marriages to expand his personal power. Through one of McIntosh's marriages, for example, Stinson became a relative of Governor George Troup. Stinson similarly enjoyed the benefits created by the marriages of McIntosh's children. One daughter married the federal interpreter to the Creeks, Stephen Hawkins, and another married David Mitchell, who worked at the Creek Agency. During the trial, kinsmen were "star witnesses" and onlookers. William R. McIntosh, Chief McIntosh, and Mitchell all attended the trial and gave legitimacy to Stinson's defense.

Not surprisingly, Stinson's defiance of federal law stemmed in large part from his kinship ties to Creek society and his assertion that he was ritually adopted into a Creek family and clan and thus naturalized as a Creek citizen. Like hundreds of other white American men in the eighteenth and early nineteenth centuries, Stinson married a Creek woman and fathered children with her. Like many other Indian countrymen in the pre-removal South, Stinson found ways to live according to the cultural and social expectations of his new family and community. After years or decades in Creek society, many Indian countrymen claimed to be "perfectly acquainted with their character, customs, laws & language." They attended and participated in the Green Corn Ceremony and other communal rituals, and they learned how to behave inconspicuously in everyday situations. Many Indian countrymen painted and tattooed their skin, dressed in traditional Creek garb, and accepted matrilineal kinship patterns and distribution of power. Like many prominent male newcomers to Creek society, Stinson married a woman from the powerful Wind Clan, and her family members arranged for him to become a trader. The Wind Clan made similar arrangements with traders in the decades that preceded Stinson's marriage, leading to generations of prominent and wealthy Creek leaders, including William McIntosh, Alexander McGillivray, Mary Musgrove Bosomworth, and William Weatherford. Furthering Stinson's interconnectedness with Creek society, he may have also been adopted into another clan, providing this trader with additional clients and protection within his village.[4]

Stinson's connections to the Wind Clan, his possible membership in another clan, and the neighbors in his village did more than protect and assist his trading venture. They also provided a means of resistance prior to the trial. Soon after the arrest, Stinson escaped. As Joseph Vallence Beven explained, "as was natural, . . . [he] fled to his brother-in-law for protection." Trading partner and in-law Chilly McIntosh and his father, Chief William McIntosh, resisted returning Stinson to Crowell or American authorities until they received an order from the Creek council. This declaration proved to be a double demonstration of self-determination whereby Stinson's family both asserted that Creeks had a right to define and protect their kinsmen and demonstrated the Creeks' ability and desire to regulate internal legal affairs. Crowell acknowledged the de facto sovereignty of the Creeks and followed a federal policy to "call on the Chiefs for as many Indians, as May be wanted for that purpose" when it is "necessary to arrest a White Man in the Creek Nation." Anything else could lead to an international incident. Crowell took this suggestion seriously, sending a message to Chief Little Prince, McIntosh's political rival, to use all of the men and force needed to apprehend the criminal. Little Prince—who had once been McIntosh's ally and partner in many diplomatic and economic deals—had increasingly opposed the McIntosh-Mitchell trade alliance. The Stinson affair provided Little Prince with an opportunity, sanctioned by the U.S. agent, to weaken McIntosh's power. When Little Prince arrived to arrest and extradite Stinson to the United States, he "found the prisoner at the house of the Indian Chief McIntosh, who with a much larger force, under [his] command, protected & defended him, & said that he was determined to prevent him from being prosecuted by the Laws of the U.S." Eventually, the order from the Creek council arrived, and Little Prince helped apprehend the accused Stinson and send him to Savannah.[5]

Details of the trial further demonstrated the interconnectedness of family and sovereignty in Native American society. Stinson's defense, in short, relied heavily on the participation and kindness of kinsmen. During the trial, Stinson admitted to his occupation as a trader and did not contest the basic facts presented by the prosecution. Instead, he proclaimed that he was a Creek and thus not subject to U.S. law. Stinson defiantly "contended that the Creek Indians were a Sovereign & independent Nation and were competent to naturalise . . . a citizen of that Nation." As a result, the case against him "did not come within the purview of the laws regulating trade & intercourse with the Indian Tribes." He presented witnesses (primarily McIntosh and Mitchell) who testified to his adoption, his Creek family, and the traditional practice of not requiring Indian countrymen to have licenses from external—that is, U.S.—governments. Stinson testified that his in-law, Indian agent David B. Mitchell, had officially advised him that the kinship ties of the intermarried white men fulfilled the function of licenses. The prosecution rejected this logic and "produced the Treaty of Fort Jackson . . . which expressly declares that the Creek Indians shall not admit among them, any persons or traders except [those who] derive their authority from the . . . U[nited] States." This, the district attorney asserted, meant that the Creeks could not accept Stinson as a trader unless he was first sanctioned by the United States, the sole arbitrating power. The judge apparently agreed. Before sending the trial to the jury, Judge Jeremiah Cuyler "stated explicitly that the Indian Tribes within the limits of the U States were not sovereign & independent . . . [and] he was Surprised to hear Gentlemen at this day contend for such doctrine." With the defense of sovereignty apparently out of the way, the judge continued by asserting his own conclusion that "it was very clear that the Def[endan]t had violated the laws of Congress." Although the judge and Indian agent refused to accept the adoption of Stinson or the sovereignty of the Creek nation, the members of the all-white Georgia jury apparently saw the situation differently. They found Stinson to be a Creek man and therefore not guilty.[6]

Many white Americans with only a cursory knowledge of Creek society recognized that kinship ties were necessary to obtain permission to live and trade among the Indians. Although the need for wives waned in the nineteenth century, traders who had wives enjoyed benefits and protections that single traders did not. As a result, Europeans and Americans who desired to become deerskin traders routinely married Creek women, often with the realization that only marital ties could provide access to native villages with immunity. In 1784, John Smyth recognized this reality during a trip through Creek country. "It is customary when a white man enters an Indian town, or nation, with intention of residing there for some time, if only a few months, for him to have a wigwam, or hut, erected, in which he lives with some squaw." Although Smyth did not spend much time among the Creeks, he could not help but observe the truism that all American traders seemed to have Indian wives. Smyth, like many other European observers, emphasized the functional and economic importance of these kinship ties. Decades earlier, John Lawson came to a similar observation, emphasizing the often short-term nature of these marital relationships. He recognized that "*Indian* Traders [who] abide amongst the *Indians* for a long space of time . . . commonly [have] *Indian* Wives, whereby they soon learn the *Indian* Tongue, keep a Friendship with the Savages; and, besides the Satisfaction of a She-Bed-Fellow, they find there *Indian* Girls very serviceable to them, on Account of dressing their Victuals, and instructing 'em in the Affairs and Customs of the Country." Indian wives performed countless other tasks for their trader husbands. They also attracted clients, helped collect debts, served as interpreters, processed deerskins, and otherwise kept their husbands apprised of the political temperament of their communities.[7]

Marital ties to Creek women frequently helped provide protection and various forms of assistance to white husbands, but these relationships alone did not make Creeks out of the newcomers. Intermarriage offered men like Stinson opportunities to attach themselves socially to a Creek clan. Although a husband could not become a member of his wife's clan, he could enjoy many of the protections and connections that a clan provided. In other words, Indian countrymen could find an acceptable temporary place in Indian society and cease to be intrusive outsiders. Because the Creeks were a matrilocal society—a society where husbands joined the households of their wives—marriages to Creek women also provided ethnic outsiders with a place to live. Not surprisingly, then, Stinson lived in his wife's village where he opened a store. By moving into her house and the village of her female relatives, Stinson, like other intermarried whites, could physically escape from the margins of Native American society, enjoy the hospitality of a Creek family, and connect to the social and kinship networks of a Creek woman.

Intermarriage did not make Indians out of white men, but adoption rituals turned newcomers into members of the Creek nation. Adoption customs predated the arrival of European traders who wanted to reside in Creek villages. Traditionally, Creeks and other southeastern Indians routinely adopted outsiders into their families. Most often, this practice provided a way of dealing with captives of war, whereby "the king, the war chief and all the men and women of the nation are assembled," before the decision to torture, kill, or adopt was made. In some instances, adoptees took on the identities of deceased native kinsmen and fulfilled their surrogate kin functions. In these instances, the newcomers were "treated as a friend and a brother," and the new families "appeared soon to love him with the same tenderness as if he stood in the place of their deceased friend."[8] In other cases, the newcomers became new members of a clan. The process of adopting outsiders occurred widely in North America and especially in the Southeast. In 1819, the National Council and Committee of the Cherokee formalized the process of adoption. In an attempt to end the practice of white men claiming marriage with an Indian women in order to claim citizenship and thus access to Indian lands, it ordered that "any white man who shall hereafter take a Cherokee woman to wife be required to marry her legally by a minister of the Gospel, or other authorized person, after procuring a license from the national clerk for that purpose." If this formal practice ensued, the man "shall be entitled and admissed [*sic*] to the privilege of citizenship." Although the Creeks neither had a comparable level of Christian influences in their community nor a national clerk to record these social transactions, they too attempted to regulate intermarriage through various treaties and laws. They also formalized the process of adoption by conducting the act in public, normally at a council in the town square.[9]

Although intermarried traders like Stinson relied heavily on the assistance and protection offered by their wives, European Americans and Creek Indians also recognized that the relationships between Indian women and European men had diplomatic functions. Many European and American officials recognized the interconnectedness of trade and "the attachment of the Indians."[10] In essence, many Americans believed that once traders became embedded in native society, they obtained disproportionate influence in the Indian community. This recognition led many officials to conclude that any effective Indian policy must include, at the least, acceptance of intermarriage with Indians. Edmond Atkin, the British superintendent of Indian affairs of the Southern District, concluded in 1755 that agents who intended to spend years among the Indians must be "permitted to do it as shall take Indian Wives; by which means our Interest among the Indians will be strengthened." Return Meigs, a U.S. Indian agent among the Cherokees, arrived at a straightforward conclusion decades later: "I encourage marriages between whitemen and Cherokee women. I always have and I always will."[11] Perhaps most notably, William Crawford, who in 1815–16 served as secretary of war under President James Madison, publicly proposed subsidizing intermarriage as a means of subduing natives and converting them to American "civilization." Many observers believed that, if a nation could create family ties with an Indian society, diplomatic alliances also would be created.

Often Europeans and Americans rejected the premise that allowing or even encouraging intermarriage would create native allies. Kinship ties, they explained, did not automatically equate with diplomatic and economic alliances. Writing under the name "Americanus," one critic characterized Crawford's proposal to subsidize Indian-white marriages as "pre-eminently ridiculous." In addition to pointing to the exorbitant cost of managing such a plan and the faulty assumptions that it could ever work, Americanus contended that even if there were hundreds or thousands of intermarriages with Indians, the plan would backfire. In his view, the only "habit acquired [by Indian society] will be the vicious habits of the frontier whites." After all, it would be impossible to persuade "the finest portion of the human race . . . the young men and young women who border on the Indian frontiers . . . to prostitute their persons, to the dirty, draggle-tailed, blanketed, half human squaws, or the filthy ferocious half naked savages." Other critics in the American South offered less severe indictments of intermarriage even as they asserted the need to regulate Indian-white marriages. French Louisiana governor Jean-Baptiste Le Moyne Sieur de Bienville, for example, recognized that restraints must be placed on his citizens who married Indian women. It "was important to bring in all the Frenchmen who are scattered among the Indians and not to authorize them to live there as libertines under the pretext that they have wives among them."[12] Unrestrained intermarriage, he recognized, could do more harm than good. As John Stuart, British superintendent to the Southern District, wrote in 1763, the "first and main step toward the right Governing of Indians and bringing them under some Police will be having Good men Traders in the different Nations subjected to good and wholesome regulations." As a result, Secretary of War Henry Knox concluded in 1789 that if the desire "to emigrate into the Indian country cannot be effectually prevented," it must be "restrained and regulated."[13] Bureaucrats and Indian agents suggested many reforms, including restricting alcohol sales, standardizing prices, limiting the number of traders, and screening the traders themselves. This ongoing struggle to regulate intermarried traders like Stinson ultimately resulted in the law that mandated that traders have licenses before they enter Creek society.

Proponents of Indian-white intermarriages had various other concerns about the relationship between kinship and diplomacy. Many feared the presence of intermarried husbands from competing nations at the same time that they viewed intermarriage as the means to obtaining native allies of their own. Arturo O'Neill, Spanish governor of Pensacola in West Florida, asserted that the southeastern Indians are "swayed generally by what the Europeans or whites advise, letting themselves be governed entirely by those who have lived with some European women of the English nation." In this phenomenon, O'Neill saw a political opportunity. "There is need that a good missionary should come promptly to make all the necessary arrangements to bring about marriages between the persons of these nations and some of our Europeans already distinguished for excessive fondness for the Indian women." The political ramifications of these "alliances" would "in a short time" result in the creation of a large congregation of "friendly Indians and mestizos."[14] These children would theoretically serve as the ideal cultural intermediaries for the connected worlds of their white fathers and Creek mothers. Kinship, therefore, could provide a means to bridge the divide between the two societies.

Agent Crowell understood the threat of Indian-white intermarriage slightly differently, seeing few opportunities and many pitfalls for U.S. diplomacy. After arresting Stinson, Crowell made the stakes of the trial clear. If intermarried white men could ignore federal rules, he explained, "there will be no licensed traders. For this plain reason, they will all have Indian wives for the sake of being irresponsible to the laws regulating trade & intercourse with the Indian tribes, and will keep Shops of Whiskey in stead of useful goods for the Indians." Marriage with Native Americans could prevent the United States from asserting control over the hundreds of white residents in Indian communities. In the aftermath of Stinson's trial, a distraught Crowell detailed the implications for Indian-white relations and the regulation of the Indian trade. "Notwithstanding the offence for which this Def[endant]t was indicted had been established by unimpeachable testimony, and the charge of the Judge to the Jury clear and conclusive, the Jury returned a verdict of Not Guilty. If so strong a case as this cannot be prosecuted to effect, it will be worse than useless to attempt the execution of the laws of the U States in the Nation."[15] In this case, the legal loophole that marriage and kinship ties provided made enforcing American laws all but impossible.

Like other Indian countrymen, Stinson recognized that he occupied a social and legal position that defied most attempts to define it. The ambiguous position of the intermarried man in Creek society led many Americans to ask as one U.S. citizen did in a letter to Secretary of State James Monroe, "In what light ought the Indian Country-men to be viewed—whether as Indians or Citizens of the United States?" Stinson may have been born in the United States, but he followed in a long line of outsiders who used their marital status or their adopted status to elude American regulations. Throughout the eighteenth and early nineteenth centuries, "renegade white men" used their relationships with Indian women to defy colonial laws. Dozens of Loyalists—like William Barnard, William Augustus Bowles, and Abraham Mordecai—found safety in Creek villages by obtaining Indian wives and embracing the political loyalties of their new communities. Fugitives from justice similarly enjoyed an ability to disappear by marrying into Creek families. One "white man named Smith" escaped from Alabama by marrying "a squaw of the Creek nation." Officials recognized that they could not arrest him, even though he continued to help his Indian neighbors commit crimes, like stealing livestock in Alabama's border towns. As an informant explained to Alabama's governor, William Wyatt Bibb, capturing him would be difficult because of the thirty to forty Indian warriors who constantly surrounded and protected him.[16]

Many fugitives decided to marry Creek women and become part of native society after their experiences among the Indians made intermarriage desirable or its necessity apparent. According to traveler Augustus Loomis, who observed the Creeks in the 1810s, these newcomers quickly found themselves immersed in Indian society: "They have come to like the Indian country and the Indian customs; and, more than that a swarm of black eyed boys and girls have sprung up around them; and they have farms and herds, which also are yearly increasing."[17] Kinship ties, whether to a clan in the Indian manner or as father to biological children in the European way, led many white newcomers to Creek villages to see themselves as belonging to Creek society.

There was yet another motivation for white men to intermarry. In the colonial era, the Creeks often evicted traders who lacked kinship ties to their community. Such was the case for "one Wright" who was arrested and sent to Augusta in 1738, for being "a lawless Person, trading among the Indians, without License, either from Carolina or Georgia." Without a wife or kinsmen to stand up for him, Wright had little chance of either getting a chief to protest on his behalf or otherwise oppose the actions of the United States. In other instances, the Creeks "burnt a trading house" that did not have the sanction or protection provided by a marriage. Similarly, Creek diplomats and warriors returned dozens of African slaves to Georgia and Alabama, even after they established residences in Creek country. When fugitive slaves obtained Creek wives, however, efforts to have them returned proved much more difficult. As a result, British, Spanish, and American officials repeatedly insisted that the Creeks were delinquent in "delivering up all prisoners, whether whites or negroes."[18] As a result, by the antebellum era, Americans recognized that kinship ties frequently led to protection by village chiefs and clan leaders.

A similar pattern emerged for licensed traders, in which the importance of kinship ties to Creek society often trumped other concerns. In 1798, the Creeks concluded that they needed to evict several traders, despite their otherwise sanctioned position in Creek society. For example, they drove Robert Kilgore out of a village because he was "an unworthy character and a vagabond, a fugitive from justice and now in the neighbourhood of Ocheubofau." The "chiefs" made their rationale for the action clear. They were "determined that no such character shall find refuge in their land." At the same time, though, Charles Weatherford avoided this fate. Although the Creeks similarly deemed him "an unworthy character and unfit to be in their land and the Chiefs had determined he should leave their land," his Creek wife's family intervened. Creek chief Efau Haujo explained that leniency would be offered "in consideration of his family on the Indian side, and of a promise made by Opoie Hutke of Ocheubofau [the chief of Weatherford's wife's village] that he will in future attend to his conduct and endeavor to make him reform his conduct and behave well in future." As a result "the Chiefs have determined to forgive the past and let him remain on his future good behavior, and if he do's misbehave again he is then to be removed without any favour or affection."[19] Kinship ties, rather than formal European- or American-sanctioned licenses, determined who could and who could not get a second chance.

While first the colonial powers and then the United States offered licenses as a means of regulating the trade, natives typically initiated intermarriages—the indigenous form of a trading license. Although the details of Stinson's marriage are unknown, the historical record contains many examples of engagements initiated by native women and very few successful attempts by white men to find Indian wives or sexual partners. Such was the case for Louis Milfort, the egocentric Frenchman who married one of the sisters of Alexander McGillivray. Although he insisted that he had an aversion to native women, he admitted to having a sexual affair with a Creek woman before accepting an offer of marriage to another Creek. In both instances, he passively responded to the decisions of the Creek women and their kin. "They had me tempted by one of the prettiest young women in the town, a maiden with an attractive face," he recalled. As Milfort explained it, the affair resulted from the actions of the female community: "The other women had clubbed together to get her a beautiful printed calico skirt, a nice chemise, silver pins, two pairs of bracelets also of silver, an enormous quantity of ribbons of all colors fastened to her hair, and five pairs of earrings which hung in graduated sizes like chains. It was in this full dress that she approached me and chose me as her partner." Milfort had little choice but to acquiesce to the woman's sexual overtures. In the aftermath of this tryst, Chief Alexander McGillivray initiated a marriage between one of his sisters and Milfort. "The friendship which binds us together," he asserted, "makes it possible for me to propose to you to marry my sister; she knows the English language and that of the savages, and thus will be able, to be sometimes of assistance to you, and serve as an interpreter for you." Milfort may have overstated his reluctance in the first sexual encounter, but his one-night stand and his marriage both adhered to social customs on the southern frontier. Benjamin Hawkins, the U.S. Indian agent among the Creeks for two decades, similarly recorded the proactive actions of Creek women to create marriages with white traders. In Hawkins's own experience regarding intermarriage, the marriage proposal occurred when a Creek woman "called at my lodgings and requested I would accept her daughter, a young widow, during my residence here, or as much longer as I thought proper."[20]

As Milfort experienced, Indian women initiated nonmarital sexual relations. When white men took the lead, it often resulted in disaster. Although few instances of the rape of Creek women have been recorded, the Creeks frequently complained about the "licentious behaviour of the traders and . . . impositions on the savages." This behavior, in part, resulted from white visitors' assumption that Creek women were easy sexual prey. As one missionary wrote: "Without any thought of shame, a Creek girl speaks of her sexual parts as casually as she would of a finger." Indeed, Creek women freely initiated sexual relations without Victorian concerns for their reputation. The forwardness of Indian women and their nonmarital sexual relationships led several European and American observers to call Indian women "whores." As a result, many white visitors falsely assumed that they could enter a Creek village and simply "lye with their Women." Yet the power that sexual relationships provided for Native Americans appeared in many descriptions of native licentiousness. "The old women who have handsome granddaughters . . . think of no support but prostituting their granddaughters or daughters," Hawkins explained. "On this they confidently rely for cloths and food and spoke of it as a cheap and easy way of acquiring both."[21] Hawkins mistook these relationships for prostitution, typifying the common belief of outsiders that Indian women were sexually available. Nonetheless, his description confirmed the ways in which Creek women initiated sexual and marital relationships on their terms and for their own purposes.

Marriage to an Indian woman and adoption into the nation did not allow an Indian countryman to act as an unrestrained free agent within Creek society. As members of a matrilineal community, Indian countrymen typically lived among their wives' families who had various interests of their own. In Stinson's case, his new Creek family found various ways to control him. Stinson's partnership with Chilly McIntosh constrained his ability to exploit fully his acceptance in Creek society. With Chilly's oversight, Stinson could neither reap all of the financial rewards of the trade nor overcharge his customers. Stinson's in-laws also insisted on various other restrictions. Chief William McIntosh, just prior to the marriage, demanded that Stinson agree to a prenuptial agreement, an innovation within Creek society. This legal pact, which was similar to other marital agreements and laws in southeastern Indian society, stipulated "he was not to take away any property should he leave her, as he brought none with him, but it was to go to his wife & children." When the marriage dissolved in the aftermath of the trial, the U.S. courts acknowledged the agreement and kept the inherited property in the hands of Stinson's Indian family. This prenuptial agreement may have led McIntosh to formulate it as a Creek national policy. In 1818, under his guidance, the Creek national council passed a law that "agreed that if a white man take an Indian woman, and have children by her, and he goes out of the Nation, he shall leave all his property with his Children for their support." Chief McIntosh and Agent Mitchell made the logic for this law explicit: "It has often happened that white men have come into our Nation poor, and taken an Indian woman to wife, by whom they have had Children, and when they have gotten their hands full, they have got tired of the Country and left their wife & Children to Suffer, which we think very unjust, and have therefore passed this law."[22] Through this policy, the Creeks formalized traditional Creek gender norms that presumed that property passed down through the maternal line.

Creek women also held the upper hand in the raising of children born to intercultural relationships. These children, who obtained their clan identities and thus their family obligations through their mothers, lived in a world defined by their matrilineage. In southeastern Indian society, maternal uncles—not biological fathers—served as male role models for Creek children. They trained boys to become hunters, disciplined them when they broke Creek rules, arranged marriages, and otherwise served the functions that biological fathers had in European society. Maternal aunts served equally important roles, augmenting the influence of mothers. Biological fathers belonged to a different clan and sometimes to a different village than their children. As a result, they had socializing roles to play for the children of their sisters rather than for their own children. In addition, the socialization of Creek children typically took place inside villages or under the supervision of clan members. This constrained the ability of white fathers to be active parents to their biological children, leading many Americans to conclude, as did Benjamin Hawkins, that "the husband [in Creek society] is a tenant at will only so far as the occupancy of the *premises* of the women."[23] These characterizations have been confirmed by twentieth-century anthropologists who concluded that "the father had no more to do with the discipline and education of his children than an alien."[24]

Although Creek families did not ignore the interests of white fathers, they did control how they socialized their children. Creek kin often allowed white fathers to teach their children the linguistic skills required to work as traders and interpreters. Although a few children of Indian countrymen attended schools in the United States and even abroad, most children obtained informal and partially "western" educations under the oversight of their Indian kin. When missionaries established schools in villages, Creek mothers limited and constrained their teaching. In 1826, Reverend William Compere complained that "another of our girls has been taken home under the pretense of visiting a sick sister." Compere knew the "real" reason for feigning sickness. "Poor girl!" he explained. "She has a mother so entirely opposed to civilized habits, that we fear it is only a trick to persuade her own child from school, who till now has been governed by her own inclinations." As a result of continuing Creek control, many children of intermarriages "spoke English well, but had not been taught to read so as to make [them] proficient."[25] Employment in the trading stores proved to be one of the most effective ways of educating the children of intermarriages. Here, too, the influence of clans could be seen, as the involvement of Creek children in trading networks resulted in certain clans obtaining further control over the lucrative trade.

Even before the birth of a generation of biracial children in the 1810s and 1820s, marital relationships with prospective traders provided the means for Native Americans to control the lucrative trade upon which the Creeks increasingly depended. While Indian women provided white husbands with essential skills and connections to their kin, they also used their marital relations to regulate the trade. As a result, Creek women obtained a tremendous amount of social and cultural power, becoming what historian Kathryn Braund called "guardians of tradition" and "handmaidens to change." Women frequently had the ability to choose what goods would enter their communities and how they would be used. Part of this control extended to the financial resources that traders often accrued. William Bartram recalled meeting an Indian trader who, though in love with his Seminole wife, was financially ruined by her practice of "drain[ing] him of all his possessions, which she dishonestly distributes amongst her savage relations." Similarly, many traders enjoyed tremendous success inside the villages only to return to American society penniless. These controls led many natives to insist that they did not need formal stores. Resident traders would serve their need. Creek chief Mico Lucko made this desire clear in a 1772 letter to the British agent in charge of trade: "We were always told that we were not to have any Traders in the woods nor any Stores in our villages." When this policy ended, and unmarried and therefore unregulated traders took over the trade, Mico Lucko and other Creeks complained that they faced unprecedented threats to their sovereignty. "Since such things has happened it is the Merchants faults and we never promised to give our Lands for debts."[26]

The decision to marry Stinson certainly had an economic rationale. Prior to the marriage, William McIntosh had secured economic advantages for his family through his relationship with Indian agent David B. Mitchell. The two dominated much of the trade through the control of the annuity, a yearly payment received largely for prior land cessions. The chief's critics, including Little Prince and Crowell, claimed that Mitchell and McIntosh distributed federal resources inequitably and to their personal financial advantage. Cronyism, not equity, determined who obtained a share of the annual payment to the Creeks. Little Prince also claimed that McIntosh and Mitchell took advantage of their literacy to cheat many Creeks out of their share of the annuity. In response, McIntosh and his allies claimed that Crowell paid the annuity to chiefs "in large bills of fifty and one hundred dollars," and only Crowell had the resources to make change at these amounts. This "compelled [most Creeks to] go to Thomas Crowell and buy domestic homespun at fifty cents per yard, of the same description of goods that General McIntosh had furnished the nation at twenty-five cents per yard only a few months ago." Mitchell lost his position as the Indian agent when evidence emerged that he planned to smuggle illegal African slaves into the United States through Florida and Creek country. When Crowell replaced Mitchell, he made it clear that he "would not join with him in cheating the nation out of their annuity," and the feud between Crowell and McIntosh began in earnest. Not surprisingly, then, McIntosh and Mitchell provided the supplies and capital needed to run Stinson's trading post. Hence Stinson's store restored McIntosh's position at the center of the Creek economy and reconnected him to American society.[27]

Stinson's Creek family also used the store for economic and political ends. The feud between McIntosh and Crowell predated Stinson's entrance into Creek society, and it continued after Stinson's trial. It eventually led Crowell to press charges against William McIntosh at the Creek's national council at Broken Arrow and then contributed to the Creek execution of William McIntosh in 1825. With this in mind, Stinson's store was not coincidentally located near Crowell's store; McIntosh apparently hoped that the store could break Crowell's hold over the trade and reduce Little Prince's political power. This goes a long way toward explaining Crowell's message to Little Prince: "If six men are not enough, send six hundred and take him by force, if he has to destroy McIntosh and his whole establishment to effect it." The message also reflected Crowell's recognition that McIntosh and Little Prince were both concerned with issues of Creek sovereignty as it related to the United States and authority within the nation as it related to its competing chiefs. "Tell him it will reflect disgrace upon him, as the head man of the nation, to suffer one chief to prevent his orders from being put into execution; and this conduct of McIntosh is quite sufficient to break him as a chief. If, however, he does suffer McIntosh to protect this man in violating the laws of the United States, his nation must suffer for it; for he may rest assured, that the Government will not put up with it." Stinson eventually may have recognized that the McIntosh family had used him for economic and political ambitions. He left his Creek wife and family and by 1827 had married a white woman in Georgia.[28]

Although the Creeks received an admission of their sovereignty and their legal ability to control who was and who was not a Creek in Stinson's trial, this reality dissipated in a few years. After the trial, especially as the prospect of forced removal became apparent, "many desperate and unprincipled white men have since the satisfaction of the treaty entered our Nation and have taken Indian wives, with the sole view of enjoying the privileges and securing to themselves the lands guaranteed to our people in the treaty." Although Creek laws and customs attempted to prevent lands and other property from passing into the hands of intermarried traders, many of the intermarried whites turned to the Alabama courts to sanction their claims. This led some federal officials to conclude that they, too, needed to restrict unmarried whites from entering Creek society. In 1830, Phillip Wager, a brevet major in the U.S. Army stationed at Fort Mitchell, issued a "proclamation, ordering all white persons, not having permits or Indian wives, within the space of 15 days, to leave the country, once known as the Creek Indian nation." This proclamation and others proved difficult to enforce, and the Creeks continued to complain that "these abandoned and desperate men are rapidly collecting among us, under colour of authority as indian countrymen, [and] are seizing [and] occupying our most valuable lands." No longer able to control these interlopers, even though they did not have the protection of a clan or the rights of a naturalized citizen, the Creeks called upon the United States. In what amounted to a remarkable admission that they lacked the ability to control their own borders, several Creek chiefs hoped that "our Great Father [the President] will order [the outsiders'] removal and for his information we subjoin the names of the most notorious and obnoxious: they annoy us much and are particularly disliked by all our people." Despite these precautions, thousands of acres were transferred to "*White Men* under the guise of *Indian Covering*."[29]

As Stinson's defense revealed, on the eighteenth-century and early nineteenth-century southern frontier, the issue of political sovereignty could not be separated from family ties. Both southeastern Indians and white southerners used parentage and spousal relationships to determine who belonged in their communities and used kinship to determine the social obligations of residents in their communities. Because kinship determined national identities and community membership, the issue of family necessarily related to the issue of sovereignty. Not surprisingly, then, Creeks and other southeastern Indians used kinship to define and defend their diplomatic interests.

While both communities understood that kinship and sovereignty were connected, their differences in regard to kinship proved more significant. While family served similar structural functions in the white South and in Indian societies, it did not work in comparable ways. The antebellum South was predominately a patriarchal society that acknowledged maternal ties at birth but emphasized paternal family name as adults. By contrast, matrilineality structured native societies, leaving issues of paternity somewhere between the realm of irrelevance and trivia. Creek children received their clan memberships and the obligations that resulted from them strictly from their mothers, making maternal uncles more important family members than biological fathers. Adoption customs further exaggerated the differences between Indian and white families. Whereas both communities had mechanisms to provide children with new parents and social identities, the white South had no equivalent to the adoption of adults into clans and families.

These distinctions in regard to kinship ensured that a diplomatic middle ground could not be created. As much as Creeks could use intercultural families to assert control in intercultural affairs, intermarriages alone could not compete with the social, economic, and diplomatic realities in the American South. Disputes like the Stinson affair reveal that differences between the two legal and cultural systems outweighed comparisons and that the federal government did not understand or want to understand these differences. As a result, Stinson's acquittal and the successful defense of Creek sovereignty hardly slowed down the subsequent erosion of Indian self-determination in the Southeast. Creeks and other southeastern Indians would use various means of resistance to protect their sovereignty, but in the end, many events, most notably the forced removal of the Creek Indians from the Southeast in the 1830s, demonstrated that these methods had failed.

Notes

1. John Crowell to John C. Calhoun, 21 August 1823, Antonio J. Waring Jr. Papers, Georgia Historical Society, Savannah; Report of Joseph Vallence Beven to George M. Troup, in *American State Papers, Class II: Indian Affairs*, 2 vols. (Washington, D.C.: Gales and Seaton, 1832–34), 2: 793.

2. Excellent works on kinship in the Southeast include Alexander Spoehr, *Changing Kinship Systems: A Study in the Acculturation of the Creek, Cherokee, and Choctaw* (Chicago: Field Museum of Natural History, 1947); Kathryn E. Holland Braund, *Deerskins and Duffels: Creek Indian Trade with Anglo-America, 1685–1815* (Lincoln: University of Nebraska Press, 1993); Tiya Miles, *Ties That Bind: The Story of an Afro-Cherokee Family in Slavery and Freedom* (Berkeley: University of California Press, 2005). Despite their respective interpretive insights, these studies do not explore the connection between kinship and tribal sovereignty. A few studies emphasize kinship ties, especially in terms of how Indian leaders used familial ties to obtain authority. For example, see Claudio Saunt, *A New Order of Things: Property, Power, and the Transformation of the Creek Indians, 1733–1816* (Cambridge: Cambridge University Press, 1999); Benjamin W. Griffith Jr., *McIntosh and Weatherford, Creek Indian Leaders* (Tuscaloosa: University of Alabama Press, 1985); Gary E. Moulton, *John Ross, Cherokee Chief* (Athens: University of Georgia Press, 1978). Rarely do works address the connections between kinship and national sovereignty in the early American South.

3. Griffith, *McIntosh and Weatherford*, 220–21; Michael D. Green, *The Politics of Indian Removal: Creek Government and Society in Crisis* (Lincoln: University of Nebraska Press, 1982), 62.

4. Testimony of William Hambly, 4 July 1825, Records of the Office of Indian Affairs, Creek Agency, 1824–76, Letters Received, 219: 902, National Archives, Washington, D.C. For a discussion of intermarriage in Creek society, see Andrew K. Frank, *Creeks and Southerners: Biculturalism on the Early American Frontier* (Lincoln: University of Nebraska Press, 2005).

5. Report of Joseph Vallence Beven, in *American State Papers, Indian Affairs*, 2: 793; John Crowell to John Calhoun, 21 August 1823, Waring Papers.

6. John Crowell to John Calhoun, 23 November 1824, Records of the Office of Indian Affairs, Creek Agency, 1824–76, Letters Received, 219: 123–26; Telemon Cuyler to John Crowell, 14 July 1825, Waring Papers; Thomas McKenney to John Crowell, 10 December 1824, Records of the Office of Indian Affairs, Letters Sent, 1: 261.

7. John Ferdinand Dalziel Smyth, *Tour in the United States of America*, 2 vols. (1784; reprint, London: Arno Press, 1968), 1: 190–91; John Lawson, *A New Voyage to Carolina*, ed. Hugh Talmage Lefler (1709; reprint, Chapel Hill: University of North Carolina Press, 1967), 192.

8. "Von Reck's Journal," in Kristian Hvidt, ed., *Von Reck's Voyage: Drawings and Journal of Philip Georg Friedrich von Reck* (Savannah, Ga.: Beehive Press, 1980), 47; interview with George Looney, 28 June 1937, Indian Pioneer Historical Collection, 55: 6500a, Grant Foreman Collection, Oklahoma Historical Society, Oklahoma City.

9. Resolved by the National Committee and Council, 2 November 1819, in *American State Papers, Indian Affairs*, 2: 283.

10. Panton Leslie & Co. to Baron de Carondelet, 2 May 1794, Ayer Collection, Newberry Library, Chicago. Lewis Cass, while governor of the Michigan Territory, for example, concluded in 1815 that "every British trader admitted into the Indian Country is in fact a British Agent." For Cass, the intransigence of Indians could be attributed to the influence of British traders who "systematically seize every opportunity of poisoning the minds of the Indians." Lewis Cass, 1815, Regulation of Indian Affairs, Ayer Collection.

11. Edmond Atkin, in Wilbur R. Jacobs, ed., *Indians of the Southern Colonial Frontier: The Edmond Atkin Report and Plan of 1755* (Columbia: University of South Carolina Press, 1954), 80; Return Meigs to Chief Chulio and Chief Sour Mush, 14 March 1808, cited in William G. McLoughlin, *Cherokees and Missionaries, 1789–1839* (Norman: University of Oklahoma Press, 1984), 69.

12. *Strictures Addressed to James Madison on the Celebrated Report of William H. Crawford Recommending the Intermarriage of Americans with Indian Tribes* (Philadelphia: Jesper Harding, 1824), 6, 10; Abstracts of Letters from Bienville to Jérôme Phélypeaux, comte de Pontchartrain, 28 July 1706, in Dunbar Rowland and Albert Godfrey Sanders, eds. and trans., *Mississippi Provincial Archives, French Dominion*, 5 vols. (Jackson: Press of the Mississippi Department of Archives and History, 1927–84), 1: 26.

13. "Observations on the Plan for the Future Management of Indian Affairs Humbly Submitted to the Lords Commissioners of Trade and Plantation," 1 December 1763, British Public Records Office, 323: 19, 20, Colonial Office, London; Henry Knox to the President of the United States, 7 July 1789, in *American State Papers, Indian Affairs*, 1: 53.

14. Arturo O'Neill to Marques de Sonora, 11 July 1787, in John Walton Caughey, *McGillivray of the Creeks* (Norman: University of Oklahoma Press, 1938), 157.

15. John Crowell to John C. Calhoun, 6 April 1824, Records of the Office of Indian Affairs, Creek Agency, 1824–76, Letters Received, 219: 78–80; John Crowell to John C. Calhoun, 23 No-

vember, 1824, Records of the Office of Indian Affairs, Creek Agency, 1824–76, Letters Received, 219: 123.

16. Gilbert Russell to the Secretary of State, 9 July 1815, in Clarence Edwin Carter, ed., *The Territorial Papers of the United States*, 28 vols. (Washington, D.C.: Government Printing Office, 1934–49), 6: 540; Andrew Jackson to William H. Crawford, 10 June 1816, in *American State Papers, Indian Affairs*, 2:110; Thomas C. Hunter to William Wyatt Bibb, 1 November 1818, in Carter, ed., *Territorial Papers of the United States*, 18: 452.

17. Augustus Loomis, *Scenes in the Indian Country* (Philadelphia: Presbyterian Board of Publication, 1816), 200–201.

18. Allen D. Candler, Kenneth Coleman, and Milton Ready, eds., *The Colonial Records of the State of Georgia*, 32 vols. (Atlanta: Franklin Printing and Publishing Company, 1904–16), 4: 166; A. S. Salley, *Journal of Colonel John Herbert, Commissioner of Indian Affairs for the Province of South Carolina, October 17, 1727, to March 19, 1727/8* (Columbia: Historical Commission of South Carolina, 1936), 16; Instructions to John Heth, an ensign in the first American regiment, 31 May 1791, in *American State Papers, Indian Affairs*, 1: 125.

19. Efau Haujo, speaker, 28 May 1798, in C. L. Grant, ed., *Letters, Journals, and Writings of Benjamin Hawkins*, 2 vols. (Savannah, Ga.: Beehive Press, 1980), 1: 177–78.

20. Louis Milfort, *Memoirs; or, A Quick Glance at My Various Travels and My Sojourn in the Creek Nation*, trans. Ben C. McCary (Savannah, Ga.: Beehive Press, 1959), 137–38; Hawkins, in Grant, ed., *Letters*, 1: 47.

21. Governor Peter Chester to the Earl of Hillsborough, 9 March 1771, in Kenneth G. Davies, ed., *Documents of the American Revolution, 1770–1783*, 21 vols. (Dublin: Irish University Press, 1972–79), 3: 65; Carl Mauelshagen and Gerald H. Davis, eds., "The Moravians' Plan for a Mission among the Creek Indians, 1803–1804," *Georgia Historical Quarterly* 51 (September 1967): 363; Candler, Coleman, and Ready, eds., *Colonial Records of the State of Georgia*, 23: 122; Hawkins, in Grant, ed., *Letters*, 2: 412.

22. John Crowell to James Barbour, 10 September 1827, Records of the Office of Indian Affairs, Creek Agency, 1824–76, Letters Received, Microcopy 234, 221: 248–49. See also Andrew K. Frank, "The Rise and Fall of William McIntosh: Authority and Identity on the Early American Frontier," *Georgia Historical Quarterly* 86 (Spring 2002): 18–48. See also Creek Agency Records, McIntosh Papers, Laws of the Creek Nation, 12 June 1818, David B. Mitchell Papers, Newberry Library.

23. Benjamin Hawkins to Thomas Jefferson, 11 July 1803, in Grant, ed., *Letters*, 2: 455.

24. J.N.B. Hewitt, "Notes on the Creek Indians," in *Bureau of American Ethnology*, bulletin 123 (Washington, D.C.: Government Printing Office, 1939), 145.

25. "Extracts from Rev. Mr. Compere's Journal, Sent to the Corresponding Secretary," 5 November 1826, in *Baptist Missionary Magazine* 7 (May 1827): 143; James Stuart, *Three Years in North America*, 2 vols. (Edinburgh, Scot.: Printed for Robert Cadell, 1833), 1: 159.

26. Kathryn E. Holland Braund, "Guardians of Tradition and Handmaidens to Change: Women's Roles in Creek Economic and Social Life during the Eighteenth Century," *American Indian Quarterly* 14 (Summer 1990): 239–58; William Bartram, in Gregory A. Waselkov and Kathryn E. Holland Braund, eds., *William Bartram on the Southeastern Indians* (Lincoln: University of Nebraska Press, 1995), 47; Mico Lucko to John Stuart, 19 April 1772, British Public Records Office, Colonial Office, 5/73.

27. Samuel Hawkins to Governor George M. Troup, 12 April 1825, in *American State Papers, Indian Affairs*, 2: 766; Questions put to the Chiefs headmen and Warriors of the Creek Nation assembled in their National Council & House at Broken Arrow by Major E. P. Gaines, 29 June 1825, Records of the Office of Indian Affairs, Creek Agency, 1824–76, Letters Received, 219: 1072.

28. John Crowell to William Hambly 22 August 1823, in Report of Joseph Vallence Beven, in *American State Papers, Indian Affairs*, 2: 793.

29. *Niles Weekly Register*, 8 May 1830; Creek Chiefs to Secretary of War, 15 November 1832, Records of the Office of Indian Affairs, Creek Agency, 1824–76, Letters Received, 223: 100; Mary Elizabeth Young, *Redskins, Ruffleshirts, and Rednecks: Indian Allotments in Alabama and Mississippi, 1830–1860* (Norman: University of Oklahoma Press, 1961), 81.

9

White Families and Political Culture
in the Old South

CHRISTOPHER J. OLSEN

~

On a hot, steamy August day in 1853, thirty-one of the eligible voters in Town-
ship Five of Rankin County, Mississippi, walked or rode to the courthouse in
Brandon, where they cast ballots to choose five school trustees. On this day,
the voting was more of a community ritual than hard-fought contest: each of
the winning candidates received between 75 and 90 percent of the vote. Many
of the voters came to support friends or family members who lived in the same
neighborhood. Among the participants were George N. Langford Sr. and his
son, George Jr., who voted together early in the morning. Two of the winning
candidates were neighbors of the Langfords. In a similar scene, on a much colder
January day in 1860, a smaller group of Mississippi voters braved the weather
and registered their unanimous support for Yancey McClung, the only candidate, as the new constable of Shongalo beat in Carroll County. McClung, thirty-
one years old, lived in his father's house and helped manage the family's slaves
and land. McClung's supporters included his father, William, his older brother,
Morgan, who lived next door, and the Gordin brothers, George, Edward, and
William. The three Gordins also owned slaves, and they lived, worked, and socialized in the same rural neighborhood as the McClungs. Of course, there were
many more famous cases of family members working to support one another's
political aspirations. In the 1850s and throughout the Civil War, in Charleston,
Washington, and Richmond, Mary Chesnut worked to advance her husband
James's political career at countless receptions and through her own friendships
and encouragement. She identified with his fortunes so much that she feared his
potential election loss would be the "defeat of my personal ambition."[1]

As suggested by these few vignettes, family and extended household relationships helped define politics in the Old South. Voting behavior is probably the most studied part of antebellum political culture, but it is just one area in which kinship played an important role. In both nuclear and extended households, and collectively in their rural neighborhoods, families also shaped officeholding and patronage, the voting process, partisan and community campaign events and rallies, and much of what we associate with "formal" or electoral politics. While families often molded individuals' political behavior and determined success, they could be, in turn, affected by politics. Political and economic success frequently came together, and extended kin groups created economic and political power blocs cemented through family ties. But family clans that lost political power could be hurt financially as well. Finally, politics became an important part of many families' social lives, not unlike church attendance, and rallies and campaign events typically included men, women, and children. The end of the campaign process, election day itself, served as an important all-male gathering of extended kin and other men in a community ritual that often helped to unify the neighborhood across class and generational lines.

The force of these extended kin and neighborhood ties were most evident in the rural Deep South and less true in urban areas where the population turned over more frequently and was more diverse in its ethnic, religious, and class composition. It was also truer in the early years of a community's settlement and less true after several generations of growth and change. The importance of families in politics, in other words, ebbed and flowed with socioeconomic conditions and across time. It was hardly a linear or uniform development, however. Long-resident families, for instance, consolidated influence over time and exerted greater control over local patronage and officeholding. In contrast, the impact of family ties and associations on voting patterns—particularly in elections beyond the local or county levels—normally faded with the passage of time as the community grew more complex and parties began to form.[2]

The role of family in southern political culture, then, was a complicated one, although in nearly every way families constituted the most basic "unit" of electoral politics. This essay aims to make clear some of the ways in which family members influenced each other's behavior, attitudes, and success, and more generally, how households and neighborhoods—often dominated by groups of extended family members—shaped the antebellum southern political culture. Finally, it also considers how politics fit into the lives of men and women in the Old South and how families could be affected by changing political fortunes.

This discussion, particularly in the areas of voting behavior and election-day rituals, focuses on Mississippi, which was reasonably representative of the

Deep South states. It was, however, more rural and less ethnically diverse than most of the South, and it was one of just two states with a slave majority in 1860. Beginning in the 1820s, many white families from the Carolinas, Virginia, and Georgia moved to the state, and by the 1840s Mississippi led the nation in cotton production. Its economy remained generally strong despite a recession in the early 1840s. By the late 1850s, however, some residents were already looking west and leaving the state. Thus there was considerable fluidity in the population as free families moved in and out. Despite these demographic trends, Mississippi's rural neighborhoods endured and retained many of their political character-istics over time. This continuity, it seems, resulted largely from the actions of extended family members and their friends who stayed in the state. The political culture, in other words, took shape through the influence of families, or groups of families, who remained in a given area for several generations.[3]

One particular feature of Mississippi politics was the frequency of elections. General elections for state, county, and local offices were held in odd-numbered years (staggered from presidential contests); beginning in 1858, county, local, and militia elections moved to even-numbered years. This meant that between 1833 (after the new constitution of 1832 took effect) and 1860 there was a general election in twenty-three out of twenty-eight years, plus all the various local, municipal, and special elections. In nonpresidential years there were, on aver-age, about fifty county and precinct offices available in every county. This pattern repeated in most of the Old Southwest, although in several states more elections were bunched with presidential contests (in even-numbered years). Mississippi, in fact, was a leader in the movement to make nearly all public officials (includ-ing judges) elected rather than appointed. In addition to frequent elections, the great majority of eligible voters participated on a regular basis. Voter turnout averaged between 70 and 85 percent in state and national elections. In Missis-sippi, roll-off (the rate of declining participation "down" the ballot) for the major county offices was negligible, typically 1–3 percent. Roll-off was actually negative about one-fourth of the time. In other words, more votes were cast for county-level than for state and national offices. After 1855, in fact, the rate of turnout for county elections greatly exceeded state and national contests.[4] Judging by voter participation, Mississippians seem to have regarded county and local politics to be at least as important as state and national elections. And in county and local elections, the family-centered, neighborhood-based, antiparty political culture was what inspired men to vote.

In bringing men to the polls and influencing their choices, women often played important roles that historians have only partly brought to light. Wives, sisters, daughters, and cousins read party newspapers and listened to speeches, discussed politics in letters, and, although seldom recorded, undoubtedly talked with the men in their families about all matters political. The extent to which women followed electoral politics varied greatly, of course—as with men. Also like men, educated and wealthier women had more chances to influence political debate and enjoyed greater access to public power. Wives of state or national politicians occasionally became very active. Virginia's James McDowell considered his wife's political advice superior because it was "always rendered from the most devoted feelings and from the *best* judgment." Like Mary Chesnut, Susan McDowell was closer to political power than most southern wives, but privately, women of all classes could affect the attitudes and behavior of men in their families.[5] Because attention to politics was not "expected" of women—and was actively discouraged by some men—a smaller proportion of women than men followed politics closely. Despite that difference, though, women—and more broadly, families—probably constitute the least carefully studied, although generally acknowledged, influence on southern men's political lives, behavior, and attitudes and on political culture generally.

In the past two decades, southern historians have helped to redefine the study of family and political history. Reassessment of the family has come from a greater emphasis on, and appreciation for, the important, often intimate personal ties that existed among extended kin. Many siblings and cousins, for instance, enjoyed special bonds that endured over decades, ties that had implications for both the actual structure of families and households and the relationships among extended kin. "It is clear, then," concluded historian Joan Cashin in an influential article, "that the planter family did not fit the nuclear model in either its residence patterns, its child-rearing methods, or the behavior of its members as manifested in relationships among cousins."[6] While much of the literature has focused on elite families, numerous studies have demonstrated that yeomen and poorer families cultivated, and benefitted from, many of the same extended familial ties as planters.[7] Most of these works on southern women and families have focused naturally on social and cultural history, particularly the functions and roles of families and gender relationships.

Over the same decades, southern historians have brought new energy to political history, but in so doing, they have not engaged much of the literature on women's and family history. This stems largely from the general preoccupation with parties, including ideology, leadership, and who voted for whom, topics that have traditionally been considered to involve just white men. Only in recent years have some historians seriously examined the participation of women in

214 Christopher J. Olsen

formal, electoral politics and considered the implications of their actions. Beginning in the 1820s, with opportunities greatly expanded in the 1840s and 1850s, southern women participated in community and party campaign functions—the barbecues, fish frys, and barn dances that filled the election calendars. They read party newspapers and wrote letters to the editor; a small number of women spoke in public and even edited newspapers. Despite the attention these political activities now receive, histories of antebellum women and politics remain largely separate.[8]

The popular conviction that parties dominated electoral politics has also limited interest in other factors operating within antebellum political culture. The argument runs that as national organizations matured, shaping public debate and voters' perceptions of what the most pressing issues were and controlling elections through nominations and supervision of polls, those institutions replaced, or superseded, kin and neighborhood loyalties as the basis for voting behavior, dispensing patronage, and so forth. The growth of parties certainly changed American political culture, particularly in the North and, to a somewhat lesser extent, the upper South. Voters responded to party appeals and symbols as each organization relied on an increasingly sophisticated network of editors and activists, men who planned campaign strategy, raised money, and bombarded potential voters with a coordinated "message." In the North, and especially New England, parties effectively controlled local elections by the 1830s (even earlier in some places) as the political culture moved from one founded on family oligarchies to one dominated by institutions.[9] Enough evidence exists, however, to question how effectively party organizations developed in the antebellum lower South. Various studies suggest that antipartyism remained an important force in regional political culture, particularly during the growing sectional crisis of the 1850s. Distrust of "professional politicians" became central to public discourse, and voters did not consistently follow party leaders.[10]

Party organizations apparently had a rather limited impact on voters in antebellum Mississippi. Their failure, in turn, meant that the state's political culture remained rooted in a family- and neighborhood-based system that operated on face-to-face relationships rather than through institutional parties. This antiparty political culture was most evident in county and local politics, but voter distrust of parties manifested at all levels. A suspicion of parties and politicians emerged in speeches, public letters and pamphlets, editorials, and private correspondence. Popular opposition to parties remained part of American politics generally, drawing particularly on revolutionary classical republican discourse, but southerners had additional reasons to distrust institutions such as political parties. Regional notions of masculinity and the ethic of honor placed a premium on men's public behavior, valuing loyalty, dependability, courage, and independence above other traits. These were the "manly qualities" that marked a man as fit for public office and that were best revealed in face-to-face encounters. Slavery also heightened the importance of loyalty to and dependability in the community, as well as ferocity and willingness to use violence if necessary. In short, in the southern context, a man's value and ability to earn respect from fellow men depended on qualities that were most easily knowable through personal interaction. In politics, this meant that parties interfered with the most vital imperatives of male culture and conflicted with the demands of honor and slavery.[11]

Mississippi's parties did have support, especially from editors, national politicians, and some core activists, but the bulk of voters chose not to follow their lead whenever possible. In national and state races in which fewer voters could know candidates personally, they often followed party labels out of necessity, although they still complained loudly about the evils of party organization. Below the state level, party activists failed to bring about county nominations or impose any regular control of local elections. Instead, most local politics revolved around networks of family, friends, and neighbors, a set of community bonds in which men relied primarily on their own and their families' reputations and resources. Thus if parties failed to develop into institutions of mass popular loyalty and had only a limited impact in the great majority of elections, the importance of families and neighborhood remained more evident.[12]

Certainly one of the most intensely studied aspects of political history has been voting behavior. Since the late 1960s, in particular, political historians have found new sources and developed new methodologies aimed at uncovering who voted for whom and why. The "new political history" gave us a much greater understanding of the social bases of party politics. Despite the ever more sophisticated use of multivariate and ecological regression, however, historians still struggle to separate the relative influences of class, ethnicity, religion, and residence among the many reasons that voters made the choices they did. Generally, historians and political scientists all contend that, in some way, family was (and is) the most important factor, but to what extent its influence was subsumed within the other variables remains debated.[13]

Many individuals remembered the decisive influence of one family member. "I found myself a democrat without being able to explain why I was of that party," remembered Mississippi politician Wiley P. Harris. "My uncle was a staunch Jackson man and I adopted his preferences without examination, . . . knowing nothing of the Force Bill, regarding 'nullification' as a heresy without knowing what it meant."[14] Most historians of the antebellum South likewise concur that residence and family shaped voting behavior and that families generally had a great influence on all political choices. But they remain conflicted about the relative importance of families and neighborhoods versus parties and ideology.[15] Of course, effective parties and neighborhood voting behavior were not mutually exclusive, and partisanship within voting districts remained common due to the efforts of party activists and the influence of important families that persisted.[16]

In Mississippi, association between voting districts and households often began with the organization of a county. Polling places tended to be country stores, churches, and especially the homes of prominent settlers. In Harrison County on the Gulf Coast, the first polling stations were the courthouse and four residences. The first Bolivar County precincts were referenced to the homes of early settlers: "The fourth district extends from Orrin Kingsley's down the river to the line between Dr. Dodd's and Colonel Field's, including all back settlements." Elsewhere in the rural South this was also typical. In Louisiana's St. John the Baptist Parish, for instance, precincts included "the plantation of Pierre Millet on the left bank of the Mississippi" and "the plantation of Mistress Widow Marcellin Haydel, on the right bank of the Mississippi."[17]

While voting frequently took place in wealthy planters' homes, election supervisors also reflected the continuing importance of families. For each polling place, the board of police (the county government) appointed three inspectors who had broad power over voter qualifications and the actual ballots. According to state law, the "inspectors shall take care that the election is conducted fairly and agreeably to law, and shall be judges of the qualification of voters, and may examine any person offering to vote." Three clerks also served, recording the names of voters and helping count ballots after the poll closed. And there was a returning officer who "shall, in the presence of the inspectors, put [each ballot] into the ballot-box." These small groups of men oversaw the right to vote in communities across the state. The boards of police chose the wealthiest planters, often longtime residents, as inspectors; returning officers were slightly younger and less prominent; and clerks included sons of the gentry and yeomen farmers. It was not unusual for fathers and sons to serve as inspector and clerk at the same precinct. And while Mississippi's wealthiest planters did not normally run for public office, many of them served as inspectors year after year. Evidently they recognized both the real and symbolic powers of guarding the right to vote.[18]

Election-day officials appointed in Bolivar County for 1855 were typical of antebellum Mississippi. Many of the county's original settlers and members of its most prominent families served as inspectors. At the third precinct, inspectors were Christopher Coffee, Joseph McGuire, and John V. Newman, all of whom owned more than fifty slaves and large tracts of prime cotton land. At the fourth precinct, Dr. John J. Ross was the poorest of the inspectors, although he owned thirty-six slaves and nearly $80,000 worth of property. Across the county, the average age of inspectors was about fifty years. Clerks, in contrast, were nearly all in their twenties, and many of them were leading planters' sons. Serving as a clerk was, for many of them, their first public responsibility in an expected lifetime of community service. Among the clerks was Robert E. Starke, twenty-year-old son of longtime state representative Peter B. Starke. The elder Starke owned nearly $200,000 in land and slaves. Other clerks were Isaac Bankston, son of Ignatius Bankston, one of the county's first settlers; James Ross, son of planter/physician John J. Ross; and young Joseph W. Elliot Jr., whose father settled Concordia Island along the great Mississippi River, in the county's first few years. Finally, there was Frank Montgomery, a future member of the board of police and son-in-law to Charles Clarke, a Civil War governor and, in 1855, the county's representative in the state legislature. Montgomery was the ideal clerk: a young, rising planter with "prospects." Serving as a clerk gave him the opportunity to meet local voters and establish himself as one of the community's leaders.[19]

Bolivar's fourth precinct offers a particularly telling case study of the ways in which families and households were central to antebellum Mississippi's political culture. The polling place was William Vick's "Nitta Yuma" plantation—literally the front veranda of the main house of one of the state's wealthiest families. Vick and his home already had a long history in young Bolivar County (it was sparsely populated until the early 1840s), having hosted the first board of police meeting and serving as an unofficial courthouse for several more years. Vick, according to one early resident, was known for his hospitality; "his home was the gathering place for the young people of the county." The three inspectors in 1855 were Vick himself and two of his fellow planters and neighbors, Christopher Field and Dr. John Ross. As each voter received the nod of approval from these three county squires, he handed his ballot to William E. Starke Jr., nephew of the aforementioned Peter B. Starke. Just twenty-two years old, William Starke already owned more than thirty slaves and several hundred acres of prime cotton land along the Mississippi River. Furthermore, his uncle Peter was a longtime acquaintance of William Vick, both of whom helped settle the area around Lake Bolivar and Bolivar's Landing. Having voted, men then recorded their names with one of the clerks, who included Robert E. Starke (Peter's son and William's cousin) and Dr. Ross's son, John Jr.[20] The arrangement on Vick's veranda surely conveyed certain messages to the community, most obviously those of power and hierarchy, introducing new residents to the county's leading men and their families while simultaneously reaffirming old friendships.

The suggestive scenes such as those from Bolivar County and William Vick's plantation, of course, also speak to the political continuity of neighborhoods. Inspectors could influence local farmers, who often depended on their wealthier neighbors' generosity or small loans at harvest time. Voters used printed ballots, but voting was far from secret; ballots printed by political parties usually varied in size and color, for instance. County and local candidates often did not appear on ballots, requiring voters to write in their selections. How many decided it was easier to announce their choices and then let one of the clerks record the candidates' names? Illiterate voters had few options. According to census figures, about 10 percent of Mississippi's adult white men were illiterate in 1850, although by a modern definition of "functional illiteracy," the rate was almost certainly at least twice that figure. In short, for a variety of reasons, it was often quite easy to establish a voter's choices, leaving poorer men vulnerable to pressure from the neighborhood's leading citizens. Tenants, the most disadvantaged voters of all, probably faced the most direct pressure. Not everyone voted alike in rural neighborhoods, but there was remarkable unanimity at the local level. How much of that came from genuine community bonding and how much from pressure by leading citizens remains difficult to know.[21]

The importance of households, families, and neighborhood associations was clear in nearly all of Mississippi's elections, but was always most evident in county and local contests. One indication was the overwhelming support that county and district candidates received in their home precincts—support from family, friends, and neighbors that was critical for success. In Mississippi's Marshall County, for instance, the 1858 elections proved typical. Five men ran for tax assessor: Thomas H. Smith, the eventual winner, received 220 of 241 votes cast in four adjacent precincts; the southeast corner of the county supported local resident B. R. Long. The other three candidates each received his highest total in the precinct nearest his home. The three candidates for surveyor similarly divided the county into geographic regions. Winner William Rudery's totals in the eastern precincts were 112 of 115 votes at Snow Creek, 31 of 37 at Hudsonville, 162 of 183 at Waterford, 117 of 118 at Cornersville, and all 86 votes at Belldazzle. Second-place J. C. Babb controlled northwestern Marshall County, winning 149 of 160 votes at Byhalia and 63 of 65 at Oak Grove. Distant third-place candidate J. G. Wilson received over 80 percent of the vote in his home precinct of Chullahoma, the largest precinct in southwestern Marshall County. The vast majority of Mississippi's county elections followed similar patterns, and voting returns from most contests showed no relationship to the party lines drawn in national elections.[22]

In a general sense, residence nearly always appears to be the most important factor influencing men's votes, although the complex networks of friends and relatives that county and local candidates relied upon are, of course, difficult to trace. One commentary on how families could be decisive came from Reuben Davis, a Mississippi politician who eventually served in the U.S. Congress. In his first campaign, Davis remembered that his friends warned him that his opponent, Thomas J. Word, would be a difficult man to beat. Known for his handsome features, Word was also a longtime resident, a polished stump speaker, and according to one resident, "a good fellow, tells a capital story, and plays the fiddle." But Davis soon met an old family acquaintance, Colonel William Duncan, who pledged the votes of his friends and family from throughout Tippah County. Davis also impressed the local Methodist minister, who appreciated the candidate's religious upbringing (Davis's father was a Baptist preacher) and took a liking to Davis's wife, a "most devout Methodist." The morning after meeting the minister, Davis remembered, "there was a large crowd at [the] tavern, most of them members of his church." Davis also made friends with the local tavern owner, who "worked for me manfully until the election." After another speech, one man told Davis that he had known his father and pledged the votes of his family and as many fellow church members as he could bring to the polls. Davis concluded, "It seemed that I was to learn on that occasion how large a part family friendship can play in such cases."[23]

Elections for local offices demonstrated even more clearly how residence determined men's votes. For the board of police and other county offices, candidates received strong support in their home precinct, but in rare instances, some recording officers separated vote totals to the subprecinct level. In those cases, the power of neighborhoods became particularly evident. In the 1855 contests for justice of the peace and constable in Amite County, votes were polled at "Smith's Box" and "Spurlock's Box" (both polling stations named for their owners). The three candidates for two justice of the peace positions were Eli S. Westbrook, Reiley Corcoran, and John C. Wilson. Westbrook and Corcoran received every vote cast at Smith's Box but none at Spurlock's; Wilson got every vote at Spurlock's and none at Smith's. For constable, the two winning candidates received all of their votes at Smith's Box, while the losing candidate received all of his votes, and all of the votes cast, at Spurlock's. In Carroll County, first district voters showed similar support for their neighbors. In the board of police contest in 1855, William McD Martin was victorious thanks to 113 of 120 votes at his home in Black Hawk precinct; his opponent, Patrick H. Brown, won every vote at his home in Greenwood. For justice of the peace, John W. McRae and Simon Lane, both from Black Hawk, won through nearly unanimous support from the voters at the two polling places nearest their homes. In Carroll County's second district—composed of three precincts: Smith's Mills, Point LeFlore, and Jefferson—no one from Point LeFlore or Jefferson even bothered to vote for constable, since all three candidates lived in Smith's Mills. In short, men voted—at least in part, if not primarily—in order to register their support for neighbors.[24]

These and countless other examples from across antebellum Mississippi underscored the continuing importance of neighborhood connections, rooted in the relationships within and between families. Of course, extra-family associations also were evident: churches, political parties, militia companies, and voluntary associations all held the loyalties of Mississippians. But judging by most men's voting behavior, neighborhoods remained the most important frame of reference. Consider the outlook of Mississippi's sometime state geologist Benjamin L. C. Wailes. A writer, naturalist, and traveler, Wailes had just recently returned from the nation's capital and Philadelphia in 1860, but when he recorded the momentous presidential election in his meticulous journal, his perspective was inevitably local: "At this precinct, Bell & Everitt received [blank space] votes."[25]

Neighborhood issues often came to the forefront of politics and public debate in antebellum Mississippi. And the confused nature of county and local contests underscores the difficulty and uncertainty of trying to link grassroots behavior to national issues or party labels. In response to a call for county partisanship, one Mississippi editor predicted (correctly) that voters would not replace neighborhood priorities with party loyalty: "All county and local interests, whether a man shall travel five miles or twenty-five miles to court all his life . . . whether the produce of the farmers shall be forwarded to market by good turnpikes or through nearly impassable bottoms, &c. . . . are all *neighborhood* questions." The impact of these local issues affected state races as well. Between 1857 and 1859, the Democratic and Know Nothing Parties in Jasper County both came apart over a dizzying combination of issues surrounding the location of the courthouse. The race for state senator from the district was even worse, involving several candidates, the Jasper courthouse dispute, the international slave trade, a Democratic tax resolution to support railroad development in the area, whether or not to use tax money to support public schools, and an ongoing controversy over ministers running for elective office. In other words, even elections for state offices that seemingly turned on questions of partisanship did not often connect to state, much less national, issues and organizations.[26] Instead, they depended upon neighborhood, friendship, and family connections and relationships.

Families could also use elected or appointed offices to gain an advantage in the local economy. Men who served as sheriffs, tax assessors, surveyors, or county legislators often had access to information before the general public and were in a position to influence local policies. When, in the 1820s, members of the Calvert-Keesee extended family moved to Tuscaloosa County, Alabama, they soon populated a range of local offices even as they prospered financially. Family members served as justice of the peace, constable, and overseer of the poor in the county's early years. Thomas Keesee, one of the family's leaders, also saw his daughter Jane marry Tuscaloosa sheriff Elias Jenkins, further extending the family's influence in local politics. Established families like the Calvert-Keesee clan could also steer favors to less wealthy relatives. Blacksmith James Hicks (who owned no slaves), for instance, was married to one of the Keesee grandchildren, and that affiliation surely helped him receive contracts for county work that netted him more than fifty dollars in fees in 1839. That county government was often held together, at least in part, by a web of extended family relationships has been demonstrated in study after study across the Old South.[27]

Beyond voting behavior, officeholding, and governance, families played a central role when communities determined voter eligibility and when local activists worked to encourage electoral participation. There was no national definition of citizenship in antebellum America, and each state set its own requirements for voting. Particularly from the 1820s forward, the national trend favored universal adult white male suffrage, and most states moved to eliminate or greatly reduce tax-paying and wealth requirements.[28]

Despite these trends, however, various impediments to voting remained in all states, most obviously age, gender, race, and residency, but also wealth in some places. In North Carolina, for instance, suffrage was still limited by class distinctions in elections for state senator until 1857. This meant that all voters cast ballots for governor and the state's lower house, but freeholders proceeded to a separate poll with separate inspectors where they exercised the more exclusive privilege of voting for senator.[29] And everywhere, poll observers—either supervisors or other citizens—could challenge a particular voter's right to cast a ballot. In Alabama, for instance, "Any person offering to vote, may be challenged by the returning officer, by either of the inspectors, or by any qualified elector." In some states (Georgia, for example), the challenged voter could take an additional oath that allowed him to vote, with his name and vote recorded in case the result was contested. Typically, though, election inspectors proceeded to an immediate interrogation. In Tennessee, inspectors asked any question they "think material to ascertain the qualifications of the person offering to vote" and "swear any bystander as to the right and qualification of such person to vote." These questions often sparked immediate debate in which the potential voter had to "defend" his age, race, or residency, often calling on family members to help his "case."[30]

When suffrage was limited by property restrictions, as in North Carolina, long and convoluted debates about deeds and titles frequently required men to provide documentation of their freehold status. Sons who worked family lands often called their fathers or uncles to testify that title to the land had been transferred legally. These debates sometimes underscored the precarious position that young, particularly unmarried, men occupied, as they needed older men to vouch for them. On the other hand, these instances also demonstrated how family members supported young men and testified to the power of family lineage. This was also true when men debated the distinctions between owning or renting from family members versus "strangers," and between holding formal title or "physical possession" of the land, which was often recognized as informal title. All of these cases underscored the central place of family members and family connections in voter eligibility, putting young men with established, successful fathers or uncles in a very strong position.

Family members also took center stage in discussions involving residency. These included cases of men who farmed lands that straddled counties or election precincts, putting their ultimate "home" in question. Some voters relied on fathers, mothers, or siblings to support their contention for residency. In contested election cases, lawyers frequently asked voters about their individual intentions and family connections: Had he always considered himself an American citizen? Had he intended to remain in the United States when he arrived? Where had he intended to make a home? Where did he sleep more than half the time? Where did he have his washing done? As one lawyer asked about a disputed voter, "Did not his mother remain in the Parish, & had she not charge of his clothing too?"[31] The answers to these questions, of course, involved families. Put simply, a husband with a family and his own household had a significant advantage over a single man when trying to establish residency or citizenship. A family "of his own" helped establish a young man as an independent head of household and a voter.

Besides the disposition of laundry, the problem that most often drew women into the process was age. Nineteenth-century Americans were notoriously vague about birth dates; many young men declared they were "about twenty-one years" old. Some brought their mothers with them to the polling place or referenced the family Bible. One stepfather revealed more about his own parenting, one suspects, than his stepson's age when he declared the boy not yet of age and "still under his control." He thought if the boy "was of age he would want to get away [from me]." Questions of residency and "householder" status called into doubt a man's personal independence. Ironically, he often needed family members, particularly his parents, to help establish his eligibility. Married men had an advantage in all of these debates, even those who still lived with parents. As historian Hendrik Hartog notes, nineteenth-century marriage was, at least in part, a "political institution" that helped a man establish himself as a "competent adult."[32]

These debates over age, residency, or freehold status manifested the tensions between southern fathers and sons as the younger generation grew to adulthood. Taught from a young age to respect and defer to elders, some young men struggled to assert themselves when it came time to make their own mark in the world. Bertram Wyatt-Brown has argued that while the ethic of honor provided rules that helped order southern society, its strictures presented men with a basic dilemma: the honor in respecting one's "betters" conflicted with the need to establish one's own place in society, which pushed men to be aggressive in search of personal aggrandizement. This tension was likewise inherent within families as a young man came of age, often needing the assistance of his father, uncle, or father-in-law to start a career or establish his own household, yet needing to demonstrate personal independence as a part of his nascent manhood. The egalitarian social and economic ideology, and to some extent reality, of antebellum America only heightened the competition for status inherent to honor and manhood.[33]

To mitigate the ever-present competitiveness, men took part in public activities and rituals that united competing generations and different classes. Some of the most important and ubiquitous were hunting, drinking, and gambling. In this context, voting too was a ritual that men, including fathers and sons, often did together—a coming-of-age moment that marked a young man as independent and sovereign, yet an act of adulthood that depended, either directly or indirectly, on his father and family. Like the Langfords who voted together in that August 1853 election in Brandon, Mississippi, fathers and sons provided perhaps the most basic family relationship that defined the Old South's political culture.[34]

Like other all-male community rituals—militia musters, slave patrols and insurrection scares, court days—voting also reinforced the essential gender division within southern (and American) society. Women participated in politics in other ways, but they could never vote. Elections could certainly be rowdy and violent, often fueled by liquor, and for many participants elections lasted most of the day and into the evening. These characteristics made election day similar to the other public events from which women were excluded. Voting was also a neighborhood event that brought together men from different classes, helping to unite white men and foster community solidarity. This imperative was always greater, of course, in the South where men were expected to protect their families from the next Nat Turner. Elections, then, helped mediate class and generational differences within every neighborhood. The franchise marked all white men, no matter how poor, with a basic equality, even if men from wealthier families dominated public office and expected (sometimes demanded) support from poor folks.[35]

Beyond disputes over age, residency, or class, contested elections also revealed a lively debate over race. Here again, family members provided critical evidence that might allow or disallow voters. In South Carolina, particularly along the coast and in Charleston, for example, voters were often challenged for being "nonwhite" and not entitled to vote. Testifying about one disputed voter, James Valentine, witness Peter Pye described him as "a very dark Mulatto," and the woman reputed to be his mother "as dark as any common negro." In contrast, Joseph Brown could "not say she was a black women—she was what I would call a mulatto." About another man, one inspector asked several witnesses, "Has not said Fitzpatrick been always looked upon as a colored man?" In defending Fitzpatrick, others asserted that he once presented a certificate attesting to his mother's "whiteness." And while several witnesses admitted that William Ferrell was "a colored man," he had always been allowed to vote because Ferrell had once produced a certificate stating that his grandmother was "a white woman and an Irish woman." One man admitted "the old woman" "had every appearance of a white woman."[36] Thus connections to women as family members—usually as wives or mothers—were important determinants of race and, therefore, of eligibility to vote.

Among all voters, the most scrutinized were men who lived or worked on the margins of the community, especially occupations that required frequent travel: stage drivers, peddlers, circuit riders, teachers, itinerant farmhands, Irish canal and ditch diggers, immigrant seamen, tenants, and the poor in general. In the end, inspectors frequently disenfranchised many of these men, either by law, personal choice, or the judgment of the community. Thus men (and occasionally women) used elections to debate and negotiate the public parameters of race, age, residency, class, and citizenship. Their testimony reveals how legal norms often conflicted or intermingled with community tradition. Local standards usually prevailed, and election inspectors enjoyed great latitude interpreting the qualifications for suffrage. Later investigations normally did not overturn the judgments made by election-day inspectors, verdicts that seemed to reflect whatever collective wisdom the community possessed on these questions. Voter eligibility for these vaguely defined requirements often turned, either directly or indirectly, on family connections or evidence from family members.

Families, particularly women, proved crucial as well to party and community organizers who hoped to lure young men to public events in order to court their votes. According to historian Elizabeth Varon, the presence of women at party events began seriously with the 1840 presidential election. Their participation lent an "air of respectability" to what were previously all-male gatherings known for liquor and general rowdiness—part of an ideal of civic duty that Varon calls "Whig womanhood." Whig leaders transformed women's attendance at party functions into a means to influence voters' choices, with mothers, sisters, and sweethearts working on their men to support the partisan cause. If Whigs pioneered this strategy in 1840, other parties quickly followed suit in the years that followed. By the 1850s, women were regular participants at all party events and regularly touted as legitimate forces in the battle for voters. This place for women (and children) was evident in many accounts from Mississippi. "There was a large number of ladies present," wrote one correspondent of a barbecue in 1856 Noxubee County, "and by mingling amid the crowd tempered that exuberance of feeling that sometimes mars festive occasions."[37]

More typically, notices that appealed to young men made it apparent that young women would be attending campaign events. In Claiborne County, Mississippi, one group of party leaders announced a barbecue in Grand Gulf for the 1851 gubernatorial campaign: "They desire that the ladies . . . shall grace the proceedings with their presence, and add to the pleasure and importance of the day." They went on to assure Claiborne's women there would be "especial preparation for their comfort and accommodation on the grounds." Even more obvious were the young men of Vicksburg, who sponsored a "Free Barbecue and Fish Fry" during the 1849 campaign. They invited all "the ladies and gentlemen of Warren county" and "hoped all will attend," but "most especially the Ladies." One group of Democrats similarly announced a barbecue to be held in early October 1855, planning for three thousand people. "Know Nothings, as well as Democrats, are invited," they said, "and especially the Ladies." Determined to attract young voters—those most likely to be uncommitted—to hear their party's message, activists emphasized the presence of young women. As one Democrat recounted the "Bran Dance at Quitman Springs" for his local newspaper, "At the usual hour, a very large crowd composed of candidates for office *and* candidates for matrimony were congregated under the spacious arbor, anxiously awaiting the first notes of the soul-stirring violin"—part political rally, part singles dance.[38]

Women also wrote letters to newspapers, debating current issues and events, and occasionally even advocating for their favorite political party. "I cannot consistently with my own inclination," wrote one Yazoo City woman, "resist the urgent pleadings of the ladies of *our* party, who are anxious that some remarks be made upon the address."[39] Her contribution to the local newspaper was part of a lengthy exchange among several women debating the Know Nothing tactic of involving young people in politics. Women also appeared as "inspiration" for whatever cause a particular group or party advocated. They marched in parades as symbols of "lady liberty," the Union, states' rights, or secession.

In one typical promotion, a group of women created some sort of award to inspire local partisans. In 1849, the Jackson (Mississippi) Democratic Ladies Association agreed to award a banner—sewn by the women themselves, of course—to the partisans of whatever county in the third district posted the greatest increase in Democratic votes from the previous year's presidential election. The banner depicted the Goddess of Liberty on one side, arrayed before a landscape of sea and mountains, pointing skyward toward a time-honored Democratic motto: "The Price of Liberty is Eternal Vigilance." "What democrat will not feel an ambition to gain this tribute of woman's esteem," a local editor proclaimed. "She is now with us in our noble battle; her prayers are offered up for our success, and we have but to do our duty to be victorious." The women presented the banner to the winning county's Democrats. The editor gushed on: "The crowd of beautiful women who will gather around that banner and uphold it, the speech that one of their number will make, and the rejoicings over our glorious victory will animate every heart with joy, [and] will be [a] welcome such as the proudest warrior might envy." The "Ladies of Jackson" eventually presented the banner to Newton County's Democrats. Isabella Matthews, daughter of Governor Joseph Matthews, complimented the winning Democrats and expressed the women's "deep and thrilling interest." After several more speeches, the men and women of Jackson dined and danced into the evening. "The bright eyes and smiles of the ladies will linger in the memories of their young chevaliers for many a day, and none will ever regret having mingled in festivities in which so much good feeling and flow of soul prevailed."[40]

By the late 1840s and 1850s, political events in the rural South occupied part of what historical sociologist Karen Hansen describes as the "social sphere" of antebellum society. Preoccupied with the private/public dichotomy that more accurately describes emerging middle-class life in the cities, historians have underappreciated the sort of events that brought together men and women of all classes and which occurred more regularly in rural areas. For rural women, the social and economic connections with the men in their families remained more important than bonds with other women. "The kinship system," writes historian Nancy Grey Osterud, "identified them as wives and mothers, daughters and sisters," and "linked women to men" in ways that "were powerful and nearly all-encompassing."[41] In the absence of strong institutions, families still provided stronger bonds for most men and women, both in public and private.

If women in antebellum New England had few chances for the sort of same-sex clubs and associations that urban, middle-class women enjoyed, consider how limited those opportunities were in the rural Deep South. For many families, campaign events came to fill that place in the "social sphere" of men, women, and even children. In that setting, families could have a great effect on men's political beliefs and behavior. Equally important, however, was the meaning that politics had for families and particularly for women. Men had numerous public events that brought them together for official or social reasons, but campaign events— especially by the 1840s—offered one of the few chances for a whole family to attend something together. This family function, of course, could include extended kin, too, making it possible for women to meet with sisters, female cousins, and in-laws, providing a social outlet for people so often isolated in their rural homes. Thus, while election day separated men and women and reinforced the great gender divide, other political activities and events brought them together.

Politics in the Old South was founded in the region's rural, kin-based neighborhoods, and even after national parties came to dominate elsewhere, they remained less effective in the South's often antiparty, family-based political culture. This was more true in the Deep South than most parts of the country and even other parts of the South. Socioeconomic, ethnic, and religious diversity, urban growth and greater population density, and a greater acceptance of institutions fueled the popularity and power of political parties. Southerners, though, demonstrated a greater reluctance to substitute institutional for personal relationships, a tendency that extended to politics. Ties between extended family members, often expressed in neighborhood and community solidarity, remained at the heart of southern politics. From voting behavior to determining the right to suffrage to identifying the most relevant public issues, families helped define the region's antebellum political culture. Looking beyond state and national politics, beyond the ideologies expressed by party leaders, and beyond the symbols and slogans reprinted by partisan editors in state party organs, and instead reexamining more closely the rich diversity of local politics sheds critical light on the enduring functions and influence of extended families, households, and neighborhoods.

Notes

1. Secretary of state records, Rankin and Carroll counties, miscellaneous returns, Mississippi Department of Archives and History, Jackson; U.S. Census, population schedule, Carroll County, Mississippi, 1860; Mary Chesnut, quoted in Elizabeth Fox-Genovese, *Within the Plantation Household: Black and White Women of the Old South* (Chapel Hill: University of North Carolina Press, 1988), 342.

2. Among studies that trace relationships between extended families and the evolution of neighborhoods, including the development of economic and political power blocs, the best examples include Christopher Morris, *Becoming Southern: The Evolution of a Way of Life: Warren County and Vicksburg, Mississippi, 1770–1860* (New York: Oxford University Press, 1995); J. William Harris, *Plain Folk and Gentry in a Slave Society: White Liberty and Black Slavery in Augusta's Hinterlands* (Middletown, Conn.: Wesleyan University Press, 1985); Robert Kenzer, *Kinship and Neighborhood in a Southern Community: Orange County, North Carolina, 1849–1881* (Knoxville: University of Tennessee Press, 1987); Orville Vernon Burton, *In My Father's House Are Many Mansions: Family and Community in Edgefield, South Carolina* (Chapel Hill: University of North Carolina Press, 1985); Edward Baptist, *Creating an Old South: Middle Florida's Plantation Frontier before the Civil War* (Chapel Hill: University of North Carolina Press, 2002); Carolyn Earle Billingsley, *Communities of Kinship: Antebellum Families and the Settlement of the Cotton Frontier* (Athens: University of Georgia Press, 2004).

3. On Mississippi's antebellum economic and social evolution, see Morris, *Becoming Southern*; Bradley Bond, *Political Culture in the Nineteenth-Century South: Mississippi, 1830–1900* (Baton Rouge: Louisiana State University Press, 1995); Porter L. Fortune, "The Formative Period," and John Edmond Gonzales, "Flush Times, Depression, War, and Compromise," both in *A History of Mississippi*, 2 vols., ed. Richard Aubrey McLemore (Hattiesburg: University of Southern Mississippi Press, 1973), 1: 251–83, 284–309; John Hebron Moore, *The Emergence of the Cotton Kingdom in the Old Southwest: Mississippi, 1770–1860* (Baton Rouge: Louisiana State University Press, 1988).

4. The material from Mississippi is drawn from manuscript election returns and some published in newspapers, proceedings of county boards of police (local government), the U.S. censuses from 1850 and 1860, and various county and local records and histories. A more complete discussion of these sources can be found in Christopher J. Olsen, *Political Culture and Secession in Mississippi: Masculinity, Honor, and the Antiparty Tradition, 1830–1860* (New York: Oxford University Press, 2000), appendix.

5. McDowell, quoted in Elizabeth Varon, *We Mean to Be Counted: White Women and Poli-*

tics in Antebellum Virginia (Chapel Hill: University of North Carolina Press, 1998), 73. See also Catherine Allgor, *Parlor Politics: In Which the Ladies of Washington Help Build a City and a Government* (Charlottesville: University Press of Virginia, 2000); Kirsten E. Wood, *Masterful Women: Slaveholding Widows from the American Revolution through the Civil War* (Chapel Hill: University of North Carolina Press, 2004).

6. Joan E. Cashin, "The Structure of Antebellum Planter Families: 'The Ties that Bound us was Strong,'" *Journal of Southern History* 56 (February 1990): 70. Also Lorri Glover, *All Our Relations: Blood Ties and Emotional Bonds among the Early South Carolina Gentry* (Baltimore: Johns Hopkins University Press, 2000).

7. Among many others, see Stephanie McCurry, *Masters of Small Worlds: Yeomen Households, Gender Relations, and the Political Culture of the Antebellum South Carolina Low Country* (New York: Oxford University Press, 1995); Victoria Bynum, *Unruly Women: The Politics of Social and Sexual Control in the Old South* (Chapel Hill: University of North Carolina Press, 1992); Harris, *Plain Folk and Gentry in a Slave Society*; Kenzer, *Kinship and Neighborhood in a Southern Community*; Burton, *In My Father's House Are Many Mansions*; Martin Crawford, "Political Society in a Southern Mountain Community: Ashe County, North Carolina, 1850–1861," *Journal of Southern History* 55 (August 1989): 373–90; Ralph Mann, "Mountains, Land, and Kin Networks: Burkes Garden, Virginia, in the 1840s and 1850s," *Journal of Southern History* 58 (August 1992): 411–34.

8. Christopher J. Olsen, "Women and Party Politics in the Old South: Mississippi in the 1840s and 1850s," *Journal of Women's History* 11 (autumn 1999): 104–25; Olsen, "'Molly Pitcher' of the Mississippi Whigs: The Editorial Career of Mrs. Harriet N. Prewett," *Journal of Mississippi History* 58 (winter 1996): 237–54; Daniel Dupre, "Barbecues and Pledges: Electioneering and the Rise of Democratic Politics in Antebellum Alabama," *Journal of Southern History* 60 (August 1994): 479–512; Varon, *We Mean to Be Counted*; Ronald P. Formisano, "The Role of Women in the Dorr Rebellion," *Rhode Island History* 44 (May 1985): 89–104; Janet L. Coryell, *Neither Heroine nor Fool: Anna Ella Carroll of Maryland* (Kent, Ohio: Kent State University Press, 1990); Jayne Crumpler DeFiore, "'COME, and Bring the Ladies': Tennessee Women and the Politics of Opportunity during the Presidential Campaigns of 1840 and 1844," *Tennessee Historical Quarterly* 51 (January 1992): 197–212.

9. Ronald P. Formisano, *The Transformation of Political Culture: Massachusetts Parties, 1790s–1840s* (New York: Oxford University Press, 1983); Alan Tully, *Forming American Politics: Ideals, Interests, and Institutions in Colonial New York and Pennsylvania* (Baltimore: Johns Hopkins University Press, 1994). On the upper South, see Daniel W. Crofts, *Old Southampton: Politics and Society in a Virginia County, 1834–1869* (Charlottesville: University Press of Virginia, 1992); Crofts, *Reluctant Confederates: Upper South Unionists in the Secession Crisis* (Chapel Hill: University of North Carolina Press, 1989), esp. chap. 2; William G. Shade, *Democratizing the Old Dominion: Virginia and the Second Party System, 1824–1861* (Charlottesville: University Press of Virginia, 1996).

10. J. Mills Thornton III, *Politics and Power in a Slave Society: Alabama, 1800–1860* (Baton Rouge: Louisiana State University Press, 1978); George C. Rable, *The Confederate Republic: A Revolution against Politics* (Chapel Hill: University of North Carolina Press, 1994); Kenneth Greenberg, *Masters and Statesmen: The Political Culture of American Slavery* (Baltimore: Johns Hopkins University Press, 1985).

11. Bertram Wyatt-Brown, *Southern Honor: Ethics and Behavior in the Old South* (New York: Oxford University Press, 1983); Edward L. Ayers, *Vengeance and Justice: Crime and Punishment in the Nineteenth-Century American South* (New York: Oxford University Press, 1985); Christopher Waldrep, *Roots of Disorder: Race and Criminal Justice in the American South, 1817–1880* (Urbana: University of Illinois Press, 1998); Olsen, *Political Culture and Secession in Mississippi*, chaps. 1 and 3.

12. For a longer discussion of these themes, see Olsen, *Political Culture and Secession in Mississippi*, chaps. 3–5.

13. One summary of this earlier literature is Ronald P. Formisano, "The New Political History," *International Journal of Social Education* 1 (January 1986): 5–21. Among many works by political scientists, see Eleanor E. Maccoby, Richard E. Matthews, and Alton S. Morton, "Youth and Political Change," in *Political Behavior: A Reader in Theory and Research*, ed. Heinz Eulau, Samuel J. Eldersveld, and Morris Janowitz (Glencoe, Ill.: Free Press, 1956), 299–307; Paul Allen Beck and M. Kent Jennings, "Family Traditions, Political Periods, and the Development of Partisan Orientations," *Journal of Politics* 53 (August 1991): 742–63.

14. Wiley P. Harris, "Autobiography of Wiley P. Harris," in *Courts, Judges, and Lawyers of Mississippi, 1798–1935*, ed. Dunbar Rowland (Jackson: Department of Archives and History and Mississippi Historical Society, 1935), 287.

15. Among many others, see Kenzer, *Kinship and Neighborhood*; Thornton, *Politics and Power*; Morris, *Becoming Southern*.

16. See esp. Shade, *Democratizing the Old Dominion*, and Thornton, *Politics and Power*.

17. John H. Lang, *History of Harrison County, Mississippi* (Gulfport, Miss.: Dixie Press, 1936), 6–9; Wirt A. Williams, ed., *History of Bolivar County, Mississippi, Compiled by Florence Warfield Sillers* (Jackson, Miss.: Delta State Teachers College, 1948), 16; Albert L. Lieutaud Collection, Tulane University Library, New Orleans. One of the most complete discussions of settlement and the evolution of neighborhoods is Morris, *Becoming Southern*; see also Joan Cashin, *A Family Venture: Men and Women on the Southern Frontier* (Baltimore: Johns Hopkins University Press, 1991); Baptist, *Creating an Old South*; Billingsley, *Communities of Kinship*; and Olsen, *Political Culture and Secession*, chap. 1.

18. William L. Sharkey et al., *The Revised Code of the Statute Laws of the State of Mississippi* (Jackson, Miss.: State Printer, 1857), 90–93. In Mississippi, the socioeconomic profile of election inspectors made them wealthier than all county and district candidates, including state representatives. See Olsen, *Political Culture and Secession in Mississippi*, chap. 6 and appendix.

19. Bolivar County, Board of Police minutes, 1854–1855; U.S. Census, population and slave schedules, Bolivar County, 1850, 1860; Goodspeed, *Biographical and Historical Memoirs of Mississippi*, 2 vols. (Chicago: Goodspeed, 1891), 1: 593.

20. Williams, ed., *Bolivar County*, 10–11, 128–29, 475.

21. On coercion, see esp. Charles Bolton, *Poor Whites of the Antebellum South: Tenants and Laborers in Central North Carolina and Northeast Mississippi* (Durham, N.C.: Duke University Press, 1994), 112–26, 180–83.

22. Secretary of state records, Marshall County, 1858, Mississippi Department of Archives and History. Also Olsen, *Political Culture and Secession in Mississippi*, chaps. 4–5.

23. Reuben Davis, *Reminiscences of Mississippi and Mississippians* (Cambridge, Mass.: Riverside Press, 1889), 66–70.

24. Secretary of state records, Amite and Carroll counties, 1855, Mississippi Department of Archives and History. Such detailed returns for state and national—normally considered partisan—elections are not generally available, and county or precinct data tend to obscure neighborhood influence. Often very small rural precincts, however, those encompassing perhaps one recognizable neighborhood, did record dramatically uneven party votes, perhaps indicating the influence of neighborhoods on partisanship. As one example, the three smallest precincts in Amite County in 1843 divided along party lines in the governor's race as follows: 67 to 5, 39 to 5, and 23 to 6.

25. Benjamin L. C. Wailes Diary, 6 November 1860, Benjamin L. C. Wailes Collection, Perkins Library, Duke University, Durham, N.C.

26. This can be traced in relevant newspapers: *Southron* (Jackson), 17 September 1847; *Eastern Clarion* (Paulding), 4 May, 1 and 8 June, 17 and 31 August, 7, 14, and 21 September 1859.

27. Billingsley, *Communities of Kinship*, chap. 4, details the connection between political and economic power within the Calvert-Keesee kinship group in several locations.

28. One summary of this period and these trends in suffrage is Alexander Keyssar, *The Right to Vote: The Contested History of Democracy in the United States* (New York: Basic Books, 2000), chaps. 1–4.

29. A good example of separate inspectors appointed for each office, and corresponding ballot boxes, is found in the John Vann Papers, North Carolina Division of Archives and History, Raleigh.

30. John J. Ormond, Arthur P. Bagby, and George Goldthwaite, *The Code of Alabama* (Montgomery, Ala.: Brittan De Wolf, 1852), 97; William A. Hotchkiss, *Codifications of the Statute Law of Georgia* (Savannah: John M. Cooper, 1845), 104; also *Code of Georgia* (Savannah: John M. Cooper, 1863), 235–37; A.O.P. Nicholson, *Statute Laws of the State of Tennessee* (Nashville: J. G. Shepard, 1846), 153.

31. South Carolina, General Assembly, Committee Reports, 1824, contested election from St. Bartholomew's Parish, microfilm, South Carolina Department of Archives and History, Columbia.

32. South Carolina, General Assembly, Committee Reports, 1848, contested election from St. James Goose Creek Parish, microfilm, South Carolina Department of Archives and History; Hendrik Hartog, *Man and Wife in America: A History* (Cambridge: Harvard University Press, 2000), 22.

33. Wyatt-Brown, *Southern Honor*, esp. part 2. More recent studies that examine the conflict between adolescence and manhood in the Old South include Robert F. Pace, *Halls of Honor: College Men in the Old South* (Baton Rouge: Louisiana State University Press, 2004); Lorri Glover, *Southern Sons: Becoming Men in the New Nation* (Baltimore: Johns Hopkins University Press, 2007). Glover argues that manhood and masculinity in the Old South need to be examined independent of honor, a paradigm that she contends has prevented southern historians from engaging men's studies. Manhood, she writes, is "less static" than honor, and southerners' understanding of manhood "included but transcended honor" (2). Nonetheless, she emphasizes that southern masculinity "required boldness and autonomy," demanded that southern boys learn to "'act the part' of men," and that a "boy became a man only when he convinced his community that he was one" (3). Furthermore, the "foundational values [of manhood] of autonomy and duty [were] taught to boys in childhood" (4). Finally, like nearly every student of southern

honor and masculinity, Glover emphasizes that manhood was precarious and earned, not conferred by being born white or wealthy: "He had to learn to perform the elaborate conventions of southern masculinity if he wanted public affirmation of his manhood" (24). These points make the distinction between manhood and honor less evident than it might seem.

34. Among a number of excellent works that examine the notion of "male bonding" rituals, see Ted Ownby, *Subduing Satan: Religion, Recreation, and Manhood in the Rural South, 1865–1920* (Chapel Hill: University of North Carolina Press, 1990); Dickson Bruce, *Violence and Culture in the Antebellum South* (Austin: University of Texas Press, 1978).

35. See Olsen, *Political Culture and Secession in Mississippi*, chaps. 1 and 6; Steven Stowe, *Intimacy and Power: Ritual in the Lives of the Planters* (Baltimore: Johns Hopkins University Press, 1987); McCurry, *Masters of Small Worlds*. One study that details the link between voting, polling places, and liquor (although in the North) is William J. Rorabaugh, "Rising Democratic Spirits: Immigrants, Temperance, and Tammany Hall, 1854–1860," *Civil War History* 22 (June 1976): 138–57. There has been more work done on northern election violence—particularly in the 1850s—than for southern violence.

36. South Carolina, General Assembly, Committee Reports, 1824, contested election from St. Bartholomew's Parish.

37. Elizabeth Varon, "Tippecanoe and the Ladies, Too: White Women and Party Politics in Antebellum Virginia," *Journal of American History* 82 (September 1995): 494–521; Varon, *We Mean to Be Counted*, esp. chap. 3; *Hinds County Gazette*, 29 October 1856.

38. *Port Gibson Herald and Correspondent*, 8 August 1851; *Vicksburg Daily Whig*, 20 October 1849; *Democrat* (Columbus, Miss.), 29 September 1855; *Democratic Banner* (Holly Springs, Miss.), 5 August 1853.

39. *Weekly American Banner* (Yazoo City, Miss.), 20 July 1855 (emphasis added).

40. *Mississippian* (Jackson, Miss.), 2 and 16 November, 19 October 1849.

41. Karen V. Hansen, *A Very Social Time: Crafting Community in Antebellum New England* (Berkeley: University of California Press, 1994), esp. chap. 1; Nancy Grey Osterud, *Bonds of Community: The Lives of Farm Women in Nineteenth-Century New York* (Ithaca, N.Y.: Cornell University Press, 1991), 1–2. Osterud refers to "patterns of sociability" instead of the "social sphere." See also Joan M. Jensen, *Loosening the Bonds: Mid-Atlantic Farm Women, 1750–1850* (New Haven: Yale University Press, 1986).

10

A View of a Will

Miscegenation, Inheritance, and Family in Civil War Era Charleston

KEVIN NOBLE MAILLARD

~

In 1861, Mary Shrine accused her "white" and recently widowed cousin, Mary Remley, of being a black slave. Were the claim true, Remley and her son and two daughters—as slaves—could not legally stand as beneficiaries of Remley's deceased husband's will, thus enabling Shrine to inherit as the legitimate next of kin. The Remleys had always believed themselves to be free white persons, and they successfully defended their status as white and free in a state court. The mere accusation of slavery, however, imperiled their social standing within the white community.

Two years later, Mary Remley's daughters revisited the interracial issue again upon the 1863 death of their brother, Paul Durbin Remley. When Philis, his slave mistress, wrote to the sisters to inform them of her master/lover's death, her notification became a crucial element in the resulting litigation, raising questions of law and memory that challenged individuals' conception of family. In Durbin's will, he disinherited his sisters in favor of his slave mistress and their two children, Charles and Cecile. His sisters objected to the trust established for Philis and contested the will.

In re Remley demonstrates how courts constructed the idea of "family" in Charleston during the Civil War era. Paul Durbin Remley had two families: a white one and a black one. In his will, he favored the latter, but in its administration, the courts favored the former. Legally privileged individuals could rely upon law to undermine the interests of blacks and aggrandize the interests of whites, particularly in establishing definitions of family. In any will dispute, the testator optimally has the testamentary freedom to decide the distribution of his or her property. However, after his or her death, others may interpret this post-humous gift decree differently. Durbin's white relatives upheld a legal definition of "family" that effectively "cut out" or weakened the testamentary interests of his black family. In looking at his will—written in 1863 and executed in 1867—law influenced not only the parties' expectations of their legitimacy to inherit but also the monetary value of the contested property.

"South Carolina," countryman F. C. Adams wrote in 1853, "pursues a course in ordinance with the misconceptions of her people; and thus she claims to carry out her ordinances without regard to the feelings, rights, justice, or stipulation of the central government with other nations." On the eve of the Civil War, this was particularly evident in the state's unusual approach to race. Unlike other slave states, antebellum South Carolina had enacted no antimiscegenation law.[1] When the state finally enacted a prohibition on interracial marriage, it coincided with the end of the Civil War and the slave regime in the South. Antebellum South Carolina recognized a level of racial intermixture that confounds contemporary understandings of racial codes in the Old South. This intriguing anomaly reveals the fluidity of antebellum racial boundaries and calls into question the purity of white and black racial categories.

In his comprehensive study on American mulattoes, Joel Williamson commented that if Freud was only generally correct, "it is safe to assume that the lines of lust in the old South ran continually and in all directions." A northern traveler in South Carolina concurred: "The enjoyment of a Negro or mulatto woman is spoken of as quite a common thing; no reluctance, delicacy, or shame is made about the matter." Indeed, in antebellum Charleston, occasional marriages occurred between persons of color and well-regarded whites.[2]

Additionally, the state offered no enunciation of racial classification, relying instead on reputation rather than descent as a measurement of racial identity. In the 1831 case of *State v. Davis/State v. Hanna,* Justice William Harper eschewed the common southern practice of fractional genealogy, or the determination of race by blood quantum. In refusing mathematical calculation as the legal definition of "mulatto," Harper instead set a precedent that classified many persons as white whom other slave states would have classified as mulatto. His vague interpretation primarily relied on physical appearance instead of descent, recognizing that "every admixture of African blood with the European, or white, is not to be referred to the degraded class."[3]

Hypodescent, or the "one drop rule," claimed no place in South Carolina's antebellum legal history. Even with proof of African ancestry, South Carolina courts still declared some persons as white. In *State v. Cantey* (1835), objectors challenged the legitimacy of two white-appearing witnesses to testify in an in-dictment for larceny. Nonwhite persons were not allowed to serve as witnesses or jurors, and worried defendants sometimes attempted to paint key witnesses as racially questionable in order to block incriminating testimony. The witnesses, who were brothers, had a white father; their mother was a "descendent in the third degree of a half breed who had a white spouse," making the witnesses one-sixteenth black. An extraordinary history of white acceptance had run long in their family. Interestingly enough, their dark-skinned maternal grandfather held the reputation of a white man, and one of their relatives of the same "ad-mixture" married into a wealthy white family and ran for the state legislature. Describing the invisibility of black blood, Justice Harper concluded, "It would be an absurdity in terms to say that such an one is, in the popular sense of the word, a person of color." Arguing that remote African ancestry did not disturb the brothers' reputation as white, Harper dismissed the case, apologizing to the gentlemen for the "unnecessary violence."[4]

Racial reputation cases, infrequent in number, left race to the mercy of the judge's gavel or to the approval of the community. Like Harper, Judge Edward Frost argued in *White v. Tax Collector* (1846) that a strict legal definition of white and black did not provide a reliable measure of citizenship. Frost calculated "honesty, sobriety, and industry, and the qualities that unite in a respectable character" in perceiving and determining whiteness. Like Harper, Frost refused to establish a doctrine of racial determination, insisting that racial identity "be decided by public opinion, expressed in the verdict of a jury."[5] His stance allowed for subjective estimations of race. The way that others remembered or perceived a person—not what the person thought of him or herself—became the juridical definition of race in antebellum South Carolina.

The intersection of race, reputation, and law arose again in the Remley fam-ily. In November 1860, Paul Remley Sr., a free white man, died in Charleston, leaving his spouse, Mary, a farm in Pennsylvania consisting of "19.5 acres of poor land but healthy with two small storm houses on it, no farm buildings, one old shed." He appointed his son, Paul Durbin Remley—commonly known as Durbin—as administrator of the estate; he assumed the role on December 1. Remley was also survived by two daughters, Elizabeth and Emma, who also shared the profits of their father's estate.[6]

Conflict arose when Durbin filed for a grant of administration of his father's will on June 3, 1861. That day, a challenger questioned his legitimacy as an admin-istrator. Mary Shrine, claiming to be Durbin's second cousin, filed a complaint in a Charleston court alleging that Durbin and his sisters were ineligible because their mother, "the supposed widow of Paul Remley," was "a colored person" and that "she was purchased by said Paul Remley as a slave." Banking on Mary Remley's social incapacity as a black woman and a slave, Shrine attempted to position herself as the only legitimate heir. If she proved Mary Remley's slave status, then Durbin and his sisters would inherit her diminished status; they would become slaves and ineligible as legal heirs.[7] Even if the Remleys considered themselves free white persons, the possible hidden condition of their mother threatened the inheritance of their father's estate. The distinctions mattered: the case would decide not only issues of race versus reputation but also legal determination of one's basic rights. South Carolina, which held jurisdiction in this case, forbade bequests to slaves.[8]

In an effort to bolster their civic legitimacy, the Remleys offered testimony from "respectable" free white persons to verify their freedom and race. They employed Charlestonian Sam Wagner to testify to Mary's whiteness. As a member of Bethel Methodist Church, Wagner testified that Paul and Mary Remley were "always recognized as white persons in the use of all the privileges of the Church." He confirmed their status as "acceptable members" and active "Class Leaders," but remained curiously silent on the church's significant black and mulatto population, which at the time constituted the majority of Charleston's black Methodists.[9]

In the absence of supporting evidence for Shrine's accusation, Wagner's single affidavit proved sufficient. Characterizing the allegation as a "question of Pedigree and legitimacy," the court postponed its decision and granted Shrine one week to corroborate her claim. When she failed to do so, the court found Durbin legally competent to administer his father's estate, qualifying its ruling by distinguishing legitimacy for administration from legitimacy for distribution. Noting that the possible truth of Shrine's claim would not greatly affect the pending grant, the court conceded that "it may become so in a progress of settlement of assets of said Estate."[10]

Legally, the court's finding rendered the issue moot, but the family continued to discuss the "great annoyance and mortification" that Shrine's assertion had caused them. In correspondence and memoranda, the older daughter, Elizabeth Remley Hubbell, refuted the claims of blackness and slavery in "a very long epistle" chronicling their family's history of respectability and, therefore, whiteness. Mrs. Hubbell asserted that her father was "not the man to lower himself by such a degrading act as is alleged"—that is, miscegenation. She viewed these charges as a "conspiracy" organized by "low people" who wished to deprive the Remley children of their inheritance, and she expressed her conviction that the "whole thing [was] gotten up by some of [Durbin's] enemies," dismissing Mary Shrine by alleging that her "mother was subject to some sort of fits."[11]

Elizabeth Hubbell drew on three primary interactions her mother had with other whites to suggest that Mrs. Remley could not have been anything other than white. First, she recalled that her mother was registered at the multiracial Bethel Methodist Church in Charleston as a "free white person," a demonstrative fact which she interpreted as conclusive proof. "Had there been any doubt of the fact," she wrote, "I imagine her name *could* not have been *entered there*." Her reliance on the church's record of its members did not account for the possibility of errors in representation. Second, Hubbell regarded her mother's wedding to her father at Bethel as proof of her whiteness, maintaining that her mother's bridesmaids were "ladies of respectability" who would not have been "intimate with a person of doubtful pretensions." Elizabeth accepted a tautology of race and reputation that equated "respectability" with whiteness and freedom and "doubtful pretensions" with blackness and slavery. She asserted: "If [Mother] had been purchased and held as a slave all these things could not have been." Lastly, she turned to her mother's parentage and upbringing, noting that her mother's mother was an orphan "brought up by strangers." Her mother's father, from Jacksonboro, South Carolina, "was of a respectable family, scarcely likely to intermarry with a low person."[12]

William Hubbell, Elizabeth Remley's spouse, rushed to her defense by composing a memorandum to his attorney that traced Mary Remley's ancestry.[13] Mr. Hubbell claimed that Mrs. Remley's mother, Leah Whitley, turned down a proposal of marriage from a man named Joseph Mitchell. In his rejection, Mitchell settled for and married another woman, Mary, who would become Mrs. Shrine's informant. Embittered, Mitchell maliciously told his spouse and others that Leah was a "colored slave." If Leah Whitley were indeed a slave, then her daughter, Mrs. Remley, would follow her condition. To disprove this allegation, Hubbell provided genealogical information about Mrs. Remley's parents, Thomas and Leah Whitley, to offer additional evidence of his mother-in-law's pedigree. Thomas Whitley, he argued, came from an English family of "respectable noble descent" and was listed in *Burke's Peerage of Landed Gentry*. In contrast, he portrayed Leah as a daughter of a fallen soldier of the Revolutionary War and a woman of unknown origins. Born from this union, Mary Whitley Remley grew to be "an exemplary moral and Christian woman" who maintained with her husband, Paul Remley, a well-known grocery store in Charleston. Even though the court had settled the legal issue regarding her status as a free white woman, the family continued to protect its political and racial status.

At the same time that Elizabeth Hubbell's 1861 letter recorded her fear of the allegation of miscegenation, her brother Durbin in Charleston generated interracial questions of his own. He died in 1863, disinheriting his white family members in favor of his black mistress—a former slave—and their mulatto children. His will was complicated by its temporal frameworks. It concerned an interracial family before the end of the Civil War and the beginning of South Carolina's antimiscegenation law—both in 1865. Durbin could have predicted a challenge from his collateral heir, his sister Elizabeth. Yet he chose to provide for his mixed race family after his death by bequeathing his property to them. Conflict arose over the probate of the will, which did not occur until after the war.

Durbin lived a quiet life as a wealthy planter in the Carolina Lowcountry. Few, if any, texts of state history record his name as a prominent figure in southern politics, agricultural affairs, or Charleston society. At the time he applied to administer his father's will in 1861, he lived on a plantation known as Remley's Point, a 305-acre plot situated in Christ Church Parish at the junction of the Cooper and Wando rivers, where he lived with his slave mistress Philis and their two children. He also owned a brick house and lot on Society Street in downtown Charleston, along with some uninhabited lots, a common practice among wealthy Lowcountry planters. State records show that he bought and sold slaves fairly regularly.[14]

No official bill of purchase exists for Philis, but census records loosely provide an understanding of who she was. In 1861, she would have been approximately eighteen years old, the mother of seven-year-old Charles and pregnant with Cecile. The 1870 census lists both her and Cecile as "black" rather than "mulatto," so we may assume that Philis and her daughter were of sufficiently dark complexion as to lead the census taker to classify them as of unmixed blood. This declaration contrasted with her private life at Remley's Point. As Remley's slave mistress, she tacitly assumed the role of spouse and paramour; he remained unmarried. As the mother of his only two children, Philis claimed a distinct role in the household. Nominally a slave but almost a spouse, she assumed an ambiguous role as both lover and servant.[15]

Interracial sex and cohabitation existed in the antebellum South within unspoken codes of behavior. Durbin could maintain Philis and their children at his plantation with impunity because her slave status eviscerated any claim of legitimacy for their sexual relationship. Even though South Carolina law allowed for interracial marriage, this proviso applied to free blacks only, preventing the legitimization of relationships between masters and slaves. Slavery precluded any legally recognized relationships, thus securing the sexual freedom of white men.

Without the marital relation, Durbin held no obligation to provide for his mistress and their children. Yet, upon his death, Durbin legitimized the relationship in his will. He died on December 25, 1863; Philis described the event in a letter as "the discharge of his Gun by shooting marsh hens in company with Major Bolks and John Antley the ball entered his lungs of which he survived 13 days after being shot." In his will, Durbin provided for Philis and their children through an annuity of $500 to be paid from the sale of his property, both real and personal. The proceeds were "to be appropriated for the use, clothing and comfort in sickness and health" for Philis and the children.[16] Durbin also rejected the interests of his white family, which he refrained from mentioning until the end of the will. He left his residual estate to his mother, Mary Remley, and upon her death to his unmarried sister Emma. At no place in the will did he mention his other sister, Elizabeth Hubbell.

He also bequeathed "his Negroes"—meaning Philis, Charles, and Cecile—to a friend "to have the labor and services of the said slaves and their issue for and during his natural life." Durbin did not intend to relegate his black family to a state of abject slavery but to place them "under the control of kind and indulgent owners, who [would], whenever the law permits manumit and make them free."[17] Under this scheme, he circumvented the legal prohibition on slave bequests and manumissions. He did not leave his property to his slave family directly but to an administrator to carry out his wishes. In this testamentary trust, his family would receive the income that Durbin could not leave to them directly because they were slaves. Additionally, while Durbin could not legally manumit the slaves in his will, he allowed for this possibility in the future.

Had Durbin left property directly to Philis, he would have placed her testamentary interests in jeopardy, considering that an 1841 prohibition on slave bequests had yet to be overturned. The Emancipation Proclamation applied to areas under Union control, so it did not free slaves in South Carolina. Not until ratification of the Thirteenth Amendment in 1865 did all slaves gain freedom. In referring to Philis and her children as slaves, Durbin presented them as favored and faithful servants instead of beloved and deserving family members. He formally maintained distance between himself and Philis. His reluctance to consider Philis and the children as free persons without restricted rights was a strategic maneuver.

The Remley case stands apart from other interracial inheritance cases because of the context of the Civil War. The period from the construction of Durbin's will to its eventual distribution encompasses tremendous social, economic, and political upheavals including the fall of the Confederacy, the Thirteenth Amendment, and the institution of antimiscegenation law—all of which transformed relationships among the story's black, white, and mulatto characters.

Hostilities between the Union and the Confederacy deterred not only the administration of Durbin's will but also communications between North and South. Years passed without hearing news from relatives in distant places. This case is no exception, and postwar letters that circulated among the members of the family demonstrate delayed notifications of salient events. A letter written by William Hubbell in 1861 was not sent until 1866 "on account of hostilities." During this same period, Mary Remley died intestate, news of which did not reach Charleston until after the war. On April 12 and May 20, 1865—soon after General Lee's surrender at Appomattox—Emma and Elizabeth wrote to Durbin to inform him of their mother's death two years earlier.

Correspondence from Charleston completed the cycle of belated information about family news. As proxy for Durbin, Philis responded to the sisters on June 1, 1865, with her own tragic news of Durbin's death, which had occurred two years prior. She expressed gratitude for their informative letter while conveying her own loneliness and depression. On both sides of the envelope, in Philadelphia and Charleston, initial and remembered reactions to family members' deaths illustrate subjective representations of the past that sparked a frenzy of responses. These death notices were not meant to incite controversy; rather, they aimed to inform the reader of a family loss and to create a forum for mutual sympathy and mourning. Unexpectedly, these letters initiated legal battles.

Philis's letter to Elizabeth, in which she conveyed her intimacy with Durbin, probably sparked the chain of events that led to the eventual inheritance dispute. She recalled in her letter:

> My Dear Mistress the morning of which he died was Christmas on that Morning he Called me to wash him saying that he felt so much better and said that he did not think that his mother was alive and was Desirous of seeing his sisters also he said on the Morning that Christmas Morning was a Mourning Day to the Family which after he called on me to give Him the Bible to read of which I did & said that he was thankful to God for his Mercies towards Him to spare his life to see that happy Morning.[18]

Philis was familiar, yet deferential, in her writing. She referred to Durbin as "My Dear Master," but she also expressed her attachment to him by admitting "you do not know how it destroyed me" and that "I truly Miss him." At the close of her letter, she begged the sisters to return to Charleston "to relieve [her] Distressing mind" and to "find a Friend." The exercise of recalling her beloved's death renewed the pain she once felt. She lamented, "I would say more but my heart ache me to think of the past or look at the present."[19] The correspondence does not evince any ill will that suggested a conflict would erupt but rather a warm familiarity with Elizabeth and Emma.

That the white sisters did not openly deny their brother's miscegenation suggests that they held no animosity toward Philis. Still, while miscegenation did not emerge as a primary objection to the will, it was present in the subtext. Counsel for the Hubbells contended that Durbin intended to spite Elizabeth and her mother by "putting the Negroes over" their interests. In the 1866 contest, the sisters challenged the will on three primary grounds: (1) that testamentary transfers to slaves were invalid; (2) that Durbin appropriated his father's estate for his own use and enjoyment; and (3) that the postwar devaluation of Durbin's estate deprived his sisters of any interest in his property.[20]

The charges were complicated further by Durbin's failure to include Elizabeth in his will. Extant documents do not record any disputes between Durbin and Elizabeth, but it is evident that between her 1861 letter and his 1863 death, something influenced him to exclude her from his will. Still, he was "Desirous of seeing his sisters" at the time of his death, as Philis wrote in her letter.

Elizabeth's scathing and condemning letter against Mary Shrine may have affected Durbin, who had a personal stake in a "degrading act" with a "low person." Her opinions of racial intermixture, which she shared with her brother, may have been a covert reprimand, demonstrating her knowledge and disapproval of his domestic arrangement. By 1861, Durbin had fathered a second child with Philis.[21] In placing his children and mistress at the center of his testamentary concerns, Durbin ensured that the taboo of miscegenation would surface in the legal channels that would execute his will. He thus called upon law to investigate, affirm, and sustain the type of interracial relationship that disgusted his sister.

Durbin's intention to establish a trust for Philis and the children immediately drew the attention of the Hubbells, who viewed the blacks as bonded persons precluded from exercising legal and economic interests. In a bill of complaint opposing Philis's interest, the Hubbells argued that permitting her to inherit was "contrary to Equity and good conscience."[22] Their focus on Philis and her children's slave status demonstrated their racially motivated objections. It may be argued that race played no role in their legal challenge, but this assertion fails upon an examination of their reliance on being free and white as evidenced in their correspondence. Had Philis been Durbin's free white wife, their challenge would not have succeeded. The Hubbells based their objection on Philis's slave (and unmarried) status in order to assert their own interests over those of the named beneficiaries.

Philis responded by asserting her rights as a free woman. In her answer to the Hubbells' complaint, she insisted upon the validity of the will by emphasizing its creation *after* the Emancipation Proclamation. Arguing for its possible validity under the regime of slavery, she emphasized that "having been actually emancipated and made free before the distribution of the estate of Paul D. Remley such bequest should be held good and valid."[23] On the strength of this claim, she succeeded in establishing her legal ability to inherit property.

The collateral heirs also viewed Philis and the children as slave property denied to them. The Hubbells not only maintained that Philis and her children were ineligible to inherit as slaves; they also asserted that Paul Remley Sr.'s death had entitled them to a share in the slave property, which Durbin "appropriated . . . to his own use and purposes." They had expected Durbin, as administrator of the estate, to convert the father's personal property into money and divide the proceeds equally among the heirs. Of this personal property, which William Hubbell estimated at $36,000, Elizabeth, Emma, and Durbin would each receive $12,000.[24]

In the interest of securing a share in Durbin's estate, the Hubbells took to heart the meaning of chattel slavery. They viewed Philis not as a fellow heir, or as part of Durbin's family, but rather as an article of property which Durbin mishandled in the administration of his father's estate. In other words, Durbin's enumeration of Philis as a beneficiary rather than as a piece of property reduced the total value of the Remley estate: "He says they are *his* slaves and then dispenses of their services as his own property to another person, exclusive of the other heirs—'*expressis imicis alterias exclusis.*' If they as he says are taken as his and dispenses of by *him as his* then he excludes the other heirs and they can [not] claim for value received by him." Even though he called them "my negroes Philis and her children," the Hubbells claimed that Philis and her children were their property as well. While they could not relegate her to slave status, they insisted on recovering the value she and her children represented.[25]

The Hubbells also argued that the Civil War caused a radical devaluation of Durbin's property. When he wrote his will after the war began, he considered his estate valuable enough to yield $500 a year for the comfort and clothing of Philis and her children, but he authorized his trustee James Gary to pay them the amount in full "if in his judgment he shall deem it judicious and proper." Since

Durbin's estimate of his finances and holdings predated the fall of the Confederacy and the collapse of its economy, the will secured his property for Philis, but could not ensure secondary bequests to his mother Mary and sister Emma. Durbin had been aware of the possible effects of the war, directing his executors to invest his money conservatively in "safe Securities, or real estate . . . until the declaration of peace between these Confederate States and the United States." Durbin's executor, Optimus Hughes, described the conditions of the estate in the aftermath of the war. Returning to Charleston after serving in the Confederate army, Hughes found all papers and accounts destroyed. He recalled the poor economic climate, saying that "everybody was oppressed with anxiety and great poverty scarcely knowing what to do to obtain food for their families."[26]

Objecting to the "fallacy of [Durbin's] expectations," the Hubbells were not "willing to bear all the losses and give her [Philis] the full measure of the legacy." In an 1866 memorandum to their attorneys, they contended: "But as to Durbin's will it was made with the view that there would be no loss in the Estate—but under the Southern Confederacy would be valuable and that he could afford to give her $500 a year on 8,000 or so absolutely out of his share—and have much left."[27] Their objection to Durbin's will focuses not only on the devaluation, then, but also on his appropriation of their father's estate. While the two sisters had moved north to Pennsylvania, Durbin remained in South Carolina, inhabiting the valuable plantation at Remley's Point and the other properties in Charleston. The sisters believed that even if Durbin's will did not make them primary beneficiaries, they deserved a share in their father's estate, which Durbin had hoarded for himself. If Durbin's executors sold the property to provide for Philis, she would take "their" property.

Based on these arguments, the collateral heirs appealed to the Equity Court to "cut the Negroes out entirely." They claimed that Durbin's bequest to his black family was "sufficient to take up the whole of his interest in his father's Estate and that there [was] nothing left for any other party." By excluding his mistress and children, the sisters hoped to erase the recorded legacy that entitled former slaves to a share in Durbin's estate. William Hubbell wrote a letter advising his attorneys to "attack . . . the validity of the will itself" and to absorb all of Durbin's interest to leave "nothing for it to take effect upon." They complained that Durbin "never wrote to them, nor sent anything during the Rebellion," and that "he never sent them a dollar." Additionally, "he did not even send his Mother money to pay his Father's funeral expenses."[28]

Durbin's white heirs most certainly knew of his interracial relationship but remained complacent until their brother affirmed that relationship in his will.

Elizabeth had clearly expressed disapproval of "questionable" family relations in her 1861 letter to her brother. Upon notice of her disinheritance, she used her leverage as a free white woman to obtain a legacy that was never meant for her. To her, the testamentary interests of Durbin's legitimate white family trumped those of his illegitimate black one. She aimed to revise history to "undo what has been done" and explicitly reject the concept of family that Durbin had recognized in his will. Finally, the Hubbells argued that Durbin's disabled condition from the gun wound made him mentally unsound. Only "with a load of shot and wad in his lungs" could Durbin spite his family in favor of slaves. According to this line of thought, respectable white persons would not knowingly relinquish their property and wealth to black slaves.[29]

Although the white collateral heirs hoped to garner sympathy from the Equity Court through their depiction of Durbin's infirmity and irresponsibility, they did not wholly exclude Philis from the will. But this nominal inclusion must not be confused with accepting her as a legitimate distributee. The Hubbells recognized Philis not as part of Durbin's family but as a servant who deserved compensation "in consideration of her attention . . . in his sickness at the Point two or three years before his death." Seeing themselves as the primary heirs, the white heirs agreed to allot $2,000 "for her comfort, when she as things proceed proves worthy of it." In stark contrast to Durbin's testamentary intent to recognize his black family, Philis received a pittance while Elizabeth, the previously disinherited sister, took the majority of his estate. The Equity Court Master approved this consolation scheme, recommending that "it be accepted as advantageous" to Philis.[30]

While court documents never mentioned the issue of miscegenation in *In re Remley*, this issue motivated the objections of the white heirs. The specter of race simultaneously characterizes this case and eludes it. It is obvious that Durbin did not marry Philis, even though Philis was technically not a slave and state law permitted interracial marriages at the time of his death. Had he married her, his siblings would not have had legal grounds to contest the will, and the combination of her free status and her freedom to marry interracially would have enabled her to inherit without restriction. Yet South Carolina law enabled the Hubbells to succeed in their will challenge because the legal system upheld the restricted notion of a white, legitimate, recognized family—because Durbin did not legally marry Philis.

State law resisted the realization of Durbin's original will. He wanted to provide for Philis and the children and leave his sister with nothing. The competing conceptions of family—his black one and his white one—found different treatments in South Carolina courts. Even though he made provisions for Philis's "use, clothing, and comfort," his testamentary maneuvering could not overcome the legal privilege accorded to free whites. His sister and her husband were able to capitalize upon the law's favoring of free persons as a way of denying any recognition of Philis as a family member. Moreover, the massive transformations stemming from the Civil War changed the composition of Durbin's estate. The Civil War, the Emancipation Proclamation, and the weakening of the southern plantocracy undermined Philis's claim to her share of Durbin's property. Durbin lived to see neither the economic devaluation of his property nor the legal wranglings that weakened his own family's testamentary interests. He did not foresee that law would force his posthumous gifts toward the family that he wished to ignore. These influences, in addition to the challenges presented by the Hubbells, precluded Philis from obtaining the legacy that Durbin had established to recognize his mixed-race family.

Notes

1. F. Colburn Adams, *Manuel Pereira; or, The Sovereign Rule of South Carolina* (Washington, D.C.: Buell and Blanchard, 1853), 13. Until 1865, the only legal prohibition against interracial sex forbade white women from participating in interracial sexual relationships that produced children. See Charles F. Robinson, *Dangerous Liaisons: Sex and Love in the Segregated South* (Fayetteville: University of Arkansas Press, 2003), 11.

2. Joel Williamson, *New People: Mulattoes and Miscegenation in the United States* (New York: Free Press, 1980), 41; Winthrop Jordan, *White over Black: American Attitudes toward the Negro, 1550–1812* (Chapel Hill: University of North Carolina Press, 1968), 41.

3. *State v. Davis/State v. Hanna*, 8 S.C. Eq. 559 (Bail. Eq., 1831).

4. *State v. Cantey*, 11 S.C. Eq. 614 (2 Hill Eq., 1853).

5. *White v. Tax Collector*, 24 S.C. Eq. 138 (3 Rich. Eq., 1846).

6. Account of Paul Remley's Estate in Pennsylvania; William Hubbell to Counsel, 8 August 1866, both in Paul Remley Estate Case Records, 1861–67, South Carolina Historical Society, Charleston.

7. In the matter of Estate Paul Remley, 18 June 1861, Paul Remley Estate Case Records. Legal definitions of children's status throughout the South followed Roman law by declaring *partus sequitur ventrem*—that children followed the condition of the mother. See Marina Wikramanayake, *A World in Shadow: The Free Black in Antebellum South Carolina* (Columbia: University of South Carolina Press, 1973), 67. A number of fictional books appealed to this white fear of sudden and unexpected relegation to slavery. In his meticulous book on mulatto imagery in Victorian fiction, Robert Mencke asks, "What threat could be more dire than that of the blood of the inferior races of the world secretly slipping into that of the mighty civilizing race of Anglo-Saxons?" Robert Mencke, *Mulattoes and Race Mixture* (Ann Arbor: University of Michigan Press, 1979), 198. Examples of such books are Rebecca Harding Davis, *Waiting for the Verdict*

(New York: Sheldon, 1868); Albion Tourgée, *Pactolus Prime* (New York: Cassell, 1890); William Dean Howells, *An Imperative Duty* (New York: Harper and Brothers, 1892).

8. The statute reads:

> Be it enacted, by the Senate and House of Representatives, now met and sitting in General Assembly, and by the authority of the same, That any bequest, deed of trust, or conveyance, intended to take effect after the death of the owner, whereby the removal of any slave or slaves, without the limits of this State, is secured or intended, with a view to the emancipation of such slave or slaves, shall be utterly void and of no effect, to the extent of such provision; and every such slave so bequeathed, or otherwise settled or conveyed, shall become assets in the hands of any executor or administrator, and be subject to the payment of debts, or to distribution amongst the distributees or next of kin, or to escheat, as though no such will or other conveyance had been made.

Act to Prevent the Emancipation of Slaves, and for Other Purposes (1841), quoted in Adrienne Davis, "The Private Law of Race and Sex: An Antebellum Perspective," *Stanford Law Review* 51 (January 1999): 224.

9. Affidavit of Sam Wagner, 27 June 1861, Paul Remley Estate Case Records. Charleston's black Methodist population in the early 1860s measured approximately six thousand in number. See Edward Lilly, ed., *Historic Churches of Charleston* (Charleston, S.C.: Legerton, 1966), 43–44.

10. In Court of Ordinary, 29 June 1861, Paul Remley Estate Case Records.

11. Elizabeth Hubbell to Paul D. Remley, 7 July 1861, Paul Remley Estate Case Records.

12. Ibid. Often census takers and keepers of official records make erroneous estimates of a person's race, thus recording some African Americans of fair complexion as "white." In sole reliance upon these subjective measures of record keeping for posterity, genealogists, historians, and other scholars may draw fatuous conclusions that have substantial effects on contemporary interpretations of racial identity. For an insightful interpretation of this problem, see Randall Kennedy, *Interracial Intimacies: Sex, Marriage, Identity, and Adoption* (New York: Pantheon, 2003), 1–12.

13. William Hubbell, Memorandum for James B. Campbell Esq. In the Matter of the Estate of Paul Remley, Deceased, on behalf of his widow Mary Remley & Children, written in 1861, but not sent "on account of hostilities" (document not shared until 9 November 1866), Paul Remley Estate Case Records.

14. Historical Overview of the 4th Avenue Tract, Remleys Point Collection, Avery Research Center for African American History and Culture, College of Charleston, S.C.; George Henry to Paul Remley, Bill of Sale for a Slave Named Amey, 9 September 1820; Paul Remley to Thomas Buller, Bill of Sale for a Slave Named Limehouse, by Trade a Bricklayer, 17 November 1830, South Carolina Department of Archives and History, Columbia.

15. The 1870 federal census lists Philis, black, as twenty-seven years old, and Cecile, black, as seven. However, litigation documents in 1866 verify Cecile being five years old. These records also make Philis a mother at age twelve. U.S. Census Bureau, 1870, South Carolina History and Genealogy Section, Charleston County Public Library.

16. Philis to Elizabeth Hubbell, 1 June 1865, Paul Remley Estate Case Records; Paul D. Remley Will, Remley's Point Collection.

17. Remley Will.

18. Philis to Hubbell, 1 June 1865.

19. Ibid.

20. William Hubbell to Messrs. Ledyard and Boulon, 9 November 1866, Paul Remley Estate Case Records.

21. Elizabeth Hubbell to Paul D. Remley, 1861, Paul Remley Estate Case Records. Legal memoranda lists Cecile as being five years old in December 1866. See Separate Answer of Cecile, 28 December 1866, Paul Remley Estate Case Records.

22. Ziba B. Oakes Bill of Complaint, 9 November 1866, Paul Remley Estate Case Records.

23. Separate answer of Philis a freed woman, South Carolina District Court, In Equity, 28 December 1866, Paul Remley Estate Case Records.

24. William Hubbell catalogued the personal property as "about 30 negroes value $25K and personal property on the farm: value $4K; Cotton $2K. He cut wood also which he had no right to do, a thousand or more cords: value $3K; Insurance stock $2K. [TOTAL] $36K." Hubbell to Counsel, 8 August 1866.

25. Hubbell to Counsel, 8 August 1866; Remley Will.

26. Remley Will; separate answer of Optimus Hughes, 24 December 1866, Paul Remley Estate Case Records.

27. Hubbell to Counsel, 8 August 1866; Hubbell to Ledyard and Boulon, 9 November 1866.

28. Hubbell to Counsel, 8 August 1866; Ziba Oakes Bill of Complaint.

29. Ziba Oakes Bill of Complaint.

30. Remley Case Masters Report, 5 July 1867, Paul Remley Estate Case Records. In the end, Philis bore the brunt of Durbin's original will. Out of the $2,000 allotted to her, all debts and legal fees were deducted, and half of this amount was given to Optimus Hughes, the administrator. Thus Philis received money, but she was required to pay the costs generated as a result of the white heirs' objections. See Order, 12 August 1867, Paul Remley Estate Case Records.

About the Contributors

Nikki Berg Burin teaches at Concordia College. Her work appears in Diana Ramey Berry, ed. *The Female Slave: An Encyclopedia of Daily Life during Slavery in the United States* (2010) and Lisa Tendrich Frank, ed., *Women in the American Civil War: An Encyclopedia* (2008).

Andrew Frank is assistant professor of history at Florida State University. He authored *Creeks and Southerners: Biculturalism on the Early American Frontier* (2005); "Taking the State Out: Seminoles and Creeks at a Transnational Moment," *Florida Historical Quarterly* 84 (summer 2005): 10–27; "Indian Re-Creation Stories," *Eighteenth-Century Studies* 35 (fall 2002): 309–13; and "The Rise and Fall of William McIntosh: Authority and Identity on the Early American Frontier," *Georgia Historical Quarterly* 86 (spring 2002): 18–48.

Craig Thompson Friend is associate professor of history at North Carolina State University. He wrote *Along the Maysville Road: The Early Republic in the Trans-Appalachian West* (2005); edited *Southern Masculinity: Perspectives on Manhood in the South since Reconstruction* (2009); and with Lorri Glover edited *Southern Manhood: Perspectives on Masculinity in the Old South* (2004).

Anya Jabour is professor of history at the University of Montana. She authored *Marriage in the Early Republic: Elizabeth and William Wirt and the Companionate Ideal* (1998) and *Scarlett's Sisters: Young Women in the Old South* (2007) and edited *Major Problems in the History of American Families and Children* (2005).

Lynn Kennedy is assistant professor of history at the University of Lethbridge. She is the author of *Born Southern: Childbirth, Motherhood, and Social Networks in the Old South* (2010).

Kevin Noble Maillard is assistant professor at the Syracuse University College of Law. His work appears in the *Michigan Journal of Race and Law, Law & Inequality*, the *American Indian Law Review*, and the *Fordham Law Review*. His current book project reviews the impact of *Loving v. Virginia* in contemporary legal and social culture.

Christopher J. Olsen is chair and associate professor of history at Indiana State University. His publications include *Political Culture and Secession in Mississippi: Honor, Masculinity, and the Antiparty Tradition, 1830–1860* (2000); and "Eliza Frances Andrews: A Southern Woman Faces the Civil War and Reconstruction," in Sarah E. Gardner and Ann Short Chirhart, eds., *Georgia Women* (forthcoming).

Emily West is senior lecturer in American history at the University of Reading. Her publications include *Chains of Love: Slave Couples in Antebellum South Carolina* (2004); "'She is dissatisfied with her present condition': Requests for Voluntary Enslavement in the Antebellum American South," *Slavery and Abolition* 28 (December 2007): 329–50; and "Tensions, Tempers, and Temptations: Marital Discord among Slaves in Antebellum South Carolina," *American Nineteenth-Century History* 5 (summer 2004): 1–18.

Kirsten Wood is associate professor of history at Florida International University. She authored *Masterful Women: Slaveholding Widows in the American Southeast from the Revolution through the Civil War* (2004). She also has published multiple articles in journals and collections, including "'Old Miss Sho' Was Good to Us . . . 'Cause She Was Raisin' Us to Wuk for Her': Widowed Planters and Paternalism in the Old South," in Winfred B. Moore, Kyle S. Sinisi, and David H. White, eds., *Warm Ashes: Issues in Southern History at the Dawn of the Twenty-first Century* (2003).

Nancy Zey is assistant professor in the Department of History at Sam Houston State University. She has authored "Children of the Public: Poor and Orphaned Minors in the Southwest Borderlands," in James Marten, ed., *Children and Youth in a New Nation* (2009).

Index

CPSIA information can be obtained at www.ICGtesting.com
Printed in the USA
BVOW07s2217050315

390307BV00005B/1/P

9 780813 036762